ALL ABOUT MARKET TIMING

The Easy Way to Get Started

OTHER TITLES IN THE "ALL ABOUT . . ." FINANCE SERIES

ALL ABOUT
MARKET TIMING

The Easy Way to Get Started

LESLIE N. MASONSON

McGraw-Hill

New York   Chicago   San Francisco   Lisbon   London   Madrid
Mexico City   Milan   New Delhi   San Juan   Seoul
Singapore   Sydney   Toronto

The McGraw·Hill Companies

6 7 8 9 0   FGR/FGR   0 9 8 7 6

ISBN 0-07-141331-6

This publication is designed to provide accurate and authoritative information in regard to the subject matter covered. It is sold with the understanding that the publisher is not engaged in rendering legal, accounting or other professional service. If legal advice or other expert assistance is required, the services of a competent professional person should be sought.
> —*From a Declaration of Principles Jointly Adopted by a Committee of the American Bar Association and a Committed of Publishers and Associations.*

McGraw-Hill books are available at special discounts to use as premiums and sales promotions, or for use in corporate training programs. For more information, please write to the Director of Special Sales, McGraw-Hill Professional, Two Penn Plaza, New York, NY 10011-2298. Or contact your local bookstore.

This book is printed on recycled, acid-free paper containing a minimum of 50% recycled de-inked paper.

Library of Congress Cataloging-in-Publication Data

Masonson, Leslie N.
    All about market timing : the easy way to get started / by Leslie N. Masonson.
      p.   cm.
    Includes bibliographical references.
    ISBN 0-07-141331-6 (pbk. : alk. paper)
    1. Investment analysis.   2. Stock price forecasting.   3. Speculation
    I. Title.

HG4529.M377   2003
332.63'2—dc21   2003005763

DEDICATION

To my beautiful wife Marilyn, the love-of-my-life, who has brought out the best in me.

To my wonderful children, Dan and Amy who have achieved their own successes.

To my confident son-in-law, Seth Reese, who has brought dedication, skill, and perseverance to a challenging profession.

To all investors all across America.

May you all benefit from the research and strategies in this book to find a smarter way to invest.

CONTENTS

FOREWORD

Market timing is not a fun vocation or avocation. It is tough and ugly. I know this well, because I've been a market timer in the trenches since 1983, both as an investor and as an advisor.

Timing requires thick skin and iron resolve. Because it is not understood, market timing is almost universally scorned on Wall Street.

Yet market timing is an important tool for investors. When it is used consistently over long periods of time, timing can dramatically improve returns while it reduces risk, as Leslie Masonson has demonstrated repeatedly in this book.

If this book is studied by the establishment financial media, it can help to reduce a tide of misguided negative articles about timing. Too many financial writers have discovered they can easily "prove" that timing doesn't work and can't possibly work. However, those authors rarely specify any measurable definition of what would be necessary for a strategy to qualify as one that "works."

I've found that timing is 100 percent successful at reducing market risk, by periodically getting investors out of the market. Every day your assets are in a money market fund, that's a day they are not at risk in the market. If timing keeps you on the sidelines 25 percent of the time, timing has reduced your risk by 25 percent.

Results from timing almost never look like returns from a buy-and-hold approach. This can be disconcerting and upsetting. But to a long-term investor, this noncorrelation amounts to a form of diversification.

Why do so many people believe that timing doesn't work? I believe the answer is twofold. First, most investors who undertake market timing are not prepared for the rigorous discipline it requires. They quickly become discouraged when they discover that timing systems are statistically "wrong" much more often than they are "right."

Second, market timing is misunderstood. No investing rule is more fundamental than this: Don't invest in something unless you understand it. I think the reason timing disappoints so many investors is that they don't understand it.

Masonson's book will help remedy that. He has put together the information and the tools that investors need to make timing work for them. He has taken a complex topic and made it accessible for real people.

The biggest problem facing most investors is that they need the potential growth they can get from owning equities—while at the same time equities are quite volatile—too much so, for most people.

As far as I know, there are only two solutions that make sense. One is to allocate as much as necessary of a portfolio to fixed-income funds. This brings stability, but at the cost of the long-term returns of equities. The second solution, the topic of this book, is market timing.

As this book shows, mechanical market timing makes it possible for investors to achieve the returns they need at lower volatility. And that makes it easier for those investors to stay the course.

Almost all my own investments are governed by market timing. Even if I could "know" that I could get a better long-term return without timing, I am just not comfortable with a buy-and-hold approach. I have worked hard all my life to accumulate assets, and I'm simply not willing to passively let the market (which, in effect, is all other investors) take them away.

This book is for investors who share my conservative approach, who believe, as I do, that hanging onto their money is as important as making it grow. In this excellent guide, those investors will find everything they need to determine if timing is for them—and if they have what it takes to be successful.

Paul Merriman

Paul Merriman is founder and president of Merriman Capital Management in Seattle, and is author of two books on investing.

ACKNOWLEDGMENTS

Writing a comprehensive book on market timing would not be possible without the expertise and involvement of many individuals and firms. Even with their assistance, I take full responsibility for any inadvertent factual errors in the book.

The following individuals provided significant input, and to them I first want to offer special thanks:

Herb Weissman devoted many pain-staking hours reviewing, editing and providing critical input to the manuscript. His clarity makes this a more readable book.

Robert W. Colby, CMT and author of *The Encyclopedia of Technical Market Indicators*, Second Edition, provided the use of his research on timing strategies from his landmark book, as well as provided critical comments on the manuscript.

Nelson Freeburg, editor and publisher of *FORMULA RESEARCH* provided the use of his research on calendar-based and presidential cycle strategies and insights on the subject of back testing.

Sy Harding, *Sy Harding's Street Smart Report*, President, Asset Management Research Corp., shared extensive information on his seasonal timing system using the MACD indicator.

Paul Merriman, President, Merriman Capital Management, wrote the foreword and whose firm provided market-timing insights, research and commentary.

Stephen Isaacs, Executive Editor, McGraw-Hill, and his talented team, for their guidance and assistance in the editing and publishing process.

I also want to thank the following organizations and individuals for their assistance, expertise, and information provided:

Active Trader magazine and Mark Etzkorn, Editor-in-Chief.
DecisionPoint.com and Carl Swenlin, founder and publisher.

Hays Advisory Group, LLC, and Don R. Hays, President and Mark Dodson.

The Hirsch Organization and *Stock Traders Almanac* and Jeffrey A. Hirsch, President and Judd Brown, Vice President.

Investor's Intelligence and Michael L. Burke, Editor and John E. Gray, President.

David Korn's Advisory Service and David Korn.

Merriman Capital Management and Dennis Tilley, Director of Research.

The MoniResearch Newsletter and Steve Shellans, President.

Prudential Securities Incorporated and Dr. Edward Yardeni.

Rydex Global Advisors, Inc. and Anna Haglund, Public Relations and Communications Manager.

Schreiner Capital Management, Inc. and Roger J. Schreiner, President.

StockCharts.com and Kellie Erlandson.

Technical Analysis of STOCKS & COMMODITIES and Jack K. Hutson, Publisher.

Theta Investment Research, LLC and Paul J. Montgomery, President.

Timer Digest and James Schmidt, Editor and Publisher.

Towneley Capital Management, Inc., and Wesley G. McCain, Chairman, and Gretchen Hartman.

UBS Americas and Karen C. Hess, Media Relations

ULTRA Financial Systems Inc. and Steve Hunter, President.

VectorVest, Inc., and Dr. Bart A. DiLiddo, Chairman and CEO, and also Linda Royer, and Mark Blake.

TradeStation (Registered trademark of the TradeStation Group Inc.) and Michael Burke, Product Manager.

INTRODUCTION

If you don't know who you are, the stock market is an expensive place to find out.

George Goodman

Did your investments get crushed in the last stock market crash?—No, not in 1929—in 2000 to 2002. Most investors got a rude awakening when they opened their year-end statements for each of the past three years—because 2000 to 2002 was only the second time in history that the market was down three years in a row.

Are you confused by the daily gyrations of the stock market? Are you upset that you lost a bundle in the past three years? Are you ready to give up on the stock market, and cash in at any price? If so, then join the club, since almost everyone is in the same boat. The talking heads on the business shows continually profess a bullish stance, no matter what the market is doing. Ignore their opinions. No one knows where the market is going tomorrow, let alone in the months and years further down the road. Just because the stock market has averaged an annual return of nearly 10.2 percent since 1926 does not mean that you can expect that rate of return to continue in the coming year or the next 5 years. Just because you may not be retiring soon does not mean that you can afford to ignore what is going on in the stock market.

If you have been investing since 1982, or perhaps since early 1995, you were probably ecstatic with your returns through the first quarter of 2000. Since then, the market has dramatically and swiftly reversed direction, and it has dropped faster than it rose. Did you sell at or near the top and put the proceeds into cash? You probably did not. Did you sell after your stocks or mutual funds fell 10 percent, then 20 percent, then 30 percent, and perhaps 90 percent in some cases? Probably not, since you thought the market would come back, as it always has.

Perhaps you followed the widely touted buy-and-hold approach. And if you are like most investors, you have no game plan for cutting your losses or taking your profits. Lacking an investing strategy and blindly following the buy-and-hold approach can lead to financial ruin. It can wipe out years of investment profits in a short time, and it can take years for your portfolio to recover, if ever. Don't fall for the buy-and-hold ruse, even though 99 percent of financial professionals tout it. This is the same crowd that tells you that dollar-cost averaging is a sound investment approach. Check it out for yourself. Has your own dollar-cost averaging worked for you?

It's great when stock prices are rising, but not so great when they continue to fall. One of the most critical rules of investing is *never* average down. It is a loser's game. Think about all the unfortunate and uninformed investors who still own Amazon, Dell, Cisco, EMC, AT&T, Eastman Kodak, Xerox, WorldCom, and Palm. Those investors got killed by continually buying more shares on the way down—or by holding on to their original shares bought at much higher prices.

IS THERE A BETTER APPROACH THAN BUY AND HOLD?

Is there a smarter way to handle your investments, to protect your profits, and to steer clear of bear markets before they decimate your portfolio? Yes. The approach is called market timing, and it works, no matter what you've heard to the contrary. This book contains compelling data on successful market-timing approaches that beat the market indexes over decades. The strategies are simple so that you can use them yourself with little work. And for those of you who prefer to have a market timer do the work for you, you'll be interested in the information provided on top-performing market-timing newsletters and market-timing advisors.

After reading this book you will understand both sides of the buy-and-hold myth and why market timing is a more sensible, risk-averse, and unemotional approach to investing in the stock market.

I do not recommend that investors buy individual stocks, ever! Stocks are simply too risky for the average investor. With the accounting scandals, SEC investigations, crooked corporate financial officers, managed earnings, and earnings targets missed by only a penny, why should you take a chance on picking the wrong stock or the right stock at the wrong time and taking a big hit? It is much more prudent, and far less risky, to invest in appropriate index funds, sector funds, or exchange-traded funds.

My objective in writing *All About Market Timing* is fourfold. First, I want to provide you with the rationale and facts indicating why market timing is a superior investment strategy compared to the ever-popular buy-and-hold strategy. Second, I want to provide you with profitable market-timing strategies that are simple to understand and easy to implement. Third, I want to help you avoid future bear markets and protect your principal. And last, I want to help you to maximize the returns that are possible to realize on your investment assets, both in good times and in bad.

WHAT IS MARKET TIMING?

Market timing can be defined as making investment buy and sell decisions using a mechanical trading strategy which employs one or more indicators and/or proven strategies. The objective of a successful market-timing system is to be invested in the market during up trends and to be either in cash (or in a short position) during down trends, especially during brutal bear markets. Market timing can be applied to all types of investments including stocks, stock and index options, mutual funds, bonds, and futures. This book therefore focuses exclusively on using timing with index funds, sector funds, leveraged funds, and exchange-traded funds. It is your choice as to which of these investments you prefer to work with because the timing principles remain the same for each of them.

Market timing is aimed at taking your emotions out of the investing equation—or at least minimizing their impact. This objective is critical to your success. Investor psychology has been studied for years, and the "herd instinct" is rampant. This urge to follow the herd plays right into your hands, because the crowd (whether individual investors or investment advisors) is characteristically wrong at *major* stock market tops and bottoms. This situation will always be with us, because the emotions of dealing with investing—fear and greed—will never change.

Market timing is not a perfect investing approach; there is no such thing. Market timing cannot predict when the market will change direction. But, if you use a reliable market-timing system and follow its signals, then you will exit the market when it begins to turn down and you will re-enter the market when it begins to turn up, all in time to maximize and protect most of your profits. A study of the performance of professional market timers by *MoniResearch Newsletter*, an independent monitoring service, found that 92 percent of the 25 timers it followed outperformed the market averages in 1987 when the DJIA dropped by 23 percent on Black October, and 96 percent did so during the declines in January 1990 and August 1992.

And in the latest time period for the year ending in September, 2002, 88 percent of classic market timers monitored beat the S&P 500 Index. Over the last five years ending on the same date, 63 percent beat the buy-and-hold strategy. And for those Nasdaq timers competing against the Nasdaq Composite Index benchmark, the numbers were even better, with 79 percent beating that index over five years, and 84 percent over the one-year time frame. These results are confirmed by *Timer Digest* publisher, Jim Schmidt, who found that 65 percent of the 100 market-timing newsletter services that he tracks beat the S&P 500 benchmark in 2000, 45 percent beat it in 2001, and 80 percent beat it in 2002. That's precisely what market timing is all about—reducing losses when a bear market strikes.

BEAR MARKETS ARE A RECURRING PART OF THE INVESTING CYCLE—YOU MUST BE PREPARED TO DEAL WITH THEM

Future bear markets will arrive like clockwork, every three to four years, on average. Avoiding these slumps is the key to protecting your hard-earned capital. Unfortunately, most investors have no clue as to the market's future direction, how the stock market really works, or how to minimize their losses. Therefore, it is not surprising that investors suffer the consequences when a bear market sneaks up and mauls them.

From 1950 to 1999, there were over a dozen bear markets, with the average one lasting 397 days, resulting in a loss in value of 30.9 percent. The average recovery period to reach the previous high was about 622 days (1.75 years) based on the S&P 500 Index.[1] Assuming the last bear market ended on October 9, 2002 the S&P 500 Index dropped 49.1 percent drop from its top on March 24, 2000 to its bottom on October 9, 2002 which lasted 941 days.

Similarly, from the market top in 2000 to the bottom on October 9, 2002, the Dow Jones Industrial Average dropped 37.8

percent (the actual top was January 14, 2000), and the Nasdaq Composite Index cratered a whopping 77.9 percent.

There will definitely be future bear markets, and if we are in a secular (long-term) bear market, then this current bear market may not have ended in 2002. Therefore, the key to investing is to preserve your capital at all costs. That means you should take prudent actions to avoid bear markets and not be invested in stocks when they occur. If you do not exit the market to protect your hard-earned money, then your profits (if there are any) and even your principal will quickly shrink. How much can you lose in the next bear market? The crash of 1929 wiped out 86 percent of the value of investors' portfolios, and the investors required 25.2 years to break even (not counting dividend reinvestment). Since then, there have been 19 bear markets, with an average loss of 33 percent, which took an average of 3.5 years to regain those losses. Not only are bear markets deadly financially, they can and do inflict significant emotional harm as well.

Intelligent investors know that bear markets are inevitable, and therefore you should either step aside, into cash or, depending on your level of risk tolerance, you should short the market using mutual funds that are specialized for investing in bear markets or exchange-traded funds. The experts tell you that no one can time the markets with consistency. Guess what? The experts are wrong again, as you shall see. This book will provide you with the information you need so that you don't have to guess or make an investing decision based on emotion or someone else's opinion of where the market is headed.

In late July 2002, Lawrence Kudlow, co-host of the *Kudlow & Cramer* show on CNBC, jokingly said that he and co-host Jim Cramer had called the 2001–2002 bear market bottom seven times, and that they will eventually get it right! But this is no joke. You can't afford to depend on someone else's guesses. You need to make your own investment decisions which you can do if you stick with the time-tested indicators and strategies which you will learn about in this book.

BEAR MARKET LOSSES ARE REAL NOT ILLUSORY

Many investors, and especially those over age 55, who have less time to recoup their stock market losses than those in their twenties and thirties, may never recover the losses they suffered in the 2000–2002 bear market. Consider the following statistics from AARP:[2]

- More than $7 trillion—equal to $25,000 for every man, woman, and child in America—went down the investment drain in the last three years.
- $700 billion in retirement savings were decimated.
- A dollar invested in a Standard & Poor's 500 Stock Index Fund in March 2000 was worth about 55 cents as of August 2002.

FORGET ABOUT DOLLAR-COST AVERAGING IN A BEAR MARKET

Dollar-cost averaging is another popular investing strategy bandied about in the canyons of Wall Street. Catherine Voss Sanders wrote an article entitled "The Plight of the Fickle Investor" in the Morningstar Investor (December 1997), and she stated: "Because emotions and hype can get in the way of smart investing, systematic dollar-cost averaging is a sound strategy. ...[I]n most cases, the dollar-cost averager is going to beat the willy-nilly investor."

To the contrary, *never* use dollar-cost averaging in a *bear* market, since it puts you on the wrong side of the trade when the market is tanking. It is the traders who are right when they say *never average down*. Take the advice of Richard Russell (*Dow Theory Letters*, 1984):

> Averaging down in a bear market is tantamount to taking a seat on the down escalator at Macy's.

Imagine buying Corning at 113 (split adjusted) on September 1, 2000, and buying more shares each month as it tanked, so that you could lower your cost basis. Corning hit a low of $1.10 on October 8, 2002. Guess what? How in the world can you ever recoup that kind of a loss?

Dollar-cost averaging in a bear market is a strategy for dummies, not for intelligent investors. That goes for stocks as well as mutual funds. There is no guarantee that your stocks and mutual funds will return to their March 2000 highs any time soon, and throwing good money into a declining fund makes no sense to me. Remember that hundreds of funds go out of existence or are merged into other funds simply because of their poor investment performance.

MOST INVESTORS ARE NOT FACING REALITY

Most investors have a similar view of the investing scene. They hold the following beliefs:

- Buying a diversified basket of stocks and holding them for the long run is the best way to invest.
- They can perform better than other investors, because they are smarter than they are.
- Buy and hold is the only rational way to invest.
- Market timing is for losers.
- Dollar-cost averaging is a good strategy.
- Financial advisors, brokers, and so-called stock market gurus should be consulted or followed to obtain the best possible investment results.
- Tax consequences should always be considered in making investment decisions.

Believe it or not, all these beliefs are false! Many intelligent individuals are not intelligent investors. In making their investment decisions, too many investors rely only on fundamental research and totally ignore the technical indicators of stock market investing. Investors must understand that their thinking may not be realistic or accurate and that they cannot be successful as investors by viewing the world through "rose-colored glasses."

Neither should you let tax consequences interfere with sensible stock market strategies. Otherwise you will end up paralyzed and confused, and you will never sell you losers or winners. Of course you can use market-timing strategies without concern in tax deferred retirement accounts because there are no tax consequences in such accounts. But, don't assume that taking profits in regular accounts, will work against you. It may or may not. But the primary concern is on protecting and preserving your capital and tax considerations are only secondary to your financial well being where the stock market is concerned. You may be intrigued by some of the statements and findings presented in this book. One of the major premises is that buy and hold is a loser's strategy—that's right, a loser's strategy. You won't see that statement very often in your perusal of the financial news. An entire chapter is devoted to debunking the buy-and-hold crowd. Another critical premise is that the safest way to invest in the stock market is to be "out" of the market in a cash account (or to be short the market), during declining periods, and to be "in" the market only during the most favorable time periods. This completely contradicts what some experts will tell you. You will hear "It's time in the market that counts, not timing the market." I will show you that the opposite is true.

INVESTORS NEED AN ACTION PLAN

Unfortunately, some investment firms do not provide fair and balanced information on investing. For example, I've come across some incomplete information in literature from Northwestern Mutual Financial Network, Merrill Lynch, Morgan Stanley, U.S. Global Investors, Invesco Funds Group, Inc., and Fidelity, to name a few. All these firms had a chart or table depicting the reduced annual returns if an investor had missed the 10 best days compared to buy and hold. They conveniently forgot to provide a chart or table showing the improved performance by missing the 10 worst days. In the latter case, the returns would be much higher if you had been out of the market. So, you are only getting half the story because these firms have a motive wanting you to stay invested at all times. For one, it reduces their overhead expenses and costs of administering the fund to have you stay put. Second, it eliminates any liquidity problems for the fund that could be caused by a large number of fund holders liquidating at the same time. If this happens, it could force the fund to sustain unwanted market losses from selling off holdings in order to meet the redemption needs of exiting fund holders.

Your financial advisor or planner, if you have one, can help you with estate planning, retirement planning, asset allocation, insurance needs, and so on. In fact, almost 75 percent of investors use advisors to provide guidance in making sense of the market moves.[3] But very few, if any, financial planners are market timers; instead, they will counsel you on investing in a diversified group of stocks or mutual funds and then leave you hanging in the breeze. That is fine advice, as far it goes. But in a bear market, the stock components will drop in value. So it is entirely up to you to protect your own portfolio.

A friend of mine attended the New York Money Show on October 23, 2002, opening day. Nine investment experts made introductory presentations about their market viewpoints and what they planned to cover in their sessions over the next few days. Guess what? The experts were almost evenly split between bulls and bears. So, bottom line as an investor relying on these "experts," you were left in a quandary as to whether you should be buying or selling. I consider such conferences as sideshows for the uninformed. You will have to make your own investment decisions to protect your money, since no one else will do it for you.

To make money and be successful in the stock market, every investor needs a plan of action based on a solid strategy that works in bull markets and especially in bear markets. This is a daunting task for any investor, since many studies have shown that the majority of investors neither equal nor beat the market averages nor do they equal the performance of the mutual funds that they've purchased. They don't because investors act emotionally, and they swing between the fear of a market downfall and the greed for making the most money during a market upswing. Eventually investors tend to buy at the top and sell at the bottom, because they invest with their stomachs instead of with their brains.

This pattern is repeated over and over, usually resulting in underperformance—that is worse than just buying and holding. DALBAR, Inc. (a leading financial-services research firm), studied the performance of mutual fund investors from January 1984 through December 2000. They found that in the year 2000 the average equity fund investor held her or his mutual funds for 2.6 years and realized an annualized return of only 5.32 percent, compared to a return 16.29 percent for the S&P 500 Index during the 17 year period studied. Clearly, individual investors are not investing with their brains.

So how should investors participate in the roller-coaster stock market without getting heart palpitations, without losing all their profits, or worse, their initial capital, and without getting physically or mentally sickened by their losses? That is what this book is about. *All About Market Timing* will provide you, whether you're a beginner or more advanced investor, with easy-to-understand, time-tested market-timing strategies that work. Timing will help you to make more accurate buy and sell decisions. No longer will you get out at the exact bottom or in at the exact top while limiting your risk at the same time.

STICK WITH THE FACTS

In this book you will see facts, information, and ideas that you most likely have not seen elsewhere. You will see why the conventional wisdom on investing is dead wrong. Following bad advice can actually cause you great financial loss and emotional distress. The problem is that you have not been given the complete story on investing and on how difficult it is to succeed over the long term. In the long run, the only thing that matters is that you have protected your money and that you've helped it grow. Letting bear markets devour your hard-earned cash does not make sense. Buy and hold does not make sense. It's like seeing a train come roaring down the tracks, and you decide to step in front of it. That's irrational and deadly, because you know the outcome.

My objective is to level the playing field and provide you with the knowledge to become a more informed, calm, and profitable investor. You have more important things to do than to be in constant turmoil about your investments and your retirement funds as you listen to the financial news each day. You can manage your portfolios in a nonemotional, methodical manner, if you put your mind to it.

Although this book is written for investors, it also provides usable strategies that financial advisors, financial planners, mutual fund managers, and brokers can use to protect their clients' capital and make it grow in both bull and bear markets. Hopefully, these professionals will embrace timing strategies, after reading this book, to use in their investment arsenal for all their clients' benefit.

HOW THIS BOOK IS STRUCTURED

All About Market Timing is a "tell-it-like-it-is" book. There is no fluff just the unvarnished truth. I am not a certified financial planner, stockbroker, portfolio manager, or investment newsletter writer. I am an individual investor, just like you, and I'm tired of being misled, by not being given the full story on investing by the Wall Street clique.

In writing this book, I have assumed that you have some knowledge of investing and index funds. My emphasis is on the importance of market timing and how to use it to improve your investment performance, while limiting your risk and protecting your principal.

The first three chapters set the groundwork for the remaining chapters. Chapter 1 focuses on how difficult it is for the investor to come out ahead in the stock market in the long run, when investors keep getting killed in the short run with periodic bear markets. In fact, in the aggregate, losses suffered in bear markets often exceed the gains earned in bull markets. Bull and bear market cycles are reviewed in detail, including secular bull and bear markets where there are long periods of time when the market does nothing and you are biding your time. That is no way to make money. Also here, the poor record of the market experts is exposed for all to see.

Chapter 2 soundly debunks the buy and hold myth. Statistics and facts are provided to show you how buy and hold is not a successful strategy in the long run because the intermittent bear markets rob you of the profits you just made and the continual impact of inflation. The complete story on missing the best days *and* missing the *worst* days will be provided. You'll be surprised by the outcome.

Chapter 3 covers everything you wanted to know about market timing but were never told by the Wall Street gurus, the financial magazine articles, or financial radio and TV shows. The critical characteristics of successful market timers are provided, as well as six key points about market timing that need to be understood. The distinction between classic market timers and dynamic asset allocators is covered. Documented examples of market timers who have been successful are mentioned to prove that market timing does work consistently in the real world.

Chapters 4 and 5 review the best vehicles to use when timing the market. Chapter 4 focuses on the advantages of market timing using index funds, sector funds, and leveraged funds. Specific fund families are named, as well as sourced for additional information. Regular mutual funds are not recommended because of their higher overall costs. Chapter 5 covers the characteristics of the relatively new exchange-traded funds and the substantial benefits they offer investors.

Chapter 6 is a fascinating chapter, chock full of sentiment and internal market indicators that can telegraph the market's health. By carefully tracking these indicators, you will see when there is a high degree of optimism or pessimism. At these extremes, the market usually reverses in the opposite direction. And as a timer, you can take advantage of those unique occurrences to get on the right side of the market rather quickly by determining the readings of all these indicators and looking for a consensus.

Chapters 7 through 11 are the heart of the book. They provide specific market-timing strategies that can be used to beat buy and hold with less risk—always a great combination. First, Chapter 7 reviews easy-to-use strategies, focusing on the best six months of the year when most of the stock market's gains are made. Certain months of the year consistently and significantly perform better than others. For example, by simply not investing in September you will significantly improve your performance.

The best six months strategy, developed in 1986 by Yale Hirsch, but not widely used by investors, has provided outstanding results compared to the worst six months since 1950. An actual investment of $10,000, in the S&P 500 Index from 1950 through 2001, using the best six months strategy, coupled with an MACD timing indicator, resulted in a gain of $1,199,247 compared to a loss of $5977 for an investment in the worst six months. And this is only the beginning of that chapter. If this fact whets your appetite, then you'll benefit tremendously from this chapter. Imagine the beauty of investing only in the months that the market makes most of its gains and being in cash for the other months! That strategy alone would have saved your stock market retirement funds from being smashed.

Chapter 8 takes seasonal investing to a higher level by providing data on best and worst years of the four-year presidential cycle. You will find out that by investing in the pre-election and election years that you can do much better than if you had invested in the postelection and midterm election years. The performance over decades has proved this strategy's powerful results on a consistent basis. And by using margin or leveraged mutual funds in the best months during the best years, your performance really skyrockets.

Chapter 9 uses a well-known, time-tested strategy that has been used by many investors. A simple moving average of a market index is used to obtain buy and sell signals. When the price of the index rises above the moving average, a sell signal is given, and when the index falls below the moving average a buy signal is given. Studies of moving averages by independent researchers will be presented to show their performance. Also, a separate 20-day moving average and a separate 25-week moving average strategy using the Nasdaq Composite Index are tested for performance over a long time frame. As you will see, both turned in an excellent performance in comparison to buy and hold.

Chapters 10 and 11 provide a market-timing approach using a percentage filter to make buy and sell decisions. Chapter 10 provides a simple strategy of buying an index fund, leveraged fund, or exchange-traded fund when a buy or sell signal is given on the Value Line Arithmetic Index. You simply buy when that index rises 4 percent from its last bottom and sell when that index drops 4 percent from its last top. It's that simple, and this strategy has proven to be successful over decades. Chapter 11 presents the same strategy, but it uses a 6 percent filter with the Nasdaq Composite and the Nasdaq 100 indexes. The Nasdaq strategy had even higher returns than the Value Line 4 percent strategy, but with more risk.

Chapter 12 provides useful information on market-timing newsletters (for example, *Timer's Digest* and *The Hulbert Financial Digest*), *FORMULA RESEARCH* (a newsletter that provides market-timing models), and Web sites (*Sy Harding's Street Smart Report*, *haysmarket focus.com, fundadvice.com, timingcube.com*, and David Korn's Advisory Service). Also included is information on market-timing advisors who manage clients' money using mutual funds as the investment vehicles. These advisors are monitored by two services: *MoniResearch Newsletter* and *Select Advisors*.

Chapter 13 provides software resources—VectorVest, ULTRA Financial Systems, and TradeStation, among others—that can be used by self-directed investors to time the market. Lastly, the epilogue offers words of encouragement to those investors considering market timing, as a viable investment strategy and summary of key points. A bibliography of books, articles and academic papers is provided for further reading and study. Important Web sites are also provided.

HOW TO USE THIS BOOK

If you are new to investing or are not familiar with market timing, then I recommend that you read the book chapter by chapter. On the other hand, if you are very experienced with the stock market and index funds, and if you are already convinced of the merits of market-timing, then I recommend that you can go directly to Chapters 7 through 11 for the recommended market-timing strategies. If you prefer subscribing to a market-timing newsletter or using a market-timing advisor instead of using a self-directed timing strategy, then Chapter 12 is for you. Those investors who prefer coming up with their own market-timing strategies or performing further testing of the strategies mentioned in this book will want to check out Chapter 13, then Chapters 7 through 11. You can read the other chapters when you have the time.

Chapter 6 is one chapter that will provide all investors with useful insight. It covers the use of ten sentiment and internal market indicators that can help you determine the market's health. Knowing this information can help you with your current investments, whether or not you plan to follow any of the strategies covered in this book. You must be on the right side of the market to make money.

Enjoy the road ahead and get ready to change the way you invest. Stay open-minded and be ready for change. I would like to hear from you with any comments about market timing or your comments on the value of this book. Please email me for more information at *lesmason@frontiernet.net*.

Leslie N. Masonson
Monroe, New York
June 2003

ENDNOTES

1. "The Upside of Down Market: What Investors Can Learn from Volatility." *Of Mutual Interest* (Invesco Funds), Summer 2001.
2. Walt Duka, "Battling Your Way Back: 50+ Americans Tell How They're Coping with Financial Losses," *AARP Bulletin Online*, September 2002.
3. "When the Going Gets Tough, the Smart Get Advice," *Of Mutual Interest* (Invesco Funds), Fall 2002.

PART 1

Market-Timing Basics

CHAPTER 1

The Stock Market = Bull Markets + Bear Markets

The first rule is not to lose. The second rule is not to forget the first rule.

Warren Buffett

In the battlefield that is the stock market, there are the quick and there are the dead!...The fastest way to take a bath in the stock market is to try to prove that you are right and the market is wrong.

William J. O'Neil (How to Make Money in Stocks, 2002), p. 54

INVESTOR PROFILES AND CONCERNS

Before diving into the intricacies of the stock market, including the occurrence of bull and bear markets, let's first begin by observing a profile of the average U.S. stock investor based on two recently conducted surveys. After understanding the makeup and views of investors, we will be in a better position to see the obstacles they face in trying to equal or beat the market's performance over the long term.

50 Percent of All U.S. Households
Hold Stocks and Mutual Funds

A comprehensive survey of investor ownership titled "Equity Ownership in America, 2002," was released in September 2002 by the Investment Company Institute (ICI) and the Securities Industry Association (SIA).[1] The survey indicated that there were an estimated 52.7 million households (49.5 percent), or 84.3 million investors, who owned stocks or equity mutual funds as of January 2002. That compares with 36.6 percent of households in 1992, and 41 percent in 1995. The survey included interviews with 4009 individuals in January and February 2002. The following are some of its key findings:

- 96 percent of equity investors are long-term investors, and 86 percent follow the buy-and-hold strategy.
- 31 percent of equity investors bought stocks during 2001, while 24 percent sold stocks.
- 36 percent of those with household income of less than $50,000 are willing to take above-average or substantial risk, for a similar gain, compared to 37 percent with income of $50,000 to $99,999, and 43 percent with higher incomes.
- 58 percent base their stock buy and sell decisions on advice from professional advisors.
- 48 percent of households holding equities do so through a retirement plan, while 44 percent originally bought equities that are not part of any retirement plan.
- 28.7 million households own stock mutual funds that are not part of any retirement plan.
- 89 percent of investors own stock mutual funds, while 49 percent own individual stocks, and 52 percent only hold mutual funds, while 11 percent only hold individual stock, and 38 percent hold both mutual funds and stocks.
- 44 percent of equity owners first bought their stocks prior to 1990, while 26 percent purchased them from 1990 through 1995.
- 65 percent indicated that saving for retirement was their most important financial goal, and 87 percent indicated that they were investing in stocks for their retirement.

- 57 percent of the investment decision making is done by co-decision makers, mostly married couples.
- 31 percent of investors use the Internet to buy and sell securities, and 46 percent use the Internet to check stock prices, while 38 percent read online publications.

For additional information about this survey, contact the ICI at *www.ici.org*, at (202) 326-5800, or contact the SIA at *www.sia.com*, (202) 296-9410.

Survey of Investors Indicates Concern about the Stock Market Decline

A more recent investor survey was conducted by CNN/USA Today/Gallup Poll by telephone on July 29–31, 2002 of 1003 adults. Some of the key findings were as follows:[2]

- 62 percent follow the stock market news closely.
- 66 percent own stock.
- 63 percent of stockholders feel that owning stocks is more of a gamble than a good investment.
- 63 percent say that "buy-and-hold" is the best strategy for them.
- 59 percent have lost money in the market over the past 12 months.
- 20 percent have sold some stock or mutual funds over the past 12 months.
- As far as the decline in the stock market is concerned, 51 percent perceive it as a major problem, while 29 percent view it as a minor problem, and 14 percent think it is a crisis.
- 34 percent feel the decline has shaken their confidence in the economy.
- 49 percent will cut back on their spending.
- 42 percent will live less comfortably than they thought they would.
- 38 percent will be unable to maintain their standard of living.
- 36 percent will now retire at a later age.

‣ 26 percent believed that the Dow Jones would recover to 11,000 within a year, 30 percent said within two years, 14 percent within three years, 16 percent in more than three years, 7 percent said never, and 7 percent had no opinion.

STOCK MARKET PERCEPTIONS

In early 2000, investors had no idea that the next three years would be horrendous. Just look at the massive devastation inflicted on investors during the period, where over $8 trillion in market value was erased in only 32 months from peak to trough. The biggest bear since the Great Depression simply mauled investors who were blindly following the buy-and-hold mantra. Unfortunately, all of those individuals who followed the buy-and-hold strategy watched helplessly as their investments got slaughtered and their egos shattered. How could this have happened?

During 1999 and 2000, the stock market was the hot topic of conversation at the supermarkets, bowling alleys, bars, and hair salons all across America, as the market soared to unprecedented heights. CNBC replaced the "soaps" as the most popular daytime entertainment medium, with its streaming stock quotes, and never-ending procession of bullish market strategists, bullish financial analysts, and bullish CEOs.

Euphoria was in the air and life was great for millions of retirees, regular folk who started investing in the past five years, and especially day traders who were racking up huge gains. But that all came to a screeching halt when the big bear started growling in the first quarter of 2000. The bear then unceremoniously clawed the market over the next three years, to prices not seen for five years.

Investors Are Too Emotional and Overconfident

The stock market is a very difficult place to make money. This is not a new thought. Over the past 100 years the stock market has been punctuated with sharp, uplifting bull markets, followed by swiftly plummeting bear markets. This cycle has happened in the past, and it will happen in the future—for after all, the markets are driven by people. Market cycles repeat themselves, just as history repeats itself. People are people, and where money is at stake they react emotionally, which usually results in bad decision making. Investors have a poor track record of making money in the market.

Numerous surveys have shown that investors buy and sell at the wrong time, and they usually buy and sell the wrong investments at the wrong time. Behavioral researchers have found that the incorrect decisions which investors are prone to make are the result of overconfidence in their investment knowledge, overtrading, lack of diversification, and incorrect forecasting of future events based on recent history. Stock market success requires that investors act independently of the crowd, while using a nonemotional, time-tested, almost mechanical investing approach. If fear and greed are not eliminated from the investing equation, then the results can be catastrophic. Unfortunately, investors will continue to make the same mistakes over and over again. That is the way it is.

Robert Safian in *Money* magazine said: "All across America, millions of people are afraid to open their account statements, afraid to look at their 401(k) balances—afraid to find out what they've lost during this long bear market and where they stand today."[3] That's a pretty sad state of affairs. But it did not have to be that way, if investors would only have had an investment plan that forced them to take profits as stocks kept going up, and they had placed stop-loss orders on their stocks to protect them as prices collapsed. But most investors froze, and did nothing until the market was well off its highs. Then, as the market hit subsequent lows in July and October 2002, investors took their billions of dollars out of equity mutual funds and began investing their money in bonds and money markets. Other investors just gave up and cashed in all their investments, having endured severe emotional and financial pain.

The vast majority of individuals are not very savvy investors, even though many have above-average intelligence and consider themselves above-average investors. They do not have the time, background, or expertise to assess the market at key turning points (for example, whether the bull market is beginning or ending). Moreover, the average investor's performance is typically worse than the appropriate market benchmark or even than the actual performance of his or her mutual funds. This outcome is a result of poor timing on entry and exit points and lack of a coherent, well-researched strategy. Most investors buy and sell on a whim, or they take advice from a friend, or they act based on hearing an "expert" giving his opinion on the market or a particular mutual fund or stock in the media.

All investors need a methodology to know when to buy and when to sell, but few if any investors have even thought about it, let alone have a methodology in place. Unfortunately, investors as a group invest and hope for the best. This approach is no way to build a nest egg for the future; but rather a recipe for financial disaster. You wouldn't leave your garden untended, since you know that weeds would grow and kill your flowers and vegetables. The same logic applies to your investments. Being proactive is better than being nonactive. That is not to say that you should be an active trader or an aggressive investor. It is saying that investing is not a static endeavor. You should watch over your investments, making adjustments as necessary to weed out the dead wood, and replacing them with more fruitful pickings. You are the best gardener for your garden of investments. Don't let the experts tell you otherwise.

Just because you bought stock in good companies doesn't mean that you made a good investment. Even the so-called blue chips have plummeted from their year 2000 highs to much lower levels by January 2003: General Electric hit $180 ($60 split adjusted) and went to $23; AOL Time Warner Inc. hit $95 and went to $11.50; General Motors hit $85 and went to $36; AT&T Corp. hit $100 and went to $19. This type of devastation doesn't have to happen to you, if you become a smarter investor going forward. Surely, by heeding the advice of the Wall Street intelligentsia, you can come out way ahead, right? Wrong! Keep reading the next section.

Market Seers Are an Embarrassing Lot

If you ask five experts where to invest, there will be six answers; the five expert opinions, plus the right one.

Jonathan Clements "Need One Expert Opinion on Investing? Here's Five." The Wall Street Journal, January 4, 2000

Business Week Forecasts

Think about all the stock market experts' market predictions you've read or heard about from 2000 through 2002. A handful of these characters have been let go or changed firms. Even well-known technicians do not have very good track records calling the market top. Let's take a look at the forecasting accuracy of the so-called prophets of Wall Street for the years 2000 through 2003. Consider the results of these seers in predicting the market indices just one year into the future.

Business Week publishes a list of the experts' individual predictions in its year-end issue. The number of prognosticators tracked by the magazine for the years 2000 through 2003 has varied between 38 to 65, with 50 being the average. This list represents a solid cross-section of the well-known market strategists. Some of the well-known names on a number of the yearly lists included Joseph V. Battipaglia, Elaine Garzarelli, Edward Yardeni, Bernie Schaeffer, Edward Kerschner, Lazlo Birinyi, Jr., Hugh Johnson, Philip J. Orlando, and Jeffrey Applegate.

Table 1-1 shows the composite results of all of their forecasts over four years for the Dow Jones Industrial Average (DJIA), the Standard & Poor's 500 (S&P 500), and the Nasdaq Composite Index. The table delineates for each year the high, low, and consensus forecast of all the forecasters for each of the three popular market averages. As you can see, starting with the first forecast for the 2000 stock market made at the end of 1999, the forecasters had a poor record. In fact, in each of the past three years their forecasts have gotten progressively worse. Forecasters, as a group, were simply overly optimistic.

There are always a few bears around, but even the bears did not predict the actual lows of the market in 2002. The most inaccurate predictions were for the Nasdaq, as the actual close compared to the consensus forecast was off by 54 percent in 2000, 84 percent in 2001, and 67 percent in 2002. In conclusion, the "best and the brightest" appeared to be not so bright or right. To be fair, their actual stock picks for their clients could have been quite different, and perhaps closer to the mark. For the sake of their clients, I hope this is so.

TABLE 1-1

Business Week Fearless Forecasts 2000 - 2003

Year	DJIA Forecast	DJIA Close	Percent Diff.	S&P 500 Forecast	S&P 500 Close	Percent Diff.	Nasdaq Comp. Forecast	Nasdaq Comp. Close	Percent Diff.
2000	14000 H			1750 H			5000 H		
	8800 L			1000 L			2000 L		
	12154 C	10788	−12.6%	1556 C	1320	−17.9%	3805 C	2471	−54.0%
2001	13050 H			1650 H			4300 H		
	8000 L			1000 L			1800 L		
	12015 C	10022	−19.9%	1559 C	1148	−35.8%	3583 C	1950	−83.7%
2002	13250 H			1535 H			2626 H		
	7200 L			920 L			1500 L		
	11090 C	8342	−32.9%	1292 C	880	−46.8%	2236 C	1336	−67.4%
2003	11400 H			1250 H			2500 H		
	7600 L			800 L			1065 L		
	9871 C	TBD		1049 C	TBD		1703 C	TBD	

Note: H is high forecast, L is low forecast, and C is for consensus forecast. TBD is to be determined.

Source: *Business Week* "Fearless Forecasts," last issue in December each year 1999–2002. Only the forecasts, not the other comparative statistics were provided by *Business Week*. Issues used were as follows: December 30, 2002, pp. 110–111; December 31, 2001, p. 81; December 25, 2000, p. 75; December 27, 1999. p. 123.

STOCK RETURNS VARY BY DECADE

Stock market returns are not consistent; in fact, they vary all over the map. That fact is what drives investors crazy. They never seem to know if they should be buying or selling. Listening to the advice and predictions of the Wall Street crowd further confuses investors. If investors are fully invested during up trends, they can experience excellent returns. Unfortunately, the down trends can take away a good portion of their gains, if they just follow the buy-and-hold approach. Consider the wide variance in average annual stock market returns during the seven decades since the 1930s, shown in Table 1-2.

The 1950s, the 1980s, and the 1990s produced above-average returns in the neighborhood of 18 percent, while on the flip side the 1930s, 1960s, and 1970s provided less-than-stellar returns, around 6 percent or less. The 1940s provided a return close to the 10.2 percent annual return of stocks between 1926 and 2002. As you can see, the 1995–1999 period was an anomaly, which produced abnormally high returns for those who stayed fully invested during that time period. Since the beginning of 1995, had those same investors

TABLE 1-2

S&P 500 Decade Performance Statistics

Decade	Average Annual Return*
1930s	−0.05 percent
1940s	9.17
1950s	19.35
1960s	7.81
1970s	5.86
1980s	17.55
1990s	18.21
Other periods:	
1995–1999	28.45
2000–2002	−14.59

*Compounded, including capital gains and reinvested dividends.

Data obtained from Ibbotson Associates. Note: Other periods data added by L. Masonson

Source: Taming a Bear Market: Investment Strategies for Turbulent Times, American Century, 2001.

been holding their stocks and mutual funds through October 9, 2002, they would have sustained substantial losses, depending upon their investment portfolio mix. (Remember that many investors had high exposure to the technology sector.)

Stock Returns from 2000 through 2002

The performance of the three major averages in the last three-year bear market was very poor. Table 1-3 shows the widespread devastation from the highs to the lows. For just the year 2000, the Nasdaq Composite Index was down 32 percent, the S&P 500 was down 23 percent, and the DJIA fell 17 percent. To be fully invested in stocks or stock mutual funds during a severe bear market is a frightening experience and one that should be avoided at all costs. Based on what you hear from the so-called experts, there is no way to know when a bear market is coming, or its duration. They keep professing that buy-and-hold is the way to go because in the long run you'll do fine. This ridiculous and costly advice will be tackled head on in the next chapter.

Stock Market Confounds
Most Investors Most of the Time

The stock market confounds most investors most of the time, and it will continue to do so in the future. That is because the markets are driven by investor psychology and perception of events. When good news comes out about a stock, sometimes its price rises, and sometimes its price falls. When the Federal Reserve FOMC (Federal

TABLE 1-3

Three-Year 2000–2002 Bear Market Performance

Index	High	Date	Low	Date	Percent Change
Nasdaq Comp.	5048.62	03/10/2000	1114.11	10/9/2002	−77.9
S&P 500	1527.46	03/24/2000	776.76	10/9/2002	−49.1
DJIA	11722.98	01/14/2000	7286.27	10/9/2002	−37.8

Open Market Committee) cuts interest rates, as it has on over a dozen occasions in the past few years, sometimes the market rises and closes up for the day, and sometimes it falls and closes down for the day. In that respect the market is unpredictable and that confuses investors, as well as the so-called professionals, although they may not admit it.

The market is a discounting mechanism and is always looking ahead, not backward in the rearview mirror. So news, whether good or bad, will impact the market in the short run. But in the long run, growth in corporate earnings and dividends, coupled with a sound economy with low interest rates and low inflation, is what will drive stock prices higher. Uncertainty caused by domestic and global political, economic, and social events will alter the market's course for days, weeks, or months, depending on the severity of the problem perceived. And when least expected by the vast majority of investors and professionals, the market will turn around and make a new bull run, with deceiving dips along the way to shake out the weak hands. And market bottoms usually occur when investor pessimism is at a low point, all the news is bad, and no one wants to own stocks anymore. Perception is what drives markets, not reality. Therefore, the market races ahead while investors are hoarding their cash.

BULL AND BEAR MARKETS

Looking back, individuals participated in a great bull run, if they were fully invested since 1982 or even since the end of 1990, or even since the beginning of 1995. From October 11, 1990 until January 14, 2000, the DJIA rose a cumulative 396 percent. From 1995 through 1999, the S&P 500 Index rose at a 28 percent annual compounded rate. In 1999 alone, the Nasdaq Composite Index jumped an astonishing 85.6 percent. That was its largest yearly increase since the index was created in 1971. Investors should have been extremely cautious in 2000, after such a huge unprecedented run-up, but they were net buyers of stock rather than net sellers right at the market top because of the unabashed euphoria and the bullish "gurus."

Unfortunately, bear markets arrive every three to five years (four years on average), and they can demolish your capital. It can then take years to get back to breakeven, assuming you have the stomach to hold at the bottom. Don't forget that a 50 percent loss in a stock or mutual funds requires a 100 percent gain, just to break even. And in the case of a 75 percent loss, a 300 percent gain is needed to break even. To recover from this magnitude of loss takes years. Most studies have shown that investors buy at market tops and sell at the bottom—just the opposite of what they should be doing. Since investing is ruled by emotions, this situation will always occur. Fear and greed are factors that are at play when humans are involved, and this fact will never change.

Stock Market Performance over 102 Years

How has the stock market performed over the last 102 years? To gain a perspective on the magnitude of bull and bear markets, consider Tables 1-4 and 1-5. This data was provided by the Hays Advisory Group, and it presents all the bull and bear markets in the twentieth century, using the DJIA as the benchmark. Neither the Standard & Poor's 500 nor the Nasdaq Composite Index has historical data that far back in time. Therefore, the DJIA was used to gather data.

Market academicians define a bear market or bull market as a decline or rise of 20 percent, respectively, in a major market index (such as the DJIA, the S&P 500, and the Nasdaq Composite Index). Table 1-4 adheres to this classification, but Table 1-5 has six time frames in which the change in percentage was less than 20 percent. Since Hays provided the data, I did not adjust it.

As Table 1-4 indicates, there have been 27 bull markets from 1900 through 2000, with an average gain of 91.5 percent and an average duration of 28.8 months (2.4 years). The average gain is skewed by the superbullish May 1926–March 1937 time frame, in which the cumulative return was over 459 percent, and the November 1990 through July 1998 time frame, where the return was 300 percent. These few outsized positive returns pumped up the average return during a bull market run to 91.5 percent. Be aware of this fact when comparing bull markets to each other.

Looking at the bear market scenario in Table 1-5 we find that there have been 28 bear markets, with an average drop of –30 percent. The largest drop ever was the –90 percent tumble from September 1929 to July 1932. The next worst was the January 1973 through December 1974 period (and February 1906 through

TABLE 1-4

Over a Century of Bull Markets

Dow Jones Industrials

START		END		LENGTH*	START	END	%CHANGE
SEPT	1900	JUNE	1901	10	54	78	44%
NOV	1903	FEB	1906	27	44	100	127%
NOV	1907	DEC	1909	26	54	100	85%
SEPT	1911	OCT	1912	14	73	94	22%
DEC	1914	NOV	1916	24	54	110	104%
DEC	1917	NOV	1919	24	68	115	69%
AUG	1921	MAR	1923	20	65	105	62%
JUN	1924	FEB	1926	21	90	170	89%
MAY	1926	SEP	1929	41	150	390	160%
JUL	1932	FEB	1934	20	40	110	175%
SEPT	1934	MAR	1937	31	85	190	124%
MAR	1938	SEPT	1939	19	100	160	60%
APR	1942	JUNE	1946	50	95	210	121%
JUN	1949	JAN	1953	43	180	295	64%
SEPT	1953	APR	1956	32	270	510	89%
OCT	1957	JAN	1960	27	410	690	68%
OCT	1960	NOV	1961	14	580	720	24%
JUN	1962	FEB	1966	45	540	1000	85%
OCT	1966	DEC	1968	27	750	975	30%
MAY	1970	JAN	1973	32	550	1050	91%
DEC	1974	SEP	1976	22	570	1025	80%
MAR	1980	APR	1981	13	750	1020	36%
AUG	1982	JAN	1984	18	790	1300	65%
JULY	1984	AUG	1987	37	1100	2750	150%
OCT	1987	AUG	1990	33	1620	3025	87%
NOV	1990	JUL	1998	92	2350	9367	300%
SEP	1998	JAN	2000	16	7400	11750	59%
OCT	2002	?	?	?	7286	?	?

27 Bull Markets
Average Length   28.8
Average Gain   91.5%   * in months

Source: Morning Market Comments, by Don Hays, August 21, 2002. Reprinted with permission of Hays Advisory Group.

TABLE 1-5

Over a Century of Bear Markets

Dow Jones Industrials							
START		**END**		**LENGTH***	**START**	**END**	**%CHANGE**
DEC	1899	SEP	1900	10	75	54	−28%
JUN	1901	NOV	1903	30	78	44	−44%
FEB	1906	NOV	1907	22	100	54	−46%
DEC	1909	SEP	1911	22	100	73	−27%
OCT	1912	JUL	1914	22	94	72	−23%
NOV	1916	DEC	1917	14	110	68	−38%
NOV	1919	AUG	1921	22	94	72	−23%
MAR	1923	JUN	1924	16	105	90	−14%
FEB	1926	MAY	1926	4	170	150	−12%
SEP	1929	JUL	1932	35	390	40	−90%
FEB	1934	SEP	1934	8	110	85	−23%
MAR	1937	MAR	1938	13	190	100	−47%
SEP	1939	APR	1942	31	160	95	−41%
JUN	1946	JUN	1949	37	210	180	−14%
JAN	1953	SEP	1953	9	295	270	−8%
APR	1956	OCT	1957	19	510	410	−20%
JAN	1960	OCT	1960	10	690	580	−16%
NOV	1961	JUN	1962	7	720	540	−25%
FEB	1966	OCT	1966	9	1000	750	−25%
DEC	1968	MAY	1970	18	975	550	−44%
JAN	1973	DEC	1974	24	1050	570	−46%
SEP	1976	MAR	1980	42	1025	750	−27%
APR	1981	AUG	1982	16	1020	790	−23%
JAN	1984	JUL	1984	7	1300	1100	−15%
AUG	1987	OCT	1987	2	2750	1620	−41%
AUG	1990	NOV	1990	4	3025	2350	−22%
JUL	1998	SEP	1998	2	9367	7400	−21%
JAN	2000	OCT	2002	30	11723	7286	−38%

28 Bear Markets
Average Length   17.3
Average Gain   −30.0%   * in months

Source: Morning Market Comments, by Don Hays, August 21, 2002. Reprinted with permission of Hays Advisory Group.

November 1907), with a drop of –46 percent. The most recent bear market, probably ending on October 9, 2002, produced a drop of –38 percent for the DJIA. But the S&P 500 Index fell –49 percent during this time frame and the Nasdaq Composite got clobbered, dropping –78 percent.

The average bear market has lasted 17.3 months. But there have been some catastrophic ones, including the 35-month bear market from September 1929 to July 1932, the 37-month bear market from June 1946 to June 1949, the 42-month bear market from September 1976 to March 1980, and of course the last 32-month bear market from January 2000 through October 2002.

Bear markets drops are much faster than bull market rises. For example, from January 1, 1991, to March 31, 2000, a period of 9.25 years, the S&P 500 rose from 330.22 to 1498.50 points, or a total gain of 1168.28 points resulting in a gain of 353 percent. In stark contrast from the end of June through the end of July 2002, the S&P 500 fell 266 points, or a loss of approximately 23 percent of that entire gain over a period of just two months. That's volatility in a bear market! The third quarter of 2002 produced the worst quarterly results in 15 years, with the major averages down 18 percent or more.

Bear Market Recoveries

Table 1-6 provides data on how long it takes to break even, assuming a buy-and-hold approach with the S&P 500 Index, once a bear market has reached bottom. Also shown is the combined time of the drop and the time to recovery. Unbelievably, it took over 25 years for buy-and-hold investors to break even from the ravages of the Great Depression. (Note, the 25 years does not include a calculation for reinvested dividends, which would have shortened the period.) Do you really want to wait this long just to get your money back, assuming you didn't sell at the bottom and didn't get back in the market? Do you think the average investor was able to take the pain of an 86 percent drop and wait 25 years? I certainly don't.

From 1956 through July 2002, the average bear market lasted 421 days (1.15 years), resulting in an average loss of 30.2 percent. The average recovery period to reach the previous high was about 639 days (1.75 years). Excluding the 2000 bear market, the average bear market lasted 364 days and lost 29.6 percent.

TABLE 1-6

Time to Recoup S&P 500 Bear Market Losses

Year Began	Percent Loss	Duration Years	Recovery Time Years	Combined Time Years
1929	−86	2.75	25.2	27.95
1933	−34	1.7	2.3	4.0
1937	−55	1.0	8.8	9.8
1938	−48	3.4	6.4	9.8
1946	−28	1.8	4.1	5.9
1956	−22	1.2	2.1	3.3
1961	−28	0.5	1.7	2.2
1966	−22	0.7	1.3	2.0
1968	−36	1.5	3.3	4.8
1973	−48	1.75	7.5	9.25
1980	−27	1.75	1.9	3.25
1987	−34	0.33	1.9	2.23
1990	−20	0.25	0.6	0.85
2000	−49	2.6	TBD	TBD

Source: Lim, Paul J., "Staying Afloat" U.S. News & World Report, Sept. 10, 2001.
The data used by USN&WR was obtained from InvesTech Research and B and A Sector Watch.
Note that the recovery time does not take into account dividends. L. Masonson adjusted 2000 data through October 2002 to be up-to-date.

Note that it took more time to recover from every bear market there has ever been than the duration of the actual bear market itself. This last bear market was the third longest in duration since the Great Depression and the worst since 1938. Investors should realize that these long bear markets will occur again in the future, so a strategy to protect principal must be in place in advance to avoid this ravaging of principal.

Percent Gain After Bear Market

The percentage gain after bear markets, can be substantial, as Table 1-7 illustrates. During the 2000–2002 bear market (not shown in the table) there have been at least five large rallies. Rallies have been persistent even during the 1930s bear market. The S&P experienced

TABLE 1-7

Recoveries After Bear Markets
Percent Gain from S&P 500 Low

Bear Market Ended	2 mos. After	6 mos. After	9 mos. After	12 mos. After
June '49	13	23	26	42
October '57	1	10	19	31
June '62	14	21	27	33
October '66	12	22	25	33
May '70	12	23	40	44
October '74	8	31	52	38
August '82	31	44	60	58
December '87	13	19	18	21
October '90	11	28	28	29
October '02	15	11	29	33
Average	13	23	32	36

Source: "Patience Will Be Rewarded," *Standard & Poors' The Outlook*, September 24, 2002.
Note: L. Masonson added data for 2002, since the low hadn't occurred when this article was written. The 15 percent gain is from the October 9, 2002, low through December 9, 2002.

five substantial advances between March 2000 and July 2003, rallying between 22 percent to 29 percent each time. Market timing can provide the tool you need to capture a fair percentage of these gains, as you shall see.

SECULAR BULL AND BEAR MARKETS

Bull and bear markets occur not only over short time frames but also over long time frames. Refer to Table 1-8, which depicts two long-term (secular) bull and two long-term bear markets for the period 1929–1999. This table was prepared by Dennis Tilley, Director of Research, Merriman Capital Management. For the entire 71-year time frame, the S&P 500 Index had an average annual return of 10.6 percent. But it was not all smooth sailing over that period. The secular bull markets from 1942 to 1965 and 1982 to 1999 produced average annual gains of 15.7 percent and 18.5 percent, respectively. But the two secular bear markets from 1929 to 1941 and 1966 to 1981 pro-

TABLE 1-8

Secular Bull and Bear Markets
Stock market returns (in percent)

	1929–1999	1929–1941	1942–1965	1966–1981	1982–1999
Type of Market	Total Period	Secular Bear	Secular Bull	Secular Bear	Secular Bull
Length in Years	71 yrs	13 yrs	24 yrs	16 yrs	18 yrs
Annualized Return of S&P500	10.6	–2.4	15.7	6	18.5
Inflation Index (CPI)	3.3	–0.8	3.1	7	3.3
S&P500 Real Return	7.1	–1.6	12.2	–0.9	14.7

Source: " Will the Bear Market Be With Us for a Long Time?" by Dennis Tilley

Director of Research, Merriman Capital Management. Article written in November 2002.

duced much lower annual average returns of –2.4 percent and 6 percent, respectively. So as you can see, there can be long periods of time when the market is flat or down.

Even in secular bull markets there are cyclical bear markets, where prices rally and falter, rally and falter, but overall no progress or negative progress is made. There are numerous opportunities to make money, assuming you have the ability and willingness to follow the markets and use a tried-and-true market-timing approach that works.

The question to ponder now is whether we have entered another secular bear market that could last 12 to 17 years. No one knows the answer. That is why it is important to have a viable investing approach. Buying and holding in a secular bear market is not a money-making approach. And inflation always eats away at whatever returns you are able to obtain. After inflation, the two previous secular bear markets had negative returns.

Michael Kahn, writing in the December 16, 2002, issue of *Barron's*, says: "Tired of waiting for a clear trend in the stock market? Get used to it. If an emerging pattern continues, the major indexes could be in for 15 years of bouncing around. That's right 15 years. Since World War II, the market has seen an 18-year rally, followed by an 18-year flat period, followed by another 18-year rally—the one ending in 2000. That means we could be about three years into the next 18-year flat spell."[4]

CONCLUSION

The stock market is not a place for amateur investors who think that they can sit back and rake in the profits, year after year with little risk. As you just saw, secular bull markets are followed by secular bear markets. The stock market is a very risky place, where investors need to be on their toes, or their feet will get burned. Long-term financial success in the stock market is difficult to attain, if not impossible, unless investors use a solid investing plan, develop strict entry and exit strategies, and have the psychological makeup to make tough decisions when conditions look the bleakest. buy-and-hold is an anachronism. As you learned in this chapter, bear markets occur often, take considerable time to come back to break even, and can result in significant financial loss and emotional distress. That is why investing in individual stocks or even stock mutual funds at the wrong time can be deadly to your wealth.

ENDNOTES

1. "Half of American Households Own Equities," Investment Company Institute, news release, September 27, 2002.

2. Dennis Jacobe, "Stock Market Decline Has Many Americans Worried," Gallup News Service, August 2, 2002. For more information on surveys, access *www.gallup.com.*

3. Robert Safian, "Taking Charge," *Money*, January 2003.

4. Michael Kahn, "Hold Your Fire, *Barron's*, December 16, 2002, p. 23.

CHAPTER 2

The Buy-and-Hold Myth

It wasn't greed that killed America's retirement savings dream. It was an irrational belief in passive, buy-and-hold investment strategies.

William E. Donoghue

THE BASICS OF BUY-AND-HOLD

Buy-and-hold is simply defined as buying a diversified portfolio of high-quality stocks, and/or a diversified group of mutual funds, and holding them for the long term—typically defined as 10 to 20 years or longer. This investing approach is well entrenched in books on investing, in mutual fund marketing literature, and in the verbiage of financial advisors, academicians, and financial journalists. As you know, it is almost impossible to change the conventional wisdom.

According to the Chicago research firm Ibbotson Associates, based on the S&P 500 Index, from 1926 to 2001, there was a 29 percent probability that that an investor would lose money in the market if he were investing for a one-year time frame. However, if he were to invest for a five-year period, the probability of loss dropped to 10 percent. For a 10-year period it dropped to 3 percent, and for a 15-year period there would be no loss whatsoever.

Translating these three numbers into actual dollar amounts: A $1000 investment in stocks over the 76-year period would have been worth $2,279,000, while a bond investment would have been worth $51,000, and T-bills would have been worth $17,000. Remember now, these results apply only if you held for 76 years!

Moreover, if the investor restricted his investments to large-cap stocks for this 76-year period, then he would have realized a compounded annual return of 10.7 percent, as compared to 5.3 percent for U.S. Treasury bonds, and 3.8 percent for T-bills.

Thus, the argument for buy-and-hold is that a long-term investor makes out well, while those in the market for short periods of time have a higher probability of loss. That is true, but bear markets can significantly reduce investors' capital. Therefore investors need a plan of action to limit those situations and preserve their capital.

From the market peak in January 2000 to its low on October 9, 2002 the mighty bear market has cost investors a whopping $8 trillion in loss in value. If you were a part of the crowd, then you stayed fully invested as you were taught to do by the proponents of the buy-and-hold philosophy, and you suffered your share of those devastating losses. Unfortunately, many investors still hold their demolished portfolios and are hoping to recoup their losses. But from the size of their losses, it seems doubtful they will ever see their money again. Many of the stocks that were purchased for $50 a share and upwards are now selling for under $10 a share.

You would think while investors were getting pummeled during that bear market that they would have the common sense and the fortitude to cut loose from buy-and-hold and bail out. But that is not what a CNN/USA Today/Gallup Poll found in a random poll of 720 investors taken on July 29–31, 2002 (when the market had already dropped by a substantial percentage for the year).

Overall, according to the survey, 63 percent of the respondents felt that buy-and-hold was the best strategy for them, 30 percent felt some other strategy which they did not name was better, and 7 percent had no opinion. As you may recall from the previous chapter, 86 percent of the respondents to the ICI/SIA 2002 survey were buy-and-holders.

Buy-and-hold is not a myth. But the fallacy is that the buy-and-hold strategy can be successfully applied to all of the stocks in your portfolio because, in practice, it only works with selective stocks. All investors should diversify to insulate themselves from the risk of any particular stock going totally sour. So, if you own a portfolio of say, ten stocks, the odds that the buy-and-hold strategy will produce positive results for all of your holdings over a period of time is probably nil. Even a few bad apples with large losses can reduce your overall return to less than you could have earned in an index fund.

So this is where the market makers get you. There are plenty of stocks in the universe for which buy-and-hold has worked well, but that is the short list and those stocks are in the minority. They cite the example of one of these stocks which has the effect of keeping you in the game all the while you are sustaining significant losses on the majority of your holdings. The myth is that if you hold on long enough despite the pain you will ultimately recoup the losses you sustained on the whole shebang. Don't bank on it, because it rarely happens.

Buy-and-Hold Arguments: Pro and Con

99 percent of the Wall Street pros, including newsletter writers, and money managers speak convincingly about the wisdom of the buy-and-hold strategy. There are numerous arguments put forth by high-level Wall Street professionals, and mutual fund executives, as to why buy-and-hold is a superior strategy compared to market timing for investors. But most of their arguments lack sufficient detail or facts to back up their claims. They may refer to one or two academic studies published in financial journals a few years ago to back themselves up. But I have read those studies and I find that the key assumptions made by the authors are not always clearly spelled out by the proponents of buy-and-hold. This leaves the investor with a problem as to the study's methodology, time frame, choice of investment vehicle, and hypothesis being tested. Let's first take some of the more popular buy-and-hold arguments, and then present the flip side to that argument.

Some arguments in favor of buy-and-hold are:

   1. No one can predict what the market will do in the future.
   Therefore, it is best to buy-and-hold good-quality stocks
   and a bevy of diversified mutual funds because good companies will always persevere in the long run.
   2. If you were out of the market and missed the 10 or 20 best
   trading days, then your average annual return would be
   much lower than if had been in the market and fully
   invested on those days under the buy-and-hold approach.
   Therefore, you must be in the market all the time so you
   don't miss the best time periods.
   3. There are no market-timing strategies that work consistently or as well as buy-and-hold over long periods of time.
   4. The famed Peter Lynch, money manager in the hey days of
   the Fidelity Magellan Fund said, "There are no market
   timers in the Forbes 400."
   5. People who need to rely on their savings and need access to
   them in the near future such as those nearing retirement age
   or those needing to finance their children's college education should be mostly out of stocks to ensure that their
   funds will be there when they need them.
   6. According to many academicians, stock prices are a "random walk," and future stock price movements cannot be
   predicted. They also argue the efficient-market hypothesis,
   which is another side of the coin and holds that all the
   information about a stock is baked into its stock price
   instantly; so that no one can consistently beat the market
   over the long term because the stock price has already taken
   it into account.
   7. I've never met a market timer who, over the long term, has
   consistently equaled or beaten the results of buy-and-hold.

   Let's take each one of these arguments and provide the coun-
terargument:

   1. No one can predict what the market will do in the future.
        It is true that no one can predict the market's future
   course. That does not mean that you just give up and keep
   your money invested *100 percent* of the time, when you
   know with *100 percent* certainty that bear markets will occur

and take away a major percentage or all of your profits
every three or four years. Buy and hold is a defeatist atti-
tude that only costs you money and grief. There is no reason to default into this defective strategy when a better one
is available. It is true that a diversified portfolio will cushion
the blow in bear markets, but in bear markets you will still
have losses in the portion invested in equities.

Buy-and-hold has had disastrous returns, even for the
well-known "nifty-fifty" stocks of the 1970s. In the 1970s
the current vogue was to invest in the fifty largest blue
chip growth companies with the expectation that they
would continue to provide investors with substantial
returns on their investments. Those who invested in Xerox
under that theory, saw their investment lose 72 percent of
its market value in the 1973–1974 bear market; and it took
them 24 years to recover their money. From October 1990
until May 1999, Xerox rose 1100 percent, but then dropped
93 percent from May 1999 through December 2000. So an
investor buying $100 worth of Xerox stock in October 1990
saw the value of his stock rise to $1,200 by May 1999, and
then saw it plummet by $1,116 in value ending up with a
loss of $16 over the 10-year period! Polaroid Corporation
lost 90 percent of its value from its peak price, and took 28
years to break even again, and then went into bankruptcy.
Avon Products stock was stagnant for 24 years, and Black
& Decker took 23 years to get back to its peak price. More
currently, Enron peaked at $90 in August 2000 and then
traded at $0.38 by year-end 2002. And hundreds of Internet
stocks and technology stocks lost 90 percent or more of
their value in just three years. Even the stable stocks and
growth stocks suffered substantial damage; witness what
happened in the banking sector, Internet sector, automobile
sector, and chemicals.

To look at the double speak of the mutual managers
you only need to know that equity mutual fund portfolio
turnover was around 15 percent in the 1950s through 1964,
rose to 48 percent in the early 1970s, to 75 percent in 1983,
111 percent in 1987, dropped back to 74 percent in
1993–1994, and rose again to 90 percent in 2000 and 111

percent in June 2002. Clearly, mutual funds managers do not practice buy-and-hold with the funds entrusted to them, but somehow find it appropriate for the individual investments of their clients. I have already stated the reason for this which is that mutual funds cannot stay in business if the fund holders embark on large-scale redemptions from their funds.

By implementing specific marketing-timing strategies, and by using specific sentiment indicators and internal market indicators, an investor can successfully time the market and avoid the major portion of down trends while being fully invested during the major portion of up trends. Chapters 4 and 7 through 11 cover this information in depth. After studying these chapters, you can make your own determination as to whether market timing or buy-and-hold is the preferred course.

2. You will miss the 10 best days.

The argument that you would have had much lower annual returns if you missed the best 10 days, 20 days, 30 days, or whatever, trading days of the year is true. But keep in mind that the 10 best days are not consecutive, but occur periodically throughout the year. Second, the purveyors of that information rarely tell you the other side of the story: that you would have had an even higher annual return if you had missed the 10, 20, or 30 WORST days. And missing the 10 worst days produces a far better overall return for you than missing the 10 best days. For the actual statistics see the section later in this chapter titled "Missing the Best and Worst Days (Months) in the Market."

3. There are no strategies that beat buy-and-hold over the long-run.

Of course there are market-timing strategies that beat buy-and-hold over the long run. But they are not discussed very much in print or on the airwaves because of the vested interest in favor of buy-and-hold. There are five strategies presented in this book (Chapters 7 through 11) that have outperformed buy-and-hold, and there are many more in print (such as in Robert Colby's book, *The Encyclopedia of*

Technical Market Indicators, listed in the bibliography) that do so by wide margins. The ones that I've chosen to present in this book have the advantage of being easy to put in practice, and they are simple strategies that have shown consistent performance over many years.

An illustration of a simple timing strategy that beats buy-and-hold is one that uses a moving average on a price chart with price crossovers above and below the moving average giving the buy and sell signals. The details are covered in Chapter 9. Let's examine investment results during the period from 1929 to 1998. Had you used a 130-day moving average on the S&P 500, and bought that index when the price crossed above that moving average, and sold that index when the price penetrated below that moving average you would have achieved an annual gain of 12.5 percent during that period. Compare that with a return of 10.3 percent for the same period for buy-and-hold with dividends reinvested. Over the 70-year period the significant difference of 2.2 percentage points a year resulted in a huge difference in total return.

4. There are no market timers among the Forbes 400 wealthiest people.

True, there probably are no timers on the Forbes 400 list. But except in some few instances, those people didn't make their vast fortunes through the stock market. They made it by founding fledgling businesses that grew into stellar companies. They have great wealth because they are the major shareholders in their own companies: Malcolm Forbes in Forbes, Bill Gates in Microsoft, and John Templeton in Templeton Funds. These people have to buy and hold or they lose their grip on the companies they own and control. It is interesting to note that when Peter Lynch was running Magellan Fund that his portfolio turnover in some of his best-performing years approached 300 percent—certainly not a buy-and-hold practitioner.

In sum, market timing is not a perfect system for making money, nor is it guaranteed. But over a 10- or 20-year period market timing can produce significant returns

exceeding buy-and-hold with less risk. And if a timer uses
leverage, the results can be outstanding, as you will see
later.

5. You need to be out of the market when you have near-term
   need for funds.

   Advising investors who will need access to their
   money in the near term to exit stocks entirely is question-
   able advice. You only want to be out of the market when a
   bear market begins or is in progress. Imagine if those individuals nearing retirement were totally out of the market at
   such a time. This would have been foolish. To the contrary
   the market is the only place to grow your funds and to keep
   up with inflation. Today, people are living longer, which
   means that they run the risk of consuming their money, if it
   isn't working at maximum capacity which means they must
   keep open the opportunity to achieve capital appreciation
   from their stock and mutual fund investments.

6. Future stock prices cannot be predicted with accuracy

   Yes, you hear the academicians profess the ran-
   dom-walk theory and the "efficient-market hypothesis"
   to bolster their case that no one can consistently outperform the market. If those two hypotheses were true,
   then only the lucky few investors would ever make any
   money in the market. Clearly, there are individuals and
   firms who do beat the buy-and-hold strategy, and with
   less risk. Chapter 12 has a listing of market timers who
   have been top performers as measured by *Timer Digest*
   and other sources. Chapters 7 through 11 provide five
   market-timing strategies that consistently beat buy-
   and-hold.

7. I never met a timer who over the long term has beaten buy
   and hold.

   I would not take at face value the statement of some
   stock market guru who says he has not met a successful
   long-term market timer because there are many of them
   around. If you are really interested in finding successful
   timers with long-term track records, you can subscribe to

Timer Digest or to *The Hulbert Financial Digest*. You could also attend the Society for Asset Allocators and Fund Timers, Inc. (SAAFTI) annual conference, where hundreds of asset allocators and market timers assemble. The contact information for SAAFTI is provided on the last page of the bibliography.

I suspect that those individuals who profess that market timing does not work are either not being totally honest with you or they have not fully tested it for themselves. As I have indicated, market timing is a threat to some people's business models. In most cases, failing to endorse market timing as a viable investment strategy is all about the dollars and cents of the antagonist, and not about the common sense of you the investor, and you can quote me on that!

More Nails in the Buy-and-Hold Casket

You won't see the title of this chapter, "The Buy-and-Hold Myth," mentioned very often on financial shows or written about in the financial press. That is because the buy-and-hold mantra has been pummeled into investors' psyches by the top Wall Street pros for decades. If the stock market rose 80 percent of the time, with corrections of 5 to 10 percent along the way, then perhaps the buy-and-hold strategy would make sense. But I will let the record speak for itself as you shall see later on.

Many individuals believe that time is on their side and no matter what happens in the short run, they will come out of it okay in the long run. Meanwhile, what do you in the short run is very important to your long-term performance. During 2002, there were numerous stories of individual investors whose portfolios dropped by 50 percent or more, and they had to go back to work or postpone their retirements. According to James Stack, editor of *InvesTech Market Analyst Newsletter* (October 1994): "The closer an investor is to retirement or needing his capital, the more dangerous a buy-and-hold strategy becomes."

Diversification through allocation of investments in a portfolio with say 60 percent stocks, and 40 percent bonds, can help reduce market risk. Overall you have less risk than the investor who is fully invested in stocks.

But the optimum scenario is to be 100 percent in stocks in bull markets to capture the highest returns for your portfolio. And to be 100 percent in cash or cash equivalents (or to be short the market) during bear markets. By watering down your portfolio with bonds, you are denying yourself the incremental profits from stocks. If bear markets are inevitable, then prepare for them, and sell your stocks and mutual funds before the bear takes hold. Consider using market timing to help you achieve that goal. That is what the heart of this book is all about—providing simple strategies to keep you on the right side of the market.

I want to emphasize here that this book and market timing are not about stock selection. The key to market timing is knowing when to enter the market and when to exit. All stocks are bad unless they go up in prices. The best stocks lose money in bear markets. At least 80 percent of stocks decline in a bear market. The art of the game is to be in the market at the right times, and to be out of the market at the right times. Picking the right stock is only secondary to this overriding principle, because a rising tide will lift all stocks and a falling tide will lower all stocks regardless of the stock you may happen to own at the time.

What leads to people's downfall in following a timing approach is, like most other things with the stock market, execution. When it is time to exit you may rationalize to yourself that this time will be different. This year the decline in the market will not happen because of certain factors, etc. Therefore, I will stay put despite the historical record and the readings of the indicators. Or, you may say that even if the market should fall, the story behind the stock is so compelling that it cannot possibly decline. This is a gambler's approach, not an investor's approach. The odds are heavily against you and you are bucking the odds. Far better to forego the profits you anticipate from that stock than for it to disappoint you and fall under the weight of the bear market. Preservation of capital is the ultimate consideration, and well worth the cost of foregone profits.

Look at Table 2-1, which provides a comparison of specific percentage allocations of stocks and bonds with their resultant risk and returns. Being 100 percent invested over the 76-year period from 1926 through 2002, each rolling 12-month period produced an average return of 13 percent with a risk of 22 percent (risk is the variability in return over the 76-year 12-month rolling periods. In this example with a return of 13 percent, the risk of 22 percent

TABLE 2-1

Percentage Mix of Stocks and Bonds
12-month rolling periods: January 1926–September 2002

Stocks/Bond Ratio	Return	Risk
100% stocks	13%	22%
90% /10%	12.20%	20%
80%/20%	11.50%	18%
70%/30%	10.90%	16%
60%/40%	10%	14%
50%/50%	9.20%	12.50%
40%/60%	8.50%	11%
30%/70%	7.90%	10%
20%/80%	7%	9.10%
10%/90%	6.50%	8.70%
100% bonds	5.80%	9%

Source: "Asset Allocation: Tips for Tending to Your Portfolio Mix," *Of Mutual Interest*, INVESCO, fall 2002. p. 5.

means that the return fluctuates between a high of 35 percent to a low of −9 percent.). A 60–40 percent split between stocks and bonds reduced the return to 10 percent from 13 percent, with risk falling from 22 percent to 14 percent. And at the other extreme, if you were all in bonds, your appreciation suffered greatly with a 5.8 percent return, and a 9 percent risk factor.

As expected, the higher the return, the higher the risk. What if I told you that you could obtain the returns of buy-and-hold (being 100 percent invested), but with half the risk. It is really simple. All you have to do is to use the "best six months" strategy, as explained in Chapter 7. You will see that you can beat buy-and-hold and be out of the market for six months in a money market account. That means that you are getting a better risk-adjusted return for your money. The sweetener is that you are accruing interest in a money market account while almost everyone else's portfolio is sinking in value.

Risk Needs to Be Taken into Account

Investors usually do not consider the risk of investing until they've lost a big chunk of their money. Unfortunately, investors are fixated on how much money they are going to make in the market, not on "how do I protect my capital from eroding." Investors may not understand that all investments are risky. The alternative is to invest in the U.S. Treasury bill, which is the safest investment there is, but the yield is pitiful compared to stocks or equity mutual funds over long time frames. Usually the more risky the investment, the greater the return. However, in a down market, the added risk results in worse-than-average returns.

Every investor has to decide, before investing in any investment vehicle, what level of risk he or she is comfortable with. For example, can an investor withstand a drop of 20 percent in his equity portfolio in a 4-week or a 52-week time frame without feeling upset and concerned? If this level of risk is unacceptable, then the investor should consider a diversified equity portfolio of index funds composed of growth and value, domestic and international, small cap and large cap. Diversification is necessary to limit the downside risk. To further reduce risk, a certain percentage of bond index funds should be included, since bond funds typically rise when stock funds decline, so there is a counterbalance.

Market timing can be successfully used with a diversified index fund portfolio to lower the risk of buy-and-hold even further. So on a risk-adjusted basis, market timing used with a diversified portfolio should be able to equal or beat buy-and-hold without a problem.

Buy-and-Hold Is Risky

Investors must understand that buy-and-hold is a very risky strategy compared to market timing. Buy-and-hold exposes investors to every twist and turn in the market, and big drops in the market can devastate the value of their portfolios. Market timing may underperform buy-and-hold in bull markets but should outperform it in bear markets. Investors who dismiss market timing as a viable investing strategy are therefore doing themselves a major disservice.

This last bear market is just one example of many over the last 100 years, where buying and holding stocks or stock mutual funds was not a wise, rational, or money-protecting strategy. Actually, it was financial suicide. Don't forget that there is something called the "opportunity cost" of money. It relates to the income foregone because an opportunity to earn income was not pursued. If you are not earning interest or capital gains on your money, then you are losing out. If you were 100 percent invested in stocks for the past three years, and you lost 50 percent of your money, then you sure got whacked. Had you sold in early 2000 instead of staying fully invested, and put your money into a money fund earning an average of 3 percent per year over the past three years, you would have been way ahead. By being fully invested you gave up the opportunity to earn an average of 3 percent a year. So in this case you lost 50 percent of your money when you could have earned 9 percent (3 percent over three years, not including compounding), so your opportunity cost was 59 percent.

Market timing is a strategy that can do that. Keep in mind the sage advice of Dan Sullivan, the editor of the *The Chartist Mutual Fund* newsletter:

> Without a set of clear and concise rules to direct them, investors do not stand much of a chance. The investor without a feasible and simple plan will almost assuredly do things which are self-defeating. A disciplined approach to the market will protect us from making decisions based solely on emotion. The inexperienced investor falls prey to the demanding pressures exerted by investing one's own money. They will jump from one investment to another, hold a losing position too long or cut a winning position too soon. They will become greedy, or impatient, or after a few set-backs they become disheartened and throw in the towel.

MISSING THE BEST AND WORST DAYS (MONTHS) IN THE MARKET

Numerous articles refer to the meager investment performance realized by the hypothetical investor who was unlucky enough to miss the best days or months in the stock market. The argument goes like this: Unless you are invested all the time using a buy-and-hold approach, you have no way of knowing when the market's best days or months will occur. Since these big up moves do not occur that often, an investor must be fully invested to take advantage of them. Unfortunately, this scenario is only half the story.

The other half of the story should be told. And that is the very positive impact of missing the worst days or months in the market.

This highly important information is rarely mentioned in the financial press. For as I have said, the whole discussion of missing the best days is contrived for the benefit of the buy-and-holder argument.

Research on Missing the Best and Worst Time Periods

Interestingly, in 1994, Towneley Capital Management, Inc., commissioned a study conducted by Professor H. Nejat Seyhun, Ph.D, at the University of Michigan School of Business Administration to research the effect of daily and monthly market swings on a portfolio's performance, for two time periods: 1926–1993 and 1963–1993. The study analyzed the best and worst days' and months' performance.

The title of his research document was "Stock Market Extremes and Portfolio Performance." The full study can be accessed at the firm's Web site: *www.towneley.com*. A few of the critical findings of the study were as follows:

- From 1926 through 1993, a capitalization-weighted index of U.S. stocks [NYSE for the entire period, ASE (American Stock Exchange) from July 1962, and Nasdaq from December 1972] gained an average of 12.02 percent annually (buy-and-hold). An initial investment of $1.00 in 1926 would have earned a cumulative $637.30.
- From 1926 through 1993, missing the 48 BEST months, or only 5.9 percent of all months, decreased the annual return to 2.86 percent from 12.02 percent, and the cumulative gain amounted to only $1.60.
- From 1926 through 1993, eliminating the 48 WORST months, or only 5.9 percent of all months, increased the annual return to 23.0 percent and the cumulative gain swelled to a total to $270,592.80.
- From 1963 through 1993, missing the best 1.2 percent of all trading days, resulted in missing out on 95 percent of the market's gains.
- From 1963 through 1993, missing the 10 best days lowered the annual return to 10.17 percent compared to 11.83 percent for buy-and-hold. But missing the worst 10 days improved the annual return to 14.06 percent.

♦ From 1963 through 1993, missing the 90 best days lowered the annual return to 3.28 percent compared to 11.83 percent for buy-and-hold. But missing the worst 90 days improved the annual return to 23.0 percent.

♦ The study clearly shows that "the returns from trying and failing to be an outstanding market timer are highly likely to be less than simply owning Treasury bills."

Will Hepburn of Cambridge Investment Research conducted additional research on the "best and worst" days. According to The Society of Asset Allocators and Fund Timers (SAAFTI), Hepburn analyzed the best and worst days data from April 1, 1984, through December 31, 2001 (see Table 2-2). During that time frame the S&P 500 Index gained an annual average 10.35 percent. Clearly, that analysis also indicates that missing the worst days is preferable to missing the best days as far as improving overall annual returns are concerned. Interestingly, missing the worst and best days still beats buy-and-hold by 3 percentage points a year.

On November 5, 2001, *Barron's* published an article titled "The Truth About Timing" by Jacqueline Doherty, which is based on a study of the five best and worst days by Birinyi Associates. The investment research firm evaluated the performance of the S&P 500 Index from 1966 through October 29, 2001, on an annual return basis each year (buy-and-hold), compared to missing the five best and worst days each year. A $1 investment at the beginning of the

TABLE 2-2

Missing the Best and Worst Days
April 1, 1984, through December 31, 2001

Number of Days	Miss Best Days	Miss Worst Days	Miss Best and Worst Days
10	8.24%	16.55%	13.25%
20	6.09%	19.12%	13.49%
30	4.30%	21.21%	13.53%
40	2.69%	23.15%	13.57%

Source: SAAFTI

period held until the end of the period was worth $11.71 (a 1071 percent gain). But missing just the five best days each year resulted in an astonishing ending value of $0.15 (an 85 percent loss), compared to a mind-boggling $987.12 (a 98,612 percent rise) by missing the worst five days each year.

This study puts another notch in the casket of the argument that missing the best days is more important than missing the worst days. It's amazing that 5 days out of 250 in the trading year, or 2 percent of the trading days a year, can have such a dramatic impact on the annual and compounded performance of investing. That is another reason why an investor should try to minimize his time in the market so that bad things do not happen to good people.

CONCLUSION

While watching CNBC on December 16, 2002, I saw an interview with Vern Hayden, Certified Financial Planner at Hayden Financial Group. when he said that buy-and-hold was no longer a viable strategy. He suggested that investors diversify their holdings and do their own asset allocation. I was encouraged to hear a financial advisor say this on the air. One can hope that he will not be the only voice of sanity on the airwaves in the future.

Buy-and-hold is a great strategy during long-term (secular) bull markets, but it is a very poor strategy during the secular bear markets, where loss of principal can be extensive while inflation eats away at what's left.

Since history shows that bear markets follow bull markets, then it is smart to sell at the end of the bull market, and put your money into money funds or other safe investment vehicles until the bear market is over. Alternatively you may wish to short the market by shorting with exchange-traded funds or by using inverse funds from a fund family like Rydex Funds.

If investors were to sit down and really think about the frequency of bull and bear market cycles, then they would realize that their inaction (for example, adopting a buy-and-hold strategy) is not an intelligent move. Therefore, the only other choice is to have a solid time-tested action plan for investing in the market. Market-timing strategies fit the bill, as will be made clear in future chapters.

CHAPTER 3

Market Timing: What You Need to Know

An investor needs to do very few things right as long as he or she avoids big mistakes.

Warren Buffett

[Learn] how to make money in bear markets, bull markets, and chicken markets.

Conrad W. Thomas

If you were to mention the words *market timing* in an innocuous discussion with your broker or financial advisor, you shouldn't be surprised to see the conversation go downhill from there. Consider that probably 99 percent of the Wall Street professionals will tell you outright that market timing does not work, period. If you were to ask these people why they feel that way, they might cite a few academic studies performed a few years ago, that have brought them to that conclusion. (The bibliography contains a number of more recent academic studies that show that market timing has value.) Or they might cite statistics from Ibottson Associates showing that over every 20-year rolling time period, the market has never gone down, as indicated in the previous chapter. Keep in mind what Aaron Levenstein said: "Statistics are like bikinis. What they reveal is suggestive, but what they conceal is vital." Even if that were true, you can't wait for five years or more to finally see your money come back from bear market lows. Long-term results cannot help you invest for the here and now, which is when you need to see your money grow.

WHAT IS MARKET TIMING?

In general, market timing is a strategy that endeavors to be fully invested in the market when it is advancing and to be all in cash or to be short when the market is declining. And that is what is different about market timing, compared to buy-and-hold. Of course, this definition applies to investing in any investment vehicle whether it be individual stocks, mutual funds, options, futures, gold or bonds. But most individuals and professional market timers use mutual funds and/or exchange-traded funds as their timing vehicle. (There will be more about these funds in Chapters 5 and 6.) Since the stock market has widely outperformed other investment assets—bonds, gold, and cash—over the long term, market timers normally concentrate on the price movements of stocks rather than any other investment choices.

Unfortunately, bear markets intercede every three or four years and cause investors to experience portfolio deterioration. An analysis of the DJIA from 1885 through 1993 found that bear markets consumed 32 percent of the time of your investment, getting back to breakeven took another 44 percent of the time, and only 24 percent of the time was spent in net bull territory.[1] That's the problem with buy-and-hold—long periods of negative or zero returns. And we haven't even factored in the opportunity cost of funds or the ravages of inflation.

The three main objectives of market timing are:

First and foremost, to preserve your capital

Second, to absolutely evade and avoid large market downturns, and

Third, to equal or exceed the performance of a buy-and-hold portfolio on a risk-adjusted basis.

The whole concept is dependent upon limiting the risk when the market begins to decline by going into cash or going short the market. Picture this. If you were in a leaking boat you'd have three choices:

1. Stay in the boat and stop the leak = Go short.

2. Get out of the boat = Switch to cash.

3. Go down with the ship = Buy-and-hold.

Do I have to ask you which is the worst choice? It's really easy to understand. What's not so easy is to execute. But we'll get to that later on in the book.

A buy-and-hold approach in equities exposes 100 percent of the invested dollars to market risk. If an investor purchases a mutual fund for $50 a share, uses a buy-and-hold strategy, and then watches as the share price fall to $5 over a three-year time frame, the investor has lost 90 percent of his or her money. A market timingapproach would have gotten the investor out of the mutual fund at a much higher price and placed his proceeds of the sale in a money market or T-bill during the downdraft. Thus the risk is reduced, because the time he was invested in the mutual fund is reduced. That is what timing is all about—reducing your risk.

CLASSIC MARKET TIMERS

There are two types of professional market timers: the classic market timers and the dynamic asset allocators. Classic market timers usually invest in mutual funds when they are invested in the market, and they move their money into a money market fund or T-bills when they are not invested in the market. A classic timer may decide to go from a cash position to a 100 percent invested position or possibly to a 25 percent invested position, in 25 percent increments, until fully invested, based upon a particular timing strategy. And he may decide to exit the same way, by selling 25 percent of the investment, in 25 percent increments. Also, some classic timers may go short instead of going into cash, to take full advantage of a market decline. Those timers who go short the market may also use leveraged funds such as Rydex Titan 500 and Rydex Tempest 500 to go 200 percent (because of the leverage) long the S&P 500 or 200 percent short the S&P 500, respectively. Or they may use unleveraged funds (such as Rydex OTC Fund and Rydex Arktos) to go long the Nasdaq 100 Index or to go short the Nasdaq 100 Index, respectively.

DYNAMIC ASSET ALLOCATORS

Dynamic asset allocators, unlike classic market timers, are always 100 percent invested in some asset class, but they spread their investments among stocks, bonds, gold, and cash in varying percentages. They either invest directly in those instruments or they use index funds, sector funds, leveraged funds, or exchange-traded funds that represent those asset classes. For those investors who prefer to always be invested with wide diversification, the asset allocation approach fits the bill nicely. And typically the overall risk of the portfolio is less than investing in one specific investment vehicle such as equities. For more information on mutual fund asset allocation, go to www.fundadvice.com and look for the "The Ultimate Buy-and-Hold Strategy."

TIMING METHODS AND BENCHMARKS

Numerous methods are available to time the market. Each professional market timer has developed a strategy based on technical indicators, price, volume, sentiment, or other variables to develop her or his timing models. Some professional timers disclose their model logic to their clients, while many others keep it proprietary. Some market timers use very simple market timing models (for example, the 100-day moving average) while others may use multiple models composed of technical indicators. The only thing that really matters is how well the market timing strategy performs against an appropriate benchmark, and the portfolio risk, as measured by the standard deviation (volatility from the average price) or ulcer index (that is, the measure of pain). If a timer is investing in the Nasdaq 100 (QQQ) listed on the Nasdaq, then the appropriate benchmark is how well the timer did compared to buying and holding of the Nasdaq 100 Index. The QQQs are composed of the top nonfinancial Nasdaq companies and trade on the AMEX. Likewise, investing in the Diamonds (DIA) listed on the AMEX (Diamonds are a composite of the 30 Dow Jones Industrials) requires a comparison with the performance of the DJIA, including dividends reinvested (called *total return* compared to nominal return – no dividends included).

The appropriate benchmark for dynamic asset allocators is more complicated than that for classic timers, since those timers may invest in multiple asset classes. In that situation, the benchmark should be a weighted average of individual benchmarks based on the asset allocation of the portfolio. For example, a portfolio composed of 25 percent equity large cap mutual funds, 25 percent intermediate bond funds, and 50 percent gold funds would use three different benchmarks appropriately weighted to provide the composite benchmark.

PERSONALITY CHARACTERISTICS OF SUCCESSFUL MARKET TIMERS

It's time to get a grip on your investment approach and reform it so that you don't have to experience fear and greed over the inevitable and numerous market roller coaster rides. Market timing can help you in developing a rational, time-tested, less risky investment methodology that will allow you to sleep at night and not worry about what tomorrow's news will bring. Is market timing perfect? Are you perfect? Of course not. No one in the market is perfect. But by putting the odds in your favor you can greatly enhance your returns and minimize your losses. In the end you will have more money in your pocket and be more savvy than 98 percent of all investors who ignore reality and ride the emotional roller coaster day in and day out.

Market timing, using the indicators and strategies detailed in this book, can work for you, only if you possess specific personality traits. If you are an impatient person, cannot stand to lose any money, expect perfection with regard to your timing system, or are always looking to change the way you invest, then self-directed market timing will not work for you. The following are the personality traits required to have a solid chance at being a successful self-directed market timer:

- **Patience, determination, perseverance, and discipline.**
  Timing the market requires patience. You cannot decide to accept some of the timing signals and ignore others, since you never know in advance which signals will lead to the most profitable trades. You must be able to sit tight and obey the timing signals after they are given, even though the market may go against you initially. You must have discipline to

follow your timing rules and you must be determined to let your timing system have sufficient time to work its wonders. Those timers that preserve are the ones that survive.

- **Self-confidence.** If you believe in the market timing approach that you've selected, and you're able to feel comfortable using that method, then you are better able to stay the course. Having a strong self image and having your ego under control are critically important characteristics that lend themselves to a successful market timing outcome.

- **Independent thinking.** You must be able to think for yourself and not be swayed by your friends, coworkers, or by popular opinion. You need to turn a deaf ear to all that noise and concentrate on your selected investment approach.

- **A realistic outlook.** Your market timing system will not equal the performance of the buy-and-hold strategy every year, especially during multiyear bull runs. That is why you need to give your timing strategy years to work. Using it for six months and then chucking it out the window is not the way to use a strategy. Moreover, you may feel concerned that only 40 to 50 percent of your trades are profitable. That's not a problem as long as the profits on your winning trades exceed the losses on your losing trading by at least a factor of 2 to 1. Moreover, you may experience runs of three to four losses in a row, and once in a while you may have 14 losses out of 15 trades. This outcome can happen, but, it is hoped, not often. As you will see with one of the timing techniques mentioned in Chapter 10 using the Value Line 4% strategy, such an unlucky streak did occur in the year 2000. Overall, market timing will minimize your loss of principal in bear markets. That's where market timing shines, and that's why you must realize that your strategy overall will beat or equal buy-and-hold with less risk.

- **Quick decision-making capability.** You must remain resolved to execute the signals given to you by your market timing system. That means you need to act on every buy-and-sell signal with your investment vehicle (for example, a sector fund, index fund, or exchange-traded fund) the day the signal is given. At the very latest, you need to act by the next day, if you cannot watch the market and anticipate the signal when it is close to triggering. If you question every signal because of emotional reasons or extraneous outside influences (say, CNBC commentary), then you will not achieve satisfactory returns. If you rationalize your decision not to honor your signals or say this time will be different, then you have compromised the timing system and you can expect that it won't work for you.

- **Emotional stability.** If you are bothered by little things, are emotional about everything, hate to be wrong, and waver in dealings with people and events, then market timing will not suit your personality. A calm, self-controlled, emotionally stable personality is what you need for market timing to succeed. You cannot let your emotions enter the investing equation, otherwise you will negate the benefit of using a nonemotional, mechanical trading system.

SIX KEY POINTS ABOUT MARKET TIMING

You should understand the following six points about market timing:

1. **Market timing has nothing to do with forecasting the market's future direction.** Samuel Goldwyn once said, "Never make forecasts, especially about the future." What you are trying to accomplish with market-timing is to equal or exceed the buy-and-hold strategy's returns with less risk, while protecting your principal from erosion, above all else. Just because you received a market-timing buy or sell signal does not mean that the market will continue in that direction for an extended period of time. Nor does it mean that the signal will be a successful one all of the time. Market timing has to do with putting the odds in your favor over multiple bull and bear market cycles. Overall you will have satisfactory or better results without having to guess where the market is going. Your signals will tell you when to buy and when to sell. That's all you need to know. Don't listen to investment gurus, the vast majority of whom have been completely wrong in their calls on the market. Just look at the December 30, 2002 *Barron's* article. Ten well-known

market strategists from leading firms were interviewed and asked for their market predictions for the upcoming year. Nine out of ten predicted a rising market. And only one predicted a drop, but he was off by 75 S&P 500 points. He predicted a close of 950 on the S&P 500, but it actually closed at 875.[2]

2. **Market timing assumes that stock prices are not random and that the stock market is not efficient.** These anomalies allow market timers to take advantage of trends in the market. Of course, academicians have written extensively about the random nature of stock prices and the efficient market hypothesis. But in the practical world of professional investment management, academic theories are just that; academic theories which cannot usually be substantiated by what goes on in actual practice.

3. **Market timing should be a mechanical, emotionless approach to investing.** Therefore, once you've decided to use a specific strategy that fits your specific temperament, take *all* the signals and monitor your performance. Once a signal is given, take it and then get ready for the next one. If the last trade was a loss, so be it. Cut your losses short and let your profits run. Small losses are good. But large losses are the killers. Ask anyone who stood pat with their investments from early 2000 through October 2002 how they would rate their investment skills. The answers would not be printable! Unfortunately, most investors don't know when to sell, don't cut their losses short, and don't use a target price. An investor needs to set a fixed exit price (for example, a fixed percent, such as 10 percent below his purchase price) to limit his losses and he needs to honor it impeccably in the same way he honors his father and mother. Investors who don't use stop-loss orders to limit their losses, and investors who are more worried about paying taxes on their gains than protecting their principal are asking for trouble and sooner rather than later, they will find it. These shortcomings are mostly psychological in nature, since taking a loss is basically admitting to yourself that your judgment was wrong and that you failed as

an investor. Another common problem is that everyone is looking to get back to breakeven after a loss. If you bought Lucent at 70 and you still held on to it when it dropped by 99 percent, then you have emotional problems that you have to overcome. No market timing strategy is going to help you unless you rid yourself of your psychological baggage.

4. **With market timing you probably will underperform in a sustained bull market.** This outcome is to be expected, if the strategy you select has periodic sell signals in an uptrending market. But with market timing you will hit the gravy train in bear markets. I will be provide you with an example of the performance of actual market timers in Chapter 12, which show that the majority exceeded buy-and-hold in the latest bear market.

5. **Market timing provides the buy and sell signals to tell you when to go long and when to go short the market.** You should understand that going short the market is the exact opposite of going long. Either strategy has the same risk, as long as you have the same tight exit rules for each one. With the availability of long and short (called inverse) mutual funds such as the Rydex Funds family, you can easily go long or short the market. You can also use exchange-traded funds called ETFs to go long or short. More is said about these funds in Chapters 5 and 6.

6. **Market timing is not magic, is not 100 percent accurate, and is not for everyone.** The market-timing strategies which will be presented in Chapters 7 through 11 have all worked in the past. They are all based on simple strategies, not complicated mathematical equations with numerous variables. Hopefully, they will continue to work in the future. Be aware that a strategy may provide profitable trades less than 50 percent of the time and still be profitable overall. Market timing requires the critical characteristics mentioned earlier. Many individual investors do not possess them and therefore should not be self-directed market timers. For those individuals, a market timing advisor may be

more appropriate. That subject is fully addressed in Chapter 12.

MARKET TIMERS HAVE SUCCEEDED IN BEATING BUY-AND-HOLD

Some market timers and market timing advisors have beaten buy-and-hold on a risk-adjusted basis for the last 10-year period and during subperiods within it, as Chapter 12 details. In that chapter there is documentation from Select Advisors, and *Timer Digest* on timers who have beaten their benchmark. Table 12-1 indicates the performance of the top timers as measured by *Timer Digest* for the last 10 years and earlier time frames. During the past five-, three-, and one-year periods, at least 10 timers beat the S&P 500 benchmark. However, over 10 years only three did so. Over the last 10 years there were 16 newsletters whose timing calls beat their benchmark.[3]

MoniResearch Newsletter monitors market timing advisors against their benchmarks. Advisors have a limited power of attorney to make buy and sell trades for an investor's account for which they charge a fee. Take a look at Table 12-2 to see advisors who performed over various time periods. Over the last 3-, 2-, and 1-year periods, most advisors beat buy-and-hold. That is how timing is supposed to perform in a bear market.

Select Advisors, also mentioned in Chapter 12, measures advisors' performance, but only has data for the past three years. They found that over the three years ending in 2002, 42 percent of 109 advisors beat their S&P 500 benchmark, 85 percent beat their Nasdaq Composite benchmark and 92 percent beat their Nasdaq 100 benchmark. For the past two years the results for 258 managers are similar at 55 percent, 72 percent, and 86 percent, respectively. And for the year 2002, for 440 managers monitored, the results are 69 percent, 79 percent, and 84 percent winners, respectively.

BEWARE OF THOSE KNOCKING MARKET TIMING

I caution you not to believe anything you hear or read about investing from anyone, unless the statement is proven to you with verifiable facts and figures. Keep in mind the following:

Nobody on Wall Street has a monopoly on truth. Market strategists don't. Money managers and investment newsletter writers don't. Brokers, financial planners and insurance agents don't. Newspaper columnists don't. So treat all financial advice with caution. Look at every investment and every investment strategy with profound skepticism. Think long and hard about every financial myth. If you do that, you will do just fine.

> *Jonathan Clements, 25 Myths You've Got to Avoid If You Want to Manage Your Money Right:The New Rules for Financial Success* (Simon & Schuster, 1999).

Financial con artists have been known to misrepresent the *true statistics* on their performance records. *The Hulbert Financial Digest* provides the annualized return of many investment newsletters, as well as their buy and sell dates, and total risk-adjusted performance. Many advertisements you see on television or in print embellish or distort the truth in a dishonest attempt to gain your business. Don't trust anyone without first checking the claims and promises against the actual performance, the references, and the Better Business Bureau.

MERRILL LYNCH CONSIDERS MARKET TIMING USELESS

Consider the full-page advertisement in the November 10, 1998, issue of The *Wall Street Journal* sponsored by Merrill Lynch. Here is the headline, which takes up one third of the page:

Timing is nothing.

The ad goes on to say: "For as long as there have been markets, investors have tried to time them—to predict the precise moment when a down market turns upward or the legs give out on a bull. Sometimes it's hubris, sometimes it's fear: watching their investments fall, even seasoned investors can lose faith in the markets and, in a moment of panic, sell.

I'll leave it up to you to decide if Merrill Lynch, just recently fined and sanctioned by the regulators, did well by its individual investors since this ad was printed. I think they missed the point that timing *is* everything, especially with regard to investments.

CONCLUSION

Market timing has long been a controversial subject, with strong views expressed on both sides of the argument. After the severe beating buy-and-hold investors have suffered from 2000 to 2002, I believe that there will be more and more individuals and institutional investors using market timing because it reduces risk, protects principal, and *is* a conservative strategy. In contrast, even with diversification, buy-and-hold is a high-risk strategy.

ENDNOTES

1. Jerry C. Wagner, "Why Market Timing Works," *The Journal of Investing*, Summer 1997.

2. Jacqueline Doherty, "How Now, Dow ?" *Barron's*, December 30, 2002, p. 17.

3. Peter Brimelow, "Bulls vs. Chartists in Head On Clash," CBS.MarketWatch, July 8, 2002.

CHAPTER 4

Ten Indicators to Determine the Market's Health

Spend at least as much time researching a stock as you would choosing a refrigerator.

Peter Lynch

I measure what's going on, and I adapt to it. I try to get my ego out of the way. The market is smarter than I am so I bend.

Martin Zweig

Wouldn't it be great to be able to discern the market's current well-being so that you could detect a change in the trend? And wouldn't you like to be able to accomplish this feat yourself without having to rely on the advice of any investment newsletter subscription or talking heads on Wall Street? Well, believe it or not, you can determine when a change in direction will likely occur, if you know what to look for and where to look. The market signals its health to those who know how to read its vital signs. This chapter will help you become a market diagnostician.

To determine the market's current "health," you need to analyze specific data that reveal the market's probable condition. That is why it is necessary to find specific indicators that have a high degree of accuracy over a long time horizon in providing guidance on the market's health and potential future direction. There are hundreds of stock market statistics and indicators that can be used to monitor the stock market's health. But the vast majority of them either fail to provide the information that we are looking for or they do not have a high degree of historical reliability.

WHAT AN INDICATOR NEEDS TO SHOW US

Our objective is, first, to determine whether the market is in a major trend (up or down) or in a "trading range" where the price vacillates back and forth between two price levels, essentially going sideways. Second, we want to know if the market is in an extremely "overbought" or "oversold" condition. An "overbought" market is one in which the market indices are at such a high price level that individual investors and market professionals are exuberantly bullish. This condition can go on for an extended period of time, as indicated by the market's huge run-up from October 1999 through March 2000, and from the lows in March 2003 through the highs in July 2003 (as of this writing). On the other hand, when the market is "oversold," it is at such a low price level that individual investors and market professionals are excessively bearish. This condition can also go on for some time before a change in trend occurs. It is critical for investors to be investing with the major trend and not against it. That is why investors have to stay alert to an impending change in the market's direction.

No one can determine exactly where and when the market will change direction but what you want to look for are indications that the market is at an extremely high or low price level, and I want to emphasize EXTREME, because when that occurs, the market usually reverses in the opposite direction. If we, as investors, can take advantage of that situation, then we are well on our way to investing profitably. That's what this chapter is all about—taking the pulse of the market to determine if it's healthy (bullish) or sickly (bearish). Either condition can be turned to your advantage if you put yourself on the right side of the market's new direction. First, we will focus first on sentiment indicators that measure the psychological framework of investors and professionals alike. Second, we will focus on the internal market indicators that measure the market's strength or weakness

The 10 indicators that we will focus on in this chapter are usually reliable in showing the condition of the market. These indicators should normally be checked weekly. However, during market extremes (e.g., January 2000, September 2001, July and October 2002, March 2003, and July 2003) they should be checked daily so that you can ascertain a better entry/exit point for your investments. In the case of all the indicators in this chapter, it is imperative to wait until the extreme reading for each specific indicator is *reversed* and the indicator begins to change direction. By acting early and not waiting for this important reversal signal, you risk the market continuing to go in its current direction for days, weeks, or months at a time.

SENTIMENT INDICATORS DETERMINE THE CONSENSUS OPINION

Be fearful when others are greedy and greedy only when others are fearful.

Warren Buffett

Sentiment measurements are useful in determining the opinion, not only of the average investor but also of the professional investment advisors and money managers. By watching the latest market calls of these market participants, and investing in the opposite direction (only during market extremes), you can become a more profitable investor. Since the consensus opinion, whether among the average investors or professionals, is usually, but not always, wrong at *extremes*, you can pinpoint the most advantageous and low-risk entry/exit points at which to invest.

Indicator #1: Investors Intelligence Advisory Sentiment Index

In 1963, Investors Intelligence, a well-known investment stock advisory service, was the pioneer in developing the first investor sentiment survey, dubbed the Advisory Sentiment Index. It has a wide following among investment professionals and market timers. The media often refers to it as the Bull/Bear Index. Each Wednesday afternoon, Investor's Intelligence releases the latest statistics on the percentage of bullish advisors and the percentage of bearish advisors among the 135 stock market advisory services that are tracked. The latest data is made available to the public the next morning.

The rationale behind gathering and publishing this bull/bear sentiment data is that advisory services, like investors, are the most bullish at market tops and the most bearish at market bottoms. We want to know this because consensus opinion, even of investment advisors, is usually wrong when the consensus reaches extreme levels. So by tracking what the majority of advisory services are telling their clients with respect to the future direction of the market, one can see when the readings are extreme and glean insight as to whether a change in the direction in the market is likely to occur. The Bull/Bear Index is therefore a contrary sentiment indicator. The weekly Investors Intelligence Advisory Sentiment Index or Bull/Bear Index can be found in various financial newspapers and on the Internet. It is carried in *Barron's* and *Investor's Business Daily.* And on the net by Investors Intelligence at *www.investorsintelligence.com*, by DecisionPoint at *www.decisionpoint.com*, and by Prudential Financial in their weekly Strategy Alert at *www.prudential-yardeni.com.*

The Bull/Bear Index is not perfect, nor does it pinpoint the exact market top or bottom. What I mean by this is that there can be a time lag lasting from a few weeks up to a few months from when the extreme reading occurs until the market reacts and actually reverses its direction. The novice will look at this reading, observe that the trend of the market has not changed and tend to conclude that this was a false signal or that this is an unreliable indicator and never use it again. This is a big mistake because this is an important indicator which tells what will happen, but it does not tell exactly when it will happen. Therefore, it is critically important for the investor to wait for the first sign of the extreme reading reversing direction before taking action. The overall record of the Advisory Sentiment Index is reasonably accurate when extreme readings are reached and reverse direction. According to Investors Intelligence, this index should be used as a confirming indicator than as a leading market indicator.

WHEN HAS THE BULL/BEAR INDEX FLASHED A SIGNAL?

Refer to Figure 4-1 from Prudential Financial to see a chart of the percentage of bullish and bearish advisors. This chart shows the weekly data from January 1994 through early January 2003.

FIGURE 4–1

Investors Intelligence Sentiment Index for Stocks

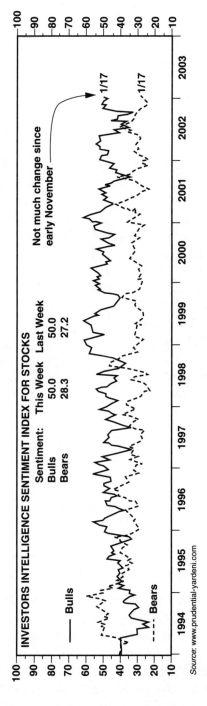

Source: www.prudential-yardeni.com

As you can see in the chart, when a reading of 55 percent or more of advisors are bullish (indicated by the solid line), we are at extreme levels of bullishness and it indicates that the market is probably going to top out soon. At the other end, if only 40 percent or preferably less of these advisors are bullish, then this is usually a bullish sign because the majority of advisors are bearish and this is a contrarian indicator.

Examples of where the Bull/Bear Index worked well with very high bullish readings of 55 percent or more occurred in April 2002, January and February 2001, January and April 2000 (at the market peak), January, February, April, and May 1999, and November and December 1998. Soon after each of these high readings, the major market indexes peaked and the market declined.

In early October 2002, the percentage of bullish advisors dropped to 29 percent, a potential signal of a probable market bottom. This very low reading was the lowest reading since 1994. And the market did rally from the October 9 low through November 27, 2002, with the Nasdaq Composite Index jumping 33.6 percent and the DJIA rising 22.6 percent.

> **KEY POINT**
>
> No indicator including the Bull/Bear Index, should be used alone to make your buy and sell decisions. It should be used as but one component of a group of indicators. When you find that a majority of the indicators line up in a bullish or bearish direction, then that is the time to carefully consider making your move. Remember that an extreme reading on each indicator must first reverse direction before you invest your money.

Indicator #2: Index of Investor Optimism: Another Contrary Sentiment Indicator

The Index of Investor Optimism has only recently been published, but the data goes back for only seven years and measures the opinions of individual investors, as opposed to the Investors Intelligence Advisory Sentiment Index which measures the opinions of the investment advisors. In its short history, when this indicator is at its low and high points it has signaled the market's major turning points very well. Started in October 1996, this survey is conducted monthly by UBS/Gallup. Approximately 1000 different randomly selected investors (with over $10,000 in investments) from across the country are surveyed each month, to assess their level of optimism or pessimism about the stock market.

Figure 4-2 shows the index readings since inception through December 2002.

As you can see, 178 was the highest reading of investor optimism, in January 2000—right at the market top for the DJIA. The previous peak in readings came in April 1999 at 168, again another high point in the market averages. Another high reading was in August 2000 at 160. The baseline reading of the index was 124 in October 1996.

What this index tells us is that investors were the most optimistic about the stock market when prices were at their highest. Is the opposite true, that when the market is at very low points, investor optimism is at a low point? Absolutely!

FIGURE 4-2

Index of Investor Optimism® October 1996–December 2002

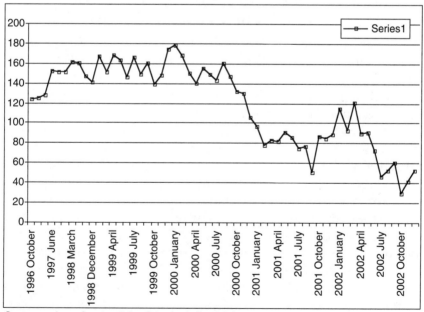

Source: www.ubs.com/investoroptimism. Data printed with permission.

The lowest readings of the Index of Investor Optimism since inception occurred first in July 2002 at 46 and last in October 2002 at 29. (The market hit a major low on October 9, 2002, and the survey was performed between October 1 and 17). Interestingly, July 2002 and October 2002 represented significant low points in the market averages. In September 2001, the reading plummeted to 50 after the 9/11 terrorist attack on the World Trade Center.

As you can surmise, this index should be interpreted as a contrary indicator. When investors are very optimistic as indicated by readings near or above 165—that is the time to consider going into cash, or to shorting the market. And when investors are very pessimistic—readings of 50 or below—that is a good time to consider going long the market. As I said before, this indicator should not be used in isolation to make buy or sell decisions but is to be used in conjunction with the other internal market indicators. In this way you are able to wait for confirmation of the future direction of the market taken from the weight of all of the indicators you are observing.

Indicator #3: The American Association of Individual Investors Survey

The American Association of Individual Investors (AAII) provides another survey of the individual investor taken from a poll of its magazine (*AAII Journal*) subscribers. This AAII data is considered a contrary indicator, since high bullish readings are considered bearish for the market's future direction and very low ones bullish.

Readings above 50 percent and certainly above 60 percent (Figure 4-3) indicate extreme readings of an overbought market. Likewise readings of 30 percent or less are considered low readings, where the market may be due for a bounce up. Remember to wait for a reversal in the extreme reading before investing. Information about the AAII investor sentiment readings are available as part of the subscription to the *AAII Journal*. This indicator is available through *Barron's*, the Hays Advisory Group (*www.haysadvisorygroup*), and DecisionPoint (*www.decisionpoint.com*), and of course from the AAII website (magazine subscribers only) at *www.aaii.com*. Some market analysts use a three- to six-week average of the readings to smooth out the results.

FIGURE 4–3

AAII Bullish Investor Sentiment 3-Week Average

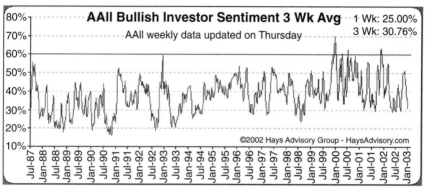

Source: Hays Advisory Group. Reprinted with permission.

Indicator #4: CBOE Options Volatility Index (VIX): The Investor Fear Gauge

Two other sentiment indicators that should be closely monitored when they are at high readings are the VIX (Options Volatility Index) and the VXN. The VIX and the VXN measure the expectations of options traders who buy and sell the options of stocks traded on the NYSE and Nasdaq, respectively. The options themselves are traded on the Chicago Board of Options Exchange (CBOE). According to their Web site *www.cboe.com:*

> VIX and VXN provide investors with up-to-the-minute market estimates of expected volatility by using real-time index option bid/ask quotes. The CBOE VIX and VXN index prices are both designed to reflect the implied volatilities of certain index options contracts; VIX is based on the prices of eight S&P 100 (OEX) index puts and calls, while VXN is based on the prices of Nasdaq 100 (NDX) options prices.

High and Low Readings of VIX

High VIX readings above 49 indicate fear among investors who are purchasing significantly more put options than call options. Put options are bets that the market will fall while call options are bets in anticipation of a market rise. There is a high correlation between VIX readings above 49 and the occurrence of market bottoms. When this indicator is at high readings, and options buyers are scared, that is bullish. So there is a inverse relationship between the extreme reading and its meaning. Again wait for a reversal from 49 or above to below 49 before investing.

But low readings of VIX below 21 do not have the same significance and should not be taken to mean that stock prices will fall. According to *Barron's*,[1] a report by Merrill Lynch's Benjamin Bowler evaluated the predictability of VIX readings on future stock market returns by looking at low VIX readings and how the market performed thereafter. He found that VIX was more reactive than predictive. Larry McMillan, an options expert, said that when VIX is low "the market does not necessarily decline. It does so only about half the time." Other market analysts have a differing view on the significance of the low VIX readings and use these readings with other indicators to time their investments in this case going to cash or shorting the market.

Recent VIX Readings

A chart of the daily close of the VIX is shown in Figure 4-4. When the VIX exceeds 49 and then declines, there is a high probability that the market has seen a bottom as it did on the following dates: October 27, 1987, August 31, 1998, October 5 to 9, 1998, September 1 and 11, 1998, September 21, 2001, July 23 and 24, 2002 (shown in Figure 4-4), and October 10, 2002 (shown in Figure 4-4). The low VIX readings on the chart (for example, below 20 in March and May 2002) do not necessarily indicate that a market top has occurred. Keep in mind, speaking statistically, even having about a dozen readings above 49 since 1987 is not considered to be statistically significant. However, used in conjunction with other indicators such as those mentioned in this chapter, those high readings can be used as an excellent guide as to the market's health.

INTERNAL MARKET INDICATORS

The key to profitable investing is to be on the right side of the market. That is the objective of market-timing strategies. Too many investors

FIGURE 4–4

VIX Index

Source: Hays Advisory Group. Reprinted with permission.

do not pay attention to what the market is saying. Instead, they prefer to read financial and investment magazines, newspapers, and newsletters and watch financial shows which transmit the market hype instead of the objective facts you need. These spin stories are misleading because all the information these investors then receive is just "noise." It has no value to the average person as to what he or she needs to know to be a more informed investor.

Instead, every investor should use a more systematic analytical approach and learn to understand what the market itself is telling them to determine if it is time to buy or sell. This goal can be easily accomplished by "putting your ear to the ground" and "listening" carefully to what the market is telling you. The market speaks loudly and clearly, not softly and surreptitiously. After reading about the internal market indicators in this section, you will come away with solid information to judge whether the market has reached a low or high point. That information alone is very useful in making your investment decision. By combining the internal market indicators with the previously discussed sentiment indicators, you will be on the right side of the market more often than not. So, let's get started.

Indicator #5: 200-Day and 50-Day
Moving Averages (dma)

Moving averages are one of the oldest tools used by investors and professionals to determine the market's underlying trend. Market technicians use various moving averages, but the ones most often used to determine the market's long-term trend are the 50-dma and the 200-dma. (If you need a detailed explanation of how moving averages work, turn to the beginning of Chapter 9 for the definition and calculation before continuing). Figure 9-1 (in Chapter 9), shows a 200-dma (the line that begins in December 1999) and a 50-dma (the lower line) on the S&P 500 index through December 2002. In simple terms, a moving average depicts the average price over a time period (say 200 days) and plots the moving average as a line on a daily price chart of the stock or index being tracked. Each day only the last 200 most current prices are used to calculate today's moving average price.

How is the moving average used? Looking at Figure 9-1, if the price of the S&P 500 index, is above its 200-dma, then the market is considered in an up trend, especially if the moving-average line is slanting upward to the right. That was the case from December 1999 through September 2000.

If the moving-average line is flat, and if the price fluctuates back and forth above and below it, then that depicts a trading range. If the S & P 500 Index is moving in a tight trading range then the moving average line may also be horizontal indicating the sideways movement. That situation did occur briefly in Figure 9-1 during the January 2002 through May 2002 timeframe. In such a case you know that the market is moving sideways and will not move up or down until there is a breakout from the trading range. In this case a breakout would have to exceed 1175 on the upside or or 1050 on the downside.

If the S&P 500 index price is below the 200-dma, and if the moving-average line is slanting downward, then that is a declining trend. That was the case from September 2000 through December 2002—a downtrend of over two years' duration. On rare occasions, prices can fluctuate by as much as 20 to 30 percent above or below the 200-dma. Consider that level to be an extreme reading, and look for the index to most likely reverse in the opposite direction.

The faster-moving 50-dma provides a better and quicker means of gauging the market's direction than the 200-dma, and thus provides earlier signals as to the market's direction. Figure 9-1 also includes the 50-dma, which has a few more jiggles than the 200-dma. There are more crossovers of price with the 50-dma. However, after the S&P's double top in late August 2000, the 50-dma gave a sell signal about two days earlier than did the 200-dma. You would have had extra money in your pocket had you acted on this signal. On other occasions, the 50-dma could provide even more of a warning.

Intelligent investors should not be waiting for any of the market averages (either the DJIA, the S&P 500, or the Nasdaq Composite Index) to penetrate its 200-dma on the downside before deciding to sell their investments. That approach can be financially ruinous, since by the time that reading occurs, their investments could be down 15 to 25 percent from their highs, especially stocks and indexes listed on the Nasdaq. I therefore recommend that you consider selling your equity investments when you see that the Index has penetrated the 50-dma instead, or even perhaps the 20-dma if you are more of an aggressive investor.

Remember, the specific moving averages provide you with a general idea as to the market's trend. Price penetration of the moving averages in either direction by itself does not warrant a buy or sell decision on your investments. Rather, it needs to be used in conjunction with the other indicators mentioned in this chapter. You will find more detailed explanations of moving averages in Chapter 9.

Indicator #6: New York Stock Exchange Bullish Percentage (NYSEBP)

Investor's Intelligence made another significant contribution to measuring market sentiment by developing the NYSE Bullish Percentage (NYSEBP) in the 1950s. The firm uses point-and-figure charts, instead of the more traditional bar charts, to track the NYSEBP percentage changes. Point-and-figure charts are used by the firm to monitor individual stocks, mutual funds, sectors, industries, and ETFs. In addition, those charts are also used to measure a stock's relative strength and other market measurements. A simple point-and-figure chart is provided in Figure 4-5. A point-and-figure chart is composed of columns of x's and o's, corresponding to increasing and decreasing prices, respectively. Neither a security's daily volume nor its prices are shown on the chart. You can find more information about these unique charts from the Websites and books listed in the bibliography.

The NYSEBP is calculated weekly and measures the percentage of NYSE stocks that have bullish point-and-figure charts. This is comparable to looking at regular bar charts that have just formed bullish patterns (e.g., breaking through double and triple tops). Figure 4-5 contains 13 years of data from January 1990 through early January 2003. The numbers in the chart represent the months of the year in each year's data. As you can see, low percentage NYSEBP readings around 24 or below which then turned up turned out to be excellent times to get into the market. The high percentage readings of 70 or over were excellent times to get out of the market, after they turned down from 70. The lowest readings occurred in October 1990, August 1998, and July, August and October 2002. These were all at significant market bottoms.

Conversely, the high readings of the bullish percentage occurred in April 1991, and August, September, and October 1997, March 1998, and April 2002, all at relative market highs.

Interestingly, at the all-time market highs in January 2000 for the DJIA and in March 2000 for the S&P 500 and Nasdaq Composite Index, the NYSEBP was at relatively low percentage bullish readings of 34. We would have expected readings in the 70 range. So realize that no indicator is ever reliable all the time. Remember to wait for extreme NYSEBP readings to reverse direction before investing.

Indicator #7: S&P 500 Bullish Percentage (SP500BP)

The S&P 500 Bullish Percentage (Figure 4-6) is another indicator along the same lines as the NYSEBP, but tracks the number of stocks in that index that have bullish patterns. Extreme low readings under 20 recorded in September 2001, July 2002, and October 2002, followed by a turn up to higher readings turned out to be excellent buying opportunities. Likewise, extreme high readings above 70 in May 2001 and March 2002 followed by a lower reading turned out to be excellent selling opportunities. Even readings above 60 with a turn-down provided good intermediate-term selling opportunities.

This chart also contains two technical indicators, MACD (Moving Average Convergence-Divergence) and RSI (Relative Strength Index), which are well known by technicians and most investors and available online. For complete descriptions of these indicators, see *The Encyclopedia of Technical Market Indicators*, by Robert Colby, which is referenced in the bibliography. You can confirm the bullish percentage moves with the indicators' high and low points.

The MACD is a momentum oscillator and uses two moving averages (usually 26-dma and 12-dma) where the longer moving average is subtracted from the shorter moving average to form a line that moves above and below zero, for the buy and sell signals.

The RSI Relative Strength Index (RSI) is another momentum oscillator that compares upward changes in closing price to downward changes in price over a selected time period, usually 14 days. One way of using this indicator is that when the oscillator moves from below 30 to above 30 on a scale of 1 to 100, that is considered a buy signal, and when it rises above 70 and then declines below 70, that is considered a sell signal.

Indicator #8: Percentage of Stocks above Their 200-Day Moving Average

Figure 4-7 is a chart of the NYSE Composite Index on the upper graph and the percentage of stocks above their 200-dma on the lower graph. The 200-dma is a long-term moving average; stocks tend to stay above or below it for extended periods during bull or bear runs. When the market peaks, you will find that 70 percent or more of all stocks on the NYSE trade above their own 200-dma. These situations occurred in February 2001, May–June 2001, and March–June 2002. When the market bottoms or is oversold you will find that only about 20 percent of all stocks are trading above their 200-dma. These situations occurred in late February 2000, late September 2001 (after the terrorism attack on New York City and Washington DC, late July 2002, and early October 2002.

When the market hit bottom on October 9, 2002, only about 20 percent of stocks were trading above their 200-dma. On November 6, when the market was up (20.4 percent for the DJIA, and 27.4 per-

F I G U R E 4–5

The NYSE Bullish % Indicator represents the percentage of stocks within the NYSE index that are short term bullish. It has signaled key trend changes in the stock market over the years through its application as a "contrary" indicator–a bullish signal is generated on an up-move from below 32% and a bearish signal from a down move from above 70%. The NYSE Bullish % Indicator was developed by Chartcraft's founder AW Cohen in the 1950s and has been widely quoted and replicated since then.

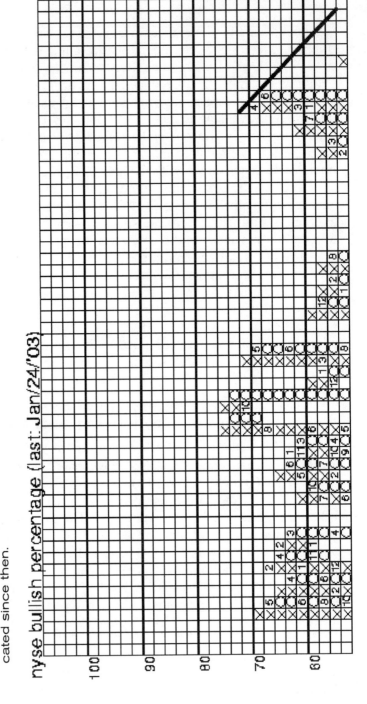

nyse bullish percentage (last: Jan/24/"03)

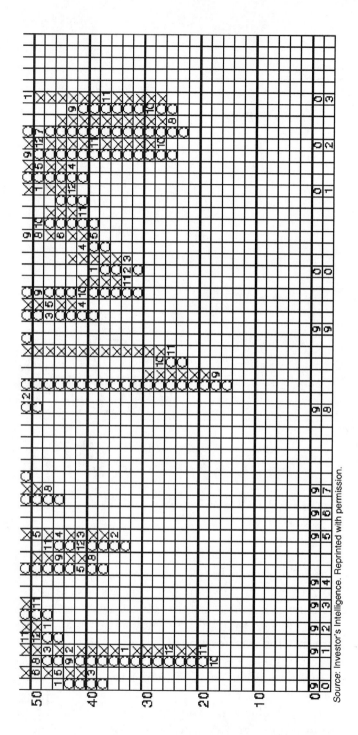

67

FIGURE 4–6

S&P 500 Bullish Percent Index

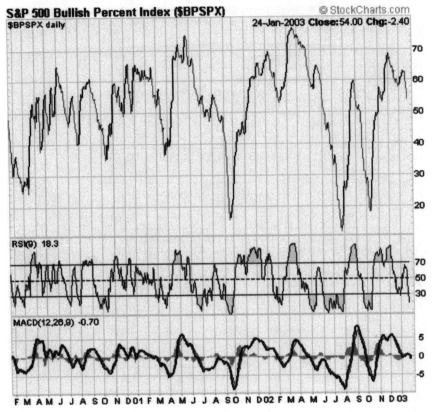

Source: Chart provided courtesy of StockCharts.com

cent for the Nasdaq Composite Index), the percentage of stocks above their 200-dma was only 25 percent. This anemic increase from the 20 percent level meant that most stocks were not really making much progress, even though the rally was quick and substantial off the bottom. This was not a positive sign of strength. The indicator peaked at around 43 percent in the first few days of 2003 but then turned down again to near 30 while the market went down.

This indicator is available on the major market indices to determine overbought and oversold conditions. DecisionPoint, at

FIGURE 4-7

Percent of NYSE Stocks Above Their 200-Day Moving Averages.

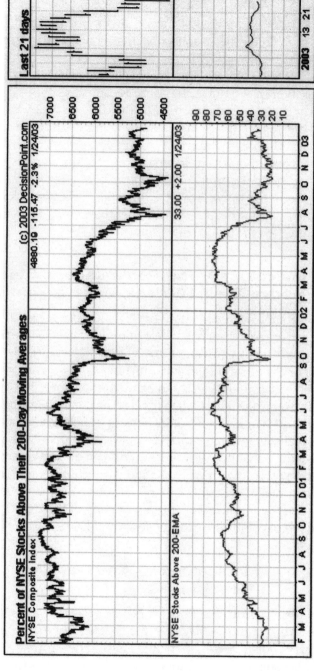

Source: Chart provided courtesy of www.decisionpoint.com.

its website, provides daily charts showing the percentage of stocks above their 200-day exponential moving average (ema), 50-day ema, and 20-day ema for the NYSE Composite Index, S&P 500 Index, DJIA, DJUA, DJTA, Nasdaq 100, and OEX. Exponential moving averages weight the more recent days more heavily than the early days in the average. For details, see Colby's book. Since the 20-day ema and 50-day ema encompass shorter timeframes than the 200-dma, the number of buy and sell signals will be more frequent, and there may be many more false signals given. You won't realize that you received a false signal until after the fact, so it is a good idea to confirm it with other indicators. So, be careful using these time frames. Also, remember to wait for the extreme reading to reverse before investing.

Indicator #9: The Percentage of Stocks above Their 10-Week Moving Average

Figure 4-8 shows the percentage of NYSE stocks above their 10-week moving average (wma) from 1996 to mid-January 2003. The 10-week moving average is equivalent to a 50-dma. When the 10-wma hits 78 percent or higher, and then starts turning down, this represents a signal to consider getting ready to exit long positions, since the market is most likely topping at that time or in the near future. Likewise, when the 10-wma bottoms at 20 percent or below, and begins to turn up get ready to go long, since the market is probably at a low point. Keep in mind that this indicator can remain at high or low points for weeks at a time before finally changing direction. So remember to use it in conjunction with the other indicators. Of the several moving average percent indicators, you can use any of these since they all do a good job of exhibiting extreme lows and highs.

Indicator #10: The Weekly New Highs and New Lows

Barron's often carries the "Weekly New Highs/Lows" of the NYSE in a table format with weekly data going back a few years. Another table they carry shows the week's new highs and new lows. In the October 21, 2002, issue of *Barron's*, there was a table with weekly data from April 14, 2000, through October 11, 2002. By simply scanning the

FIGURE 4-8

NYSE Stocks Above Their 10-week Moving Average.

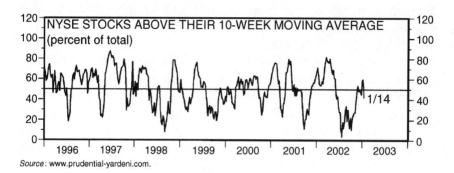

Source: www.prudential-yardeni.com.

columns, it is easy to spot extreme readings. For example, when weekly lows were over 900, as they were in the weeks ending October 11, 2002 (962 new lows), July 26, 2002 (1131), and September 21, 2001 (1035), those were excellent times to go long the market.

On the other hand, when weekly highs hit over 600 as they did in the week ending December 29, 2000 (663), and March 8, 2002 (614) that indicated a potential market high and time to sell or go short. Moreover, when new highs are scarce, the weekly reading of between 60 to 80 portends that the market bottom has probably been reached. This occurred in the weeks ending April 21, 2000 (61 highs), September 14, 2001 (63), July 26, 2002 (60), August 2, 2002 (78), and October 11, 2002 (77) all of which turned out to be excellent buying opportunities.

CONCLUSION

By tracking the 10 market indicators covered in this chapter, you should be able to assess the market's overall health. It is only when extreme readings occur on a majority of the sentiment and internal indicators at the same time, and they reverse their direction, that you can assume that the probability is that the market's direction is about to change. In some cases, it is only a matter of days before the trend changes after a consensus of extreme readings occur. Keep in mind that sometimes it may take a few weeks or a few months before the market actually changes direction. That is why it is important to look at all the indicators to get the overall view of the market. These indicators can be helpful to all investors, whether or not they decide to use the market-timing strategies presented in later chapters. An investor who wants to go long the market or short the market with a basket of stocks or mutual funds should make sure the market's health has been adequately assessed.

For those investors who want to track each of these indicators, I have provided Table 4-1 which is a summary of these indicators with their key numbers for bullish or bearish readings. In addition, the last column is labeled "assigned value." I arbitrarily assigned a –1 to each indicator that was bearish and a +1 to an indicator that was bullish. By tabulating all the indicators, you can get a reading on the market's health. An overall reading of 7 or higher, for example, would indicate that most indicators are now bullish and a –7 would indicate the opposite. Keep in mind that this is just an example of how to tabulate the indicators and not a precise methodology. Remember that being on the right side of a trending market and minimizing your risk are both critical elements in building wealth.

ENDNOTE

1. "The Volatile Truth: A Low VIX Isn't Always a Sell Signal," *Barron's*, March 18, 2002, p. MW15.

TABLE 4-1

Ten Market Indicator Components and Bullish/Bearish Readings

Indicator Component Name	Data Frequency	Originating Source	Data Availability	Key Numbers	Bullish or Bearish	Assigned Value
SENTIMENT INDICATORS						
1. Investor's Intelligence Sentiment Index	Weekly	II*	II, DecisionPoint, IBD, Barron's, etc.	Bullish Advisors 55% bullish 35% bullish	Bearish Bullish	−1 1
2. Index of Investor Optimism	Monthly	UBS/Gallup	www.gallup.com (around 25th of month)	> 165 <=50	Bearish Bullish	−1 1
3. AAII Investor Surveys	Weekly	AAII	AAII, DecisionPoint, Barron's Mkt Lab sect.	Bullish Investors >50% bullish <30% bullish	Bearish Bullish	−1 1

TABLE 4-1

(Continued)

Indicator Component Name	Data Frequency	Originating Source	Data Availability	Key Numbers	Bullish or Bearish	Assigned Value
INTERNAL MARKET INDICATORS						
4. CBOE Volatility Index (VIX)	Daily	www.cboe.com	www.cboe.com, WSJ, Barron's, many charting services on net	>49 <20†	Bullish Bearish	1 −1
5. 50-dma and 200-dma	Daily	Calculated Value	IBD, DecisionPoint, etc.	Price Above both Price Below both	Bullish Bearish	1 −1
6. NYSE Bullish %	Daily	Calculated Value	InvestorsIntelligence.com www.dorseywright.com	<24% >70%	Bullish Bearish	1 −1
7. S&P 500 Bullish %	Daily	Calculated Value	www.stockcharts.com, www.dorseywright.com	>70% <20%	Bearish Bullish	−1 1
8. Percent of NYSE stocks above 200-dma	Daily Weekly	Calculated Value	IBD, DecisionPoint, other sources	>70% <20%	Bearish Bullish	−1 1
9. Percent of NYSE Stocks above 10-wma	Weekly	Calculated Value	prudential-yardeni.com other sources	>80% <20%	Bearish Bullish	−1 1
10. NYSE Weekly New Highs and New Lows	Weekly	NYSE	WSJ, IBD, Barron's, DecisionPoint, Hays Advisory Group, many financial sites such as finance.yahoo.com	>600 new highs <80 new highs	Bearish Bullish	−1 1

* II = Investors Intelligence

† Use only as a confirming indicator, since not as accurate on bearish calls. Refer to discussion of this indicator in this chapter.

CHAPTER 5

Specialized Mutual Funds

Index, Sector, and Leveraged Funds

> Warren Buffett says that indexing is the best approach to the stock market for 99 percent of all investors.
>
> *Lewis Schiff and Douglas Gerlach,* The Armchair Millionaire, *2001, p. 125.*

To successfully pick stocks that make you money is not easy. The odds are heavily stacked against you. Another difficulty is determining exactly when to buy and sell your stocks. Moreover, if your stock portfolio is not diversified, you may be inadvertently exposing yourself to more risk than you intended to take.

Bad news about your stock, its industry group, or even a competitor's stock can result in large down moves, and it can decimate your stock's price by 25 to 50 percent almost overnight. To avoid potential losses that can occur at any time for any reason, the astute investor will steer clear of individual securities entirely. Simply put, the risks are too high with respect to the rewards. If the vast majority of professional money managers with the financial credentials and experience cannot consistently pick a stock portfolio that does better than a comparable benchmark index, then how do you expect to do it?

Instead of investing in individual stocks, consider investing in a portfolio of diversified mutual funds: these could be index funds, sector funds, and exchange-traded funds which represent a wide range of indexes. You should understand each of these investment vehicles, and then you need to decide for yourself which ones you feel comfortable investing in, based upon your risk tolerance. This chapter will cover the basics on index, sector, and leveraged funds, while the next chapter covers exchange-traded funds. If you decide to use any of the market-timing strategiesprovided in Chapters 7 through 11, then your best choice, from a risk-reward standpoint, is to select investment vehicles covered in this chapter and the next one.

INDEX FUNDS

An index fund is a specialized type of mutual fund holding specific stocks that exactly mirror the make up of an existing stock market index. Because of this, the index fund's performance will replicate the performance of the index it is mimicking. In 1971, Wells Fargo Investment Advisors marketed the first index fund to institutional investors. In 1976, John C. Bogle, founder of the Vanguard Group, marketed to retail investors the Vanguard Index 500 Trust, which is composed of stocks in the S&P 500 index. Index funds represent approximately 10 percent of the total U.S. stock market capitalization of all mutual funds. In 2002, of all equity funds inflows, almost 60 percent of new investor money went into index funds.[1] Index funds slightly underperform the index they are copying. This is because, unlike the index itself, the funds incur operating and administration costs which slightly reduces their performance.

Fidelity Spartan 500 Index (FSMKX) owns securities that reflect the S&P 500 Index, each stock held by the fund being in the same proportion as it is in the S&P 500 Index. If the S&P 500 moves up or down 15 percent, this Fidelity fund will move in lock-step with it and go up or down close to 15 percent. For example, for the year 2002, FSMKX dropped 22.17 percent, compared to the S&P 500's drop to 22.10 percent, the .07 percentage point difference being the result of internal fund expenses and administrative fees.

Many index funds are available from mutual fund families. They cover all the major indexes, including the Wilshire 5000, Russell 2000, MSCI (Morgan Stanley Capital International) EAFE (Europe, Australasia, Far East), and 10-year bonds. Index funds are passively managed and portfolio changes are rare. As a result administrative costs are held to a minimum. Compare this situation to that with ordinary mutual funds that are actively managed, and portfolio turnover averages between 50 percent to over 200 percent a year, depending on the fund. The average diversified mutual fund has turnover averaging 111 percent per year, with a 1.46 percent annual expense ratio, according to Morningstar.[1] All this trading eats into the funds performance, as trading fees mount up.

Indexes are used as benchmarks against which to compare the performance of a specific mutual fund or category. For example, if a fund invests in large capitalization-weighted stocks, then the S&P 500 Index is used as the benchmark. Mutual fund managers consistently try to beat the benchmark index, but over many years they are hard pressed to do this. They find it difficult, because their loads (if charged), cash drag (when the fund is not fully invested), expense ratios, 12b-1 fees, portfolio turnover, trading costs, and tax inefficiencies eat into their performance. These factors result in underperformance.

Key Factors in Selecting an Index Fund

When selecting an index fund to invest in when applying market timing and a buy-or-sell signal is given, make sure you take into account the following factors:

1. *Minimum investment amount.*   Some funds have minimums of $1000, while others may require $5000, $10,000, or even higher amounts.

2. *Annual expense ratio.*   The lower the ratio, the better. A ratio below 0.20 percent is best. Typical mutual funds have an average expense ratio about 1.46 percent. That means that 1.46 percent of your investment is going toward paying the fund's overhead each year, in addition to any load or commissions you pay on purchasing or exiting the fund. Index funds should have ratios below 0.50 percent.

3. *Deadline for making a trade.*   The later in the day the trade deadline is, the better. If you plan to make a buy-or-sell decision on a particular day, having the ability to make a phone call or perform the transaction on a fund's Web site up until the 4 P.M. EST market close is very desirable. Calling after the close will result in getting the next day's closing price, which may or may not be in your favor.

4. *Maximum number of trades permitted over a 12-month period.*
   The more the allowable number of trades, the better. Most
   funds are very stringent about the number of trades permitted, and almost all fund families do not cater to market
   timers. Make sure you can make at least four transactions a
   year. The optimal situation is being permitted to have
   unlimited trades.
5. *Redemption fees.* Some funds levy charges of approximately
   0.5 percent to 1 percent, if a fund is redeemed within 30
   days to 180 days.

If none of the families you investigate offer the features mentioned above, then consider the Rydex Funds, ProFunds, and
Potomac Funds families, which are geared toward traders and market timers. Their annual expense ratios and minimum investments
may be higher than those of other families, but they provide a wide
selection of funds. More detailed information about these funds is
provided in the upcoming section on leveraged mutual funds.

If you are a subscriber to Morningstar online (*www.
morningstar.com*) or its *Morningstar Mutual Funds* publication (available in most libraries), you can check out and compare all index
funds at once, instead of going to each of the family Web sites
or receiving their material in the mail. Another comprehensive
resource is the Web site *www.indexfunds.com*.

Market Timing with Index Funds

When using market timing to make buy and sell decisions, you can
invest in any index fund. For example, if are interested in investing in
large-capitalization stocks or the market as a whole, you can select an
index fund that tracks the S&P 500 or the Wilshire 5000 (total stock
market).

Of course, if you prefer to invest in other market indexes such
as a small-cap or value fund index, that's easy to do. To spread
your risk, you may want to select 5 to 10 diverse index funds (for
example, large-, mid-, or small-cap growth; large-, mid-, or small-
cap value, or international funds). This approach is similar to
building a diversified stock portfolio, except in the case of index
funds there could be thousands of stocks represented in the index

funds you select. This broad diversification will work in your favor to cushion any severe corrections, but it does not mean that you have no risk. There is always risk in the stock market. Only cash or U.S. government money market funds offer no risk, but cash decays with inflation, and currently the short-term interest rates are hovering around 1 percent.

Morningstar offers a tool called Instant X-Ray to help you determine the portfolio composition of your mutual fund. (This tool is available, without charge, from the company's Web site: *www.morningstar.com*). Your objective should be to minimize overlapping of the holdings of the mutual funds you invest in, to provide the most diversification as possible. All you have to do is put in the ticker symbols of your funds and the program does the rest.

Remember that almost all fund families frown upon market timers (except Rydex, ProFunds, and Potomac), and they may limit the number of trades that can be made in a year to four or less. So make sure you check out their transaction limit, and avoid a fund family, if it does not offer the number of transactions required by the timing strategy you select.

SECTOR FUNDS

Sector funds are a popular subset of mutual funds. As the name implies, a sector fund limits the stocks it owns to companies in a particular segment of an industry. Common sectors include technology, biotech, consumer cyclicals, financial services, precious metals, real estate, and medical equipment. Sector funds avoid the need for you to purchase a group of individual stocks if you want to participate in that industry and thereby avoid incurring multiple brokerage commissions. A large number of stocks in a sector fund portfolio offers some diversification by company. But if the entire sector is having difficulties, you can still suffer a major loss.

Typically sector funds have higher volatility, higher portfolio turnover, and potentially higher returns and losses than a diversified stock fund. They do because sector funds are highly concentrated in one or a few related industries. These funds, therefore, should be used by only the more experienced and venturesome investors with a higher risk tolerance. Keep in mind that some industry sectors might excel in bear markets, such as natural resources and gold. So depending upon the market's trend, the right sectors need to be chosen, otherwise large losses may result. Interestingly, in 2002 not one of the S&P sector categories made it into the plus column. This may be a rare occurrence, but it can happen.

Fidelity is well known for being the pioneer in sector funds; they dub their sector funds Fidelity Select Portfolios. Their first few sector funds came out in July 1981, with additional funds being launched in the mid-1980s, and a few more added in the last few years. Currently, the Select Portfolios consist of 41 sector funds and one money market fund. This large selection makes Fidelity the largest sector fund player in the industry.

Fidelity Select funds have a 3 percent front-end load. But the fee can be avoided, if you stay within the Select funds when you sell one fund to buy another. There is also a 0.75 percent redemption fee, and a $7.50 exchange fee, if you sell before 30 days. Fidelity does not encourage market timing, and it may restrict your trading, if you trade too often. One benefit of investing in sector funds is Fidelity's practice of pricing these funds every hour. So investors who call at 9:40 A.M., for example, receive the 10:00 A.M. price. This practice offers great flexibility in a volatile market.

Additionally, Fidelity offers investors the ability to short 11 of its Select Portfolios. So in a bear market this option should prove useful. Hourly pricing is available with these funds as well. Individual Select Portfolios have up years and down years. Therefore, any investment in these type of funds must be based on a well-conceived and consistently performing strategy. Complete information about these funds is available at *www.fidelity.com* or by calling Fidelity at 800-343-3548. Other mutual funds families that offer sector funds include Vanguard (*www.vanguard.com*), INVESCO (*www.invesco.com*), Rydex (*www.rydexfunds.com*, 17 sectors), and ProFunds (*www.profunds.com*, 21 leveraged sector funds).

Market Timing with Sector Funds

Sector funds offer the experienced and aggressive investor a way to capture significant profits, but only when these funds are purchased and sold at the right time. Timing is extremely critical with these funds; otherwise, you could suffer losses from which you might take years to recover. Bad earnings or a killer bear market can decimate any sector fund, even if it contains so-called high-quality stocks. In bear markets most sectors get hit hard, except for the gold sector, which usually excels. So sector funds should only be used with specific buy-and-sell rules to protect your principal. After reviewing the timing strategies presented in Chapters 7 through 11, you can select one that you feel will work with a group sector funds.

> **Warning**: It is solely up to you to select the most appropriate strategy for investing in the sector funds that you may want to invest in, as well as to have predetermined stop-loss price points in mind to limit your losses. You must use specific buy-and-sell rules so that you protect your principal, at all costs. Remember that you cannot usually place stop-loss orders with mutual funds; therefore you should make sure that you track the prices daily. These are not the types of funds you buy and put away forever.

LEVERAGED FUNDS

Leveraged funds make more exaggerated moves than the indexes that they track. Prior to the inception of the Rydex Funds in 1993, an investor had no way of obtaining leverage on mutual fund investments, without resorting to margin (if offered on mutual funds by the brokerage firm). And margin interest would be accruing every day, eating into any gains. Traders and market timers were therefore pleased when Rydex offered funds with leverage.

Rydex Funds: First Inverse and Leveraged Funds

Leveraged funds provide returns of between 25 percent to 100 percent more than the nonleveraged funds. These funds have betas between 1.25 to 2.00. That means that your risk rises as well. For bullish investors who want leverage, the Rydex Nova fund tracks the S&P 500 Index with a beta of 1.5. Thus, every 1 percentage point move in the S&P means a 1.5 percentage point move in Nova. If the S&P 500 rises 10 percent, then Nova would theoretically rise 15 percent. I use the word *theoretically* because the percentage may not be exactly 15 percent, although it should be very close to it. However, if the S&P falls instead of rising, this fund will lose money 1.5 times as fast. So timing the purchase and sale of these funds is critical to capital preservation.

For bears, the Rydex Ursa fund tracks the inverse of the S&P 500, with a beta of 1.0. Thus, every 1 percentage point drop in the S&P means a 1.0 percentage point drop in Ursa. If the S&P 500 Index falls 10 percent, then Ursa should drop about 10 percent.

Nova's annual expense ratio is 1.16 percent and the minimum investment to open an account for a self-directed investor or for a retirement account is $25,000. Some of the brokerage firms that offer the Rydex funds may have lower minimums. For example, investing through a registered financial advisor drops the initial investment to $15,000. Ursa's annual expense ratio is 1.31 percent and the opening account details are the same.

Rydex currently offers 34 funds in four major categories. Table 5-1 provides their names by type of fund. Currently, Rydex offers eight leveraged funds on the long side, and two inverse (short) leveraged funds. Three funds are inverse funds without leverage. Also, Rydex offers 21 long funds without leverage, of which 17 are sector funds. The performance statistics of all Rydex funds for the year ending December 2002 are shown in Table 5-2.

Rydex's Dynamic Funds offer the most leverage of all its funds, with a beta of 2.0. So you'd better be on the right side of the market with these leveraged funds, otherwise you double your losses. The four funds are as follows:

- Rydex Titan 500 Fund: 200 percent of the daily performance of the S&P 500.
- Rydex Tempest 500 Fund: 200 percent of the inverse performance of the S&P 500.
- Rydex Velocity 100 Fund: 200 percent of the daily performance of the Nasdaq 100.
- Rydex Venture 100 Fund: 200 percent of the inverse performance of the Nasdaq 100.

On March 17, 2002, Rydex added the Sector Rotation Fund, which invests in the strongest sectors. Each month, the managers quantitatively rank 59 industries and buy the strongest ones, based on price momentum, and sell the weaker ones. Thus, an investor can gain the benefit of investing in the strongest sectors by purchasing one fund, assuming that this approach works.

TABLE 5-1

Rydex Fund Family

Category	Long	Long Leveraged	Inverse	Inverse Leveraged
26 Quantitative Funds	OTC 17 Sectors U.S. Gov't Money Market	Nova Mekros Medius U.S. Gov't Bond	Ursa Juno Arktos	
2 International Funds		Large-Cap Europe Large-Cap Japan		
4 Dynamic Funds		Titan 500 Velocity 100		Tempest 500 Venture 100
2 Strategic Funds	Sector Rotation Core Equity			

Source: www.rydexfunds.com. Printed with permission

On September 30, 2002, Rydex, launched a multiinvestment style fund called the Rydex Core Equity Fund. The fund invests across the large-cap value, mid-cap value, small-cap value, large-cap growth, and mid-cap growth style boxes. The fund automatically rebalances the portfolio to maintain a roughly equal weighting in each of the five categories.

For additional information on Rydex Funds, call 800-820-0888 or access their Web site at *www.rydexfunds.com*. Some investment firms offering access to Rydex Funds include Fidelity, TD Waterhouse, Charles Schwab, Vanguard Brokerage Services, ML Direct, T. Rowe Price, Dreyfus Brokerage Services, Scottrade and Ameritrade.

ProFunds

ProFunds opened its doors in 1997, in direct competition with Rydex Funds. ProFunds offers 47 index-based funds (not including their 46 variable insurance ProFunds), more than any other mutual fund firm. The funds the family offers include:

- 15 bullish funds
- 6 bearish funds
- 21 sector funds
- 1 money market fund

TABLE 5-2

Rydex Fund Performance – Year Ending December 31, 2002
SEC Standardized Annual Total Returns (as of 12/31/02)

DYNAMIC FUNDS

FUND NAME	YTD**	4th QTR	1 YEAR	3 YEAR	5 YEAR	S.I.*	Inception
Titan 500-RYTNX	1.13%	13.69%	-46.60%	N/A	N/A	-38.28%	05/19/00
Tempest 500-RYTPX	-2.79%	-19.40%	37.48%	N/A	N/A	27.56%	05/19/00
Velocity 100-RYVYX	8.90%	32.85%	-68.47%	N/A	N/A	-70.81%	05/24/00
Venture 100-RYVNX	-11.41%	-37.07%	50.92%	N/A	N/A	16.52%	05/23/00

BENCHMARK FUNDS

FUND NAME	YTD**	4th QTR	1 YEAR	3 YEAR	5 YEAR	S.I.*	Inception
OTC-RYOCX	4.86%	17.47%	-38.55%	-37.07%	-1.39%	9.76%	02/14/94
Arktos-RYAIX	-5.62%	-18.72%	35.46%	24.43%	N/A	-12.55%	09/03/98
Nova-RYNVX	0.90%	11.30%	-35.09%	-25.95%	-7.41%	6.95%	07/12/93
Ursa-RYURX	-1.25%	-9.12%	22.23%	18.64%	3.45%	-4.19%	01/07/94
Bond-RYGBX	-1.77%	-1.02%	19.02%	13.31%	6.43%	5.74%	01/03/94
Juno-RYJUX	1.26%	0.49%	-16.73%	-10.02%	-3.51%	-3.95%	03/03/95
Mekros-RYMKX	-0.98%	7.78%	-33.70%	N/A	N/A	-22.66%	11/01/00
Medius-RYMDX	-0.97%	7.05%	-27.40%	N/A	N/A	-22.46%	08/16/01

STRATEGIC FUNDS

FUND NAME	YTD**	4th QTR	1 YEAR	3 YEAR	5 YEAR	S.I.*	Inception
Sector Rotation-RYSRX	0.13%	0.00%	N/A	N/A	N/A	-22.20%	03/17/02

INTERNATIONAL FUNDS

FUND NAME	YTD**	4th QTR	1 YEAR	3 YEAR	5 YEAR	S.I.*	Inception
Large-Cap Europe-RYEUX	-4.97%	12.48%	-30.99%	N/A	N/A	-31.71%	05/08/00
Large-Cap Japan-RYJPX	4.17%	-5.88%	-20.73%	N/A	N/A	-38.98%	05/08/00

SECTOR FUNDS

FUND NAME	YTD**	4th QTR	1 YEAR	3 YEAR	5 YEAR	S.I.*	Inception
Banking-RYKIX	1.72%	3.63%	-1.98%	3.76%	N/A	-4.40%	04/01/98
Basic Materials-RYBIX	-0.94%	8.83%	-13.58%	-11.97%	N/A	-8.68%	04/01/98
Biotechnology-RYOIX	4.82%	4.65%	-45.56%	-16.49%	N/A	6.56%	04/01/98
Consumer Products-RYCIX	-0.41%	3.96%	-3.58%	-6.54%	N/A	-5.54%	07/06/98
Electronics-RYSIX	2.57%	16.19%	-49.16%	-33.45%	N/A	-4.01%	04/01/98
Energy-RYEIX	-3.30%	10.27%	-13.22%	-2.53%	N/A	-1.81%	04/21/98
Energy Services-RYVIX	-3.47%	13.27%	-10.36%	-4.74%	N/A	-10.01%	04/01/98
Financial Services-RYFIX	1.11%	4.99%	-15.94%	-3.78%	N/A	-4.01%	04/02/98
Health Care-RYHIX	2.07%	3.38%	-20.05%	-2.88%	N/A	-1.81%	04/17/98
Internet-RYIIX	10.02%	32.15%	-43.49%	N/A	N/A	-56.29%	04/06/00
Leisure-RYLIX	-2.88%	-2.04%	-15.31%	-18.44%	N/A	-9.25%	04/01/98
Precious Metals-RYPMX	2.91%	12.34%	48.24%	11.22%	3.32%	-4.89%	12/01/93
Retailing-RYRIX	-0.72%	0.85%	-23.44%	-15.65%	N/A	-3.60%	04/01/98
Technology-RYTIX	4.73%	23.33%	-40.38%	-36.28%	N/A	-6.76%	04/14/98
Telecommunications-RYMIX	3.61%	36.36%	-43.04%	-43.17%	N/A	-19.28%	04/01/98
Transportation-RYPIX	-3.78%	6.53%	-13.01%	-5.52%	N/A	-11.66%	04/02/98
Utilities-RYUIX	1.80%	5.48%	-32.37%	N/A	N/A	-16.51%	04/03/00

Quarter End After Tax Performance
* Since Inception Annualized
** As of 01/23/03
*** SI Cumulative Return for RYMDX
Source: www.rydexfunds.com. Printed with permission

ProFunds minimum initial investment is $15,000 for self-directed individual investors or $5000 for investors working through an affiliated investment advisor. That is $10,000 lower than Rydex's minimums in both cases. To provide leverage, ProFunds not only invests in securities, but it may also invest in futures contracts, options on futures contracts, swap agreements, options on securities and indices, U.S. government securities, repurchase agreements, or combinations of these instruments.

The performance statistics of each of the ProFunds is provided on its Web site at *www.profunds.com*. ProFunds can be purchased directly from the firm or at the following firms: Accutrade, Ameritrade, Charles Schwab, Fidelity Investments, Scottrade and TD Waterhouse.

Market Timing with Leveraged Funds: Be Very Careful

Using leveraged funds and making a lot of money is the ultimate goal for seasoned market timers. Initially, investors just starting out with market-timing strategiesmay not want to jump right into leveraged funds. Until the investor feels comfortable with his market timing strategy, his rules for cutting loses, including the use of stop-loss orders, and his performance against a suitable benchmark, the use of leveraged funds, should probably be delayed. A novice market timer using leverage can get destroyed in a month, if the market turns against him, and if he does not get out immediately with a small loss. Losses of 50 percent and higher can easily occur with the 2.0 beta funds.

After investors have profitably used market timing for a few years they may want to consider investing in leveraged funds, but only with the minimal account size, at the beginning. After six months, more funds can be added. Slow and steady wins the race with these enhanced funds. Your main concern is minimizing your losses and protecting your capital, not maximizing your profits. That gain will come, it is hoped, if you have the proper timing model in place and if you follow your game plan.

Leveraged funds offer market timers who get on the right side of the market a powerful vehicle for participating in both bull and bear markets. For aggressive investors who are able to control their risk, leveraged funds can lead to tremendous returns. Of course, more reward means more risk. When you read the chapters on specific market timing strategies, you will be provided with statistics on leveraged returns, so that you can see their significant dollar impact over time.

ENDNOTES

1. Morningstar Mutual Funds, December 21, 2002.
2. Norris Floyd, "Investors, Bruised, Hope It's Over," The New York Times, January 2, 2003 p. C1.

CHAPTER 6

Exchange-Traded Funds

Quite often, when someone says something won't work, what they really mean is, "I can't make it work!"

John K. Sosnowy, SAAFTI Conference, May 1996.

ETF BASICS

Exchange-traded funds (ETFs) are relatively new, and currently only 1 percent of investor assets are invested in them. Most of the players are frequent traders, not buy-and-hold investors. As investors become more familiar with the characteristics of ETFs, they will draw assets away from conventional mutual funds and index funds.

In the United States, there are about 125 ETFs valued at over $105 billion, representing popular indexes, international indexes, and various sectors of the market. This valuation is still a pittance compared to the $6 trillion invested in mutual funds. Almost all ETFs are listed on the American Stock Exchange (AMEX), except for three international ETFs listed on the NYSE and two listed on the Nasdaq. A listing of AMEX-listed ETFs can be found at *www.amex.com*, along with other useful information.

According to the AMEX, the official definition of ETFs is "registered investment companies under the Investment Company Act of 1940, which have received certain exemptive relief from the SEC to allow secondary market trading in the ETF shares. ETFs are index-based products, in that each ETF holds a portfolio of securities that is intended to provide investment results that, before fees and expenses, generally correspond to the price and yield performance of the underlying benchmark index."

In 1993, the AMEX listed the first ETF: the Standard & Poor's Depositary Receipt (SPDR), pronounced "spider." It exactly mirrors the movement of the S&P 500 Index. Its ticker symbol is SPY. There are also ETFs that track the DJIA, called "Diamonds"; the Nasdaq 100 (QQQ), called "Cubes"; the largest 1000 U.S. incorporated companies, known as the Russell 1000 (IWB); and many other industry sectors and indexes. For example, there are nine Select Sector SPDR Funds corresponding to specific sector indexes. The AMEX lists 31 international-oriented ETFs and 69 domestic ETFs on its Web site.

The most heavily traded ETFs are as follows:

SPY. SPDR Trust Series securities, SPDRs: Pooled investments that track the price and yield of the S&P 500 Index.

QQQ. The Nasdaq-100 Trust Series I: A pooled investment that tracks the price and yield of the Nasdaq 100 Index.

DIA. Diamonds Trust Series I: A pooled investment that tracks the price and yield of the DJIA.

MDY. SPDR Trust series: S&P 400 Mid-cap.

iSHARES. Pooled-securities with an open-ended investment structure issued by Barclays Global Investors. There are over 50 different iShares index funds that trade like stocks. Each share tracks a specific portfolio. For a complete description, check out the iShares Web site at *www.ishares.com*.

MERRILL LYNCH HOLDRS

Another instrument similar to ETFs, called HOLDRS (HOLding Company Depositary ReceiptS), was created by Merrill Lynch and also trades on the AMEX. The HOLDR portfolio represents ownership in the common stock of American Depositary Receipts of specific companies. They have features similar to ETFs.

Almost all the 17 HOLDRS are sector funds, concentrated in one industry, and they may contain only 20 stocks. Such a concentration can be risky, if you are long a sector when it is crashing. Of course, if you are short the ETF, you will reap the rewards of a bearish price trend. A listing of the current HOLDRS with their ticker symbols, and component securities, can be found at *www.holdrs.com*.

One limitation of HOLDRS is that they must be bought or sold in 100-share lots, while ETFs can be purchased in odd lots. Also, the HOLDRS portfolios never add or delete stocks unless the company disappears in an acquisition or goes bankrupt. That may not contribute to price stability. The opposite could be true. We need price stability and predictability and not just "portfolio" stability.

ETFs have been developed for the following types of portfolios:

- Stock indexes (for example, total market, large-cap growth, and small-cap value)
- Industry sector–specific stock indexes (for example, technology, financial, real estate, and telecommunications)
- International and country-specific equity indexes (for example, Latin America, Europe, Singapore, and Australia)
- Fixed income indexes (for example, short- and long-term Treasury bonds and corporate bonds)
- Specialty indexes (for example, Fortune 500 and Dow Jones U.S. Stock Market)

ETF BENEFITS

ETFs are viable and useful investment vehicles for the following reasons:

- **Transparency.** You have the ability to replicate a particular index with a single EFT purchase.
- **Liquidity.** Trades can be made any time during the day so that you obtain the current price at the time you place your order and are not stuck with an end of day price, as is the case with mutual funds. Thus, the investor is not at the

mercy of the market for the entire day and can liquidate a position at any time for any reason. This flexibility is critical in times of volatile, panicky, or news-driven markets.

♦ **Low costs.** Expense ratios and management fees are much lower than with regular mutual funds and usually a few basis points (.01 = 1 basis point) lower than index funds. No analysts or investment managers need to be paid; however, there is a brokerage commission each time an ETF is bought or sold. A discount or online broker can be used to keep the commission below $10 for each trade. SPDRs, for example, have an annual expense ratio of just 0.12 percent, and Barclay's iShares S&P 500 have a ratio of 0.18 percent. The Vanguard 500 Index Fund annual expense ratio is 0.18 percent per year compared with the SPDR's ratio of 0.12. On a $10,000 initial investment that works out to an annual savings of only $6 for the ETF. Remember that among mutual funds families, Vanguard is known to have extremely low fees, while other fund families have significantly higher expense ratios.

Active traders pay commissions whenever they trade an ETF. So, having an index fund with low expenses and the ability to do active trading could be comparatively cheaper. But most index funds do not allow more than four exchanges a year. Still, four exchanges could work fine for some of the less active market-timing strategies recommended in Chapters 7 through 11.

♦ **Tax efficiency.** ETFs are more tax-efficient than a comparable mutual fund, as they involve lower capital gains and less portfolio turnover so are more tax efficient. You pay capital gains only when you sell your ETF. With mutual funds you have to declare capital gains, when they are declared by the fund, even though you never sell the fund. Owners of ETFs have capital gains or losses only when an ETF transaction is closed. If there are no closing trades, then there are no capital gains or losses. By contrast, mutual funds pass on the capital gains and losses realized within the fund to their shareholders who must declare these gains and losses.

- **Flexibility for implementing trading strategies.** ETFs can be purchased on margin and sold short. Also, limit and stop orders can be placed. These capabilities are not present with mutual funds. An ETF is considered a passive investment like an index fund. Portfolio turnover is minimal, except when certain issues are replaced when they are replaced in the underlying index. Investors can buy and sell ETFs at any time during trading hours. Moreover, an EFT can be shorted without having to wait for an uptick in price before the order is executed, as is the case with common stocks.

  A short sale is the opposite of buying a stock or EFT. The seller, in effect, borrows the stock or ETF from the brokerage firm hoping to repurchase it later at a lower price and repaying the broker with the stock purchased at the lower price. The objective in short selling is to make money when the price drops. If a stock sold short drops in price the shares are bought back at a lower price, generating a profit for the investor. But if the share price rises instead of falls, the investor suffers a loss, since he has to buy back the shares at a higher price.

- **Diversification.** ETFs are composed of a portfolio of stocks, thereby substantially reducing overall risk compared to buying a individual stocks. Of course, the specific ETF purchased may be more risky than another ETF, depending upon its portfolio mix and volatility.

- **Favorable interest income and dividends.** Dividends declared on stocks or interest paid on bonds held in the ETF will be passed on to shareholders.

ETF RISKS

Of course, like any investment, ETFs have specific risks:

- **Market risk.** Like stocks and mutual funds, the price fluctuates throughout the day, sometimes with wide price swings, depending upon many variables.

- **Net asset value risk.** The price may not trade at exactly the net asset value; instead, it may be a bit higher or lower, depending on conditions of the market. In the case of the most active ETFs, there is a minimal, if any, difference in price between the net asset value and the market price. Any wide differences would be observed, and big institutional traders and hedgers would step in to take advantage of the situation, thereby rapidly closing any price gap.

- **Bid/ask price spread.** Depending on the volume of transactions, some ETFs may have higher price spreads between the bid and ask price, thereby resulting in higher transaction costs. The spread is minimal (e.g., a few pennies) on the more active ETFs.
- **Sector risk.** If an EFT is sector-specific, then variables specific to that sector can greatly influence the price of all its portfolio components.

MARKET TIMING WITH ETFs

ETFs offer advantages over index funds that make them more attractive and liquid for investors who are looking to time the market. ETFs are more diversified than individual stocks and have advantages over mutual funds, as well. Investors can be more aggressive and buy and sell industry-sector ETFs, taking into account the cautions raised in the previous chapter with sector funds. And ETFs are a great tool to develop a balanced investment portfolio because of the array of choices. However, ETFs are not leveraged, so an investor would have to use a margin account to obtain leverage and incur margin interest until the ETF position is closed. In contrast, leveraged funds (for example, selected Rydex Funds) offer leverage on both the long and short sides of the market.

The most popular ETFs to use for market timing are the QQQs and SPYs. They each have huge trading volume, offer minimal bid/ask spreads, and represent a very significant specific market segment. For those investors who want more risk, numerous ETF sectors can fill the bill, such as the nine SPDR sectors. Refer to the AMEX Web site (*www.amex.com*) for further details.

CONCLUSIONS

ETFs are relatively new investment vehicles that offer outstanding flexibility and wide-ranging options. Market-timing strategies can be easily implemented with these hybrid mutual funds. Best of all, ETFs can be bought and sold any time throughout the day, and they can be easily shorted. But if you want to leverage ETFs, you'll need to open a margin account and pay the margin interest until the transaction is closed out.

PART 2

Market-Timing Strategies

CHAPTER 7

Calendar-Based Investing
The Best Six Months Strategy

The only thing that works is to let the market indices tell you the
time to enter and exit. Never fight the market—it's bigger than
you are.

William J. O'Neil, How to Make Money in Stocks

BACKGROUND

Investing based on using the calendar has intrigued investors, market technicians, and other investment professionals for years. For
the most part, the broadcast media has mentioned seasonal investing strategies on occasion, but they have not given it the attention
it deserves. Therefore, most investors may have heard something
about it but not taken it seriously or done any homework on the
topic. As it turns out, that lack of initiative was probably a huge
mistake, because careful analysis of seasonal investing strategies
reveals their superiority to buy-and-hold over a long time period.

Over the years, many academic studies have been done on the
seasonal influences on stock market returns. This chapter will present a few of the more profitable strategies that have worked in the
past but also in the present. Excluding the worst-performing
months, staying out of the market and into cash, is an excellent

strategy. It not only reduces risk but also provides better-than-average risk-adjusted returns.

Investing during specific months each year is an example of a seasonality pattern that will be covered in detail in this chapter. According to *The Wall Street Journal*,[1] Ned Davis Research found that since 1950, on average, stocks have gone up 8 percent from the beginning of October through the end of April but have increased only 1 percent from the beginning of May through the end of September.

That firm found that investing $10,000 from the fourth trading day in May, through the last trading day in September of the following year (or a continuous period of 6 months), from 1950 through 2000, resulted in a miniscule total gain of $2977 for that entire period. However, entering into the market every October 1 and exiting the following May 3 resulted in a total gain of $585,909.[2]

Look at Table 7-1 to get an inkling as to the best-performing consecutive months. Note that the period November through January offers the highest return compared to any other three consecutive months.

SO, WHAT SHOULD YOU DO? Should you be skeptical or should you think that maybe this year will be different and fight the facts by investing contrary to what the past has clearly taught you? You should if you want the odds to be against you. You

TABLE 7-1

Best Consecutive Three-Month Periods For S&P 500 Index
[average cumulative change 1928–2002 (Oct.)]

Period	Change, %
Nov., Dec., Jan.	3.8
June, July, Aug.	3.5
Dec., Jan., Feb.	3.1
Oct., Nov., Dec.	2.5
Average 3 months	1.8

Source: Standard & Poor's, *The Outlook*, November 6, 2002.

should if you're in the market to gamble away your money for the thrill of it.

Investing is a serious business, not a game. You can't make money at it if you're going to invest your money on a lark. You need to go with the high probabilities you know about from the proven past performance and never fall into the trap that this time, it will be different.

A research paper entitled "The Halloween Indicator, Sell in May and Go Away: Another Puzzle" (September 1999) by Sven Bouman, ING Investment Management, Netherlands, and Ben Jacobsen, Faculty of Economics and Econometrics, University of Amsterdam, also weighed in on the best and worst months.

Is the presence of the November–April period of stock market strength simply a manifestation of the U.S. economy, banking system, and markets? Not at all. Bouman and Jacobsen discovered that stock prices rose more sharply in the November–April time period than in the corresponding May–October period in 36 of 37 countries. This effect has occurred in the U.K. stock market since 1694. They found no evidence that this phenomenon can be explained by the January effect, stock market crash of 1987, dividend payment seasonality, or time-varying risk parameters. The main reason turns out to be the extent and timing of vacations. For example, summer vacations in Europe have a strong seasonal effect on financial markets.

HISTORICAL PERSPECTIVE

Let's take a look at the individual monthly performance of the S&P 500 Index over the past 50 years. Mark Vakkur, M.D, a psychiatrist by training, and a stock and options trader, has analyzed the historical data.[3] His findings are depicted in Table 7-2. This table provides the monthly performance of the S&P 500 Index (excluding reinvested dividends) from 1950 through March 2002, divided into two time frames. Clearly there are specific strong and weak months. January, April, July, November, and December have been the best-performing months from 1950 through 1995. Excluding July, *the continuous months of November through January are the best ones*, with an average gain of 1.58 percent per month. By including

February, March, and April, the performance falls to 1.19 percent, but it is still positive.

Now let's look at the more recent time period, from 1996 to March 2002 in Table 7-2. The best-performing months are January, March, April, June, October, November, and December. March, June, and October have now emerged as strong months. Five months—March, April, June, October, and November—have provided higher performance in the most recent six-year period compared to the prior period. Except for June, these are all months in the October–April time frame.

According to the August 21, 2001, issue of the *FORMULA RESEARCH* newsletter, edited and published by Nelson Freeburg,

TABLE 7-2

Monthly Performance of S&P 500
S&P 500 Monthly Prices
1950–March 2002

| Month | Average Monthly Gain, % | | Difference |
	1950–1995	1996–Mar. 2002	
January	1.55	1.31	−0.24
February	0.37	−0.87	−1.24
March	0.76	1.76	1.00
April	1.23	2.75	1.51
May	0.16	0.35	0.19
June	0.08	2.31	2.22
July	1.29	−0.63	−1.92
August	0.39	−3.24	−3.63
September	−0.60	−0.15	0.45
October	0.45	2.64	2.19
November	1.43	3.50	2.07
December	1.77	1.77	0
Average	0.74	0.95	0.21
Nov.–Jan. only	1.58	2.14	0.56
Nov.–Apr. only	1.19	1.63	0.44
May–Oct. only	0.29	0.21	−0.08

Note: Bolded numbers are the best performing monthly.

Source: "Mark Your Calendars: Stock Market Seasonality," Mark Vakkur, M.D., *Active Trader*, September 2002, p. 96–97. © *Active Trader* Magazine. All Rights Reserved.

a longtime trading systems developer who uses rigorous statistical testing on timing models: "Since 1950 there have been 34 declines of at least 10 percent in the Dow Jones Industrials. In thirty-one of these cases, key portions of the pullback—often the brunt of the sell-off—occurred during the May–October period. Twelve declines took place entirely within the bearish period. The record since 1900 shows more 'crashes,' 'massacres,' and 'panics' in October than in any other month. Of the 34 corrections cited above, fully twelve ended in October."

Freeburg goes on to say "over 90 percent of the net gain in the Dow since 1950 came in just 40 months, a mere 8 percent of the time span." Furthermore, "to a remarkable extent almost all the stock market's advance since World War II came at a specific, recurring time of the year."

History indicates that there is a consistent nonrandom period of strong and weak months. The risk-averse investor can take advantage of this strategy, especially in retirement accounts, where there are no capital gains implications for selling. As we'll see throughout this chapter, specific strategies will be provided to capitalize on these strong and weak monthly patterns.

BEST SIX MONTHS STRATEGY

Astute investors should consider seasonal patterns since they have stood the test of time. The first seasonal strategy we will cover—the *best six months strategy*—has the following characteristics:

- There are only two signals a year—one buy and one sell.
- The buy signal is close to November 1, and the sell signal is near April 30.
- The annual rate of return exceeds buy-and-hold, on a risk-adjusted basis.
- The strategy misses the brunt of bear markets, since it is not invested in the weakest half of the year but instead is invested in the strongest months of the year.
- This strategy provides 50 percent less risk than buy-and-hold.
- The time required to implement the strategy is minimal (about an hour a year).

These attributes should whet most investors' appetites because all the research data over the past 50 years supports it. That evidence is what this chapter is all about. I will present the findings of well respected researchers who have rigorously evaluated the data. So, let's begin the journey of understanding how successful the seasonal investing strategy can be, and why you may want to use it with your hard-earned cash.

Very few simple timing strategies have such a long-term track record as does the best six months strategy developed in 1986 by Yale Hirsch. (I'll refer to it as the BSM or best six months, strategy.) It was first published in The Hirsch Organization's 1987 edition of the *Stock Trader's Almanac*. It has been tweaked a bit over the years by his son Jeff Hirsch, and is updated annually in each year's edition of the almanac. Moreover, the BSM's current buy-and-sell signals are provided in real time to subscribers of their monthly newsletter *Stock Trader's Almanac Investor* newsletter, as well as via their subscriber email service.

The BSM strategy's buy-and-sell rules are simple: invest in the stock market (for example, a S&P 500 Index fund) on November 1 of each year, and then sell on April 30 of the following year (and go into cash equivalents—a money fund or T-bills), until November 1 of the next year when the next investment is made.

According to the *Stock Trader's Almanac 2003* (page 50), from 1950 through 2001, an initial investment of $10,000 produced a total *loss* of $77 for the entire May–October time period.[4] This compares with a *gain* of $457,103 when the investor was investing in the November–April period. The strategy assumed that the funds were invested in the DJIA.[5] Clearly, the months selected for investing play a significant role in the total return over that extensive time period. On page 52 of the almanac, the same strategy is tested, but in conjunction with a technical indicator known as the Moving Average Convergence-Divergence (MACD), based on the work of Sy Harding. Using the MACD's buy signal near November and sell signal near April, you would have realized a gain of $1,199,247 for the DJIA from November through May, in the same period 1950–2001 while the May through November showed a loss of $5977. Clearly this strategy almost tripled the previous strategy's return. Sy Harding's contribution to seasonal timing is covered in detail in the next section of this chapter.

Keep in mind that, for an investor who had been using the BSM strategy, the worst market meltdowns would all have been avoided:

- The October 28 and 29, 1929, crash, in which the DJIA dropped 25.2 percent
- The October 19, 1987, stock market crash, in which the DJIA plunged over 508 points, dropping 22.6 percent
- The 555-point drop on October 27, 1997 (–7.2 percent)
- The 513-point drop on August 31, 1998 (–6.4 percent)
- The 357-point drop on August 27, 1998 (–4.2 percent)
- The 1370-point drop between September 10 and 21, 2001 (–14.3 percent), after the terrorist attack on the World Trade Center and Washington, DC
- The 1651-point, third-quarter 2002 (–17.9 percent) decline

Jeff Hirsch used this same BSM strategy but substituted the Nasdaq Composite Index instead of the DJIA to see how that index performed. Since that index began in 1971, Hirsch ran the numbers from 1971 through year-end 2001. He found that an $10,000 initial investment in 1971 mushroomed to $230,066 in 2001, if invested during the best six-month period, compared to a only slight gain of $734 if it was invested during the opposite six months.[6] Clearly, there is seasonality in the stock market, and it worked on this index as well, which further adds to its validity.

Using Ultra 7, a software program developed by Ultra Financial Systems (see Chapter 13 for more details on the program), I ran the BSM and the WSM (worst six months) strategy against the DJIA from 1950 through January 17, 2003, to update the results. (The S&P 500 reinvested dividends were included in these results, since there was no DJIA dividend data captured in Ultra 7). The performance statistics over that time period are as follows:

Strategy Tested	Compounded Total Gain	Annualized Total Return	Time Invested
BSM	61,894%	12.88%	49.3%
WSM	900%	4.43%	50.6%
BUY-AND-HOLD DJIA	5,130%	7.74%	100.0%

An investment in the DJIA fared 12 times better than buy-and-hold and 69 times better with the WSM strategy than with buy-and-hold.

Sy Harding's Street Smart Report Seasonal Timing Strategy

Sy Harding, the founder and president of Asset Management Research Corporation, publishes the *Sy Harding's Street Smart Report* newsletter and offers the Street Smart Report at Web site (*www.StreetSmartReport.com*). Harding is also the author of *Riding the Bear: How to Prosper in the Coming Bear Market*, a paperback book that predicted the latest bear market.[7]

Harding's research for a strategy that would allow an investor to continue to make gains in the bear market he anticipated, led him eventually to seasonality. Building on the pioneering work on seasonality of Yale Hirsch, Ned Davis, and Norman Fosback, Harding recognized that the market does indeed have a favorable season and an unfavorable season, but his additional research convinced him that the beginning of those seasons varies quite widely from year to year. Rather than being an even-keeled six-months-in, six-months-out situation, he claims the market's favorable season can vary from as few as four months to as many as eight months.

His initial research first led him to use the next-to-last trading day of October as a strictly calendar-based entry, and the fourth trading day of May as the optimum calendar-based exit. But his research also led him to believe that the calendar alone could not produce optimum results.

His Seasonal Timing Strategy (STS) incorporates the Moving Average Convergence-Divergence (MACD) a short-term momentum reversal indicator to better pinpoint the entries and exits. The indicator is used to determine if a rally has begun prior to the arrival of the calendar-based entry date. If so, the "buy signal" of the MACD indicator is used to provide an early entry, rather than waiting for the actual calendar date. However, if the MACD indicator remains on a sell signal when the calendar-based entry date arrives, the rule is to delay the entry until the MACD indicator does trigger a buy signal.

If the MACD indicator triggers a sell signal prior to the arrival of the calendar date in the market's favorable season, that signal is used as the exit signal rather than waiting for the calendar-date. However, if MACD is still on a buy signal when the calendar date arrives, the investor simply waits until it does trigger a sell signal before exiting.

Figure 7-1 shows Harding's STS applied to the DJIA, from 1998 through 2002, a period that encompassed very different market conditions: two years of an unusually strong bull market and three years of a devastating bear market.

> *Note: Many free charting services available on the Internet such as www.bigcharts.com or www.stockcharts.com can plot the MACD indicator against any index, mutual fund, or ETF.*

FIGURE 7-1

Chart of STS from 1998 through 2002 with MACD signals

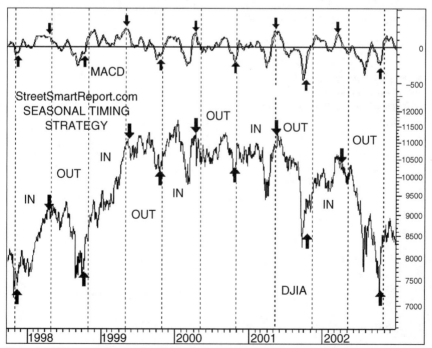

Source: Asset Management Resource Corp. Reprinted with permission.

The dotted vertical lines in the chart are what would have been the calendar-based entries and exits. The arrows show the actual entries and exits of the strategy (as triggered by MACD). Harding points that the many short-term signals of MACD throughout the year are ignored until within a week or two of the approaching calendar date. This means that the investor buys on the first MACD buy signal that takes place (or is already in place) on or after October 16 and, on the exit, the first MACD sell signal that takes place (or is already in place) on or after April 20.

Table 7-3 shows the conversion of the STS signals shown in Figure 7-1 to end-of-year numbers, for comparison of returns on an annual basis. Harding notes that the performance shown for the four years of 1999 through 2002 is the performance of the actual *Street Smart Report* newsletter STS portfolio, which used various index funds in the favorable seasons. In order to arrive at a five-year compounded return, the performance for 1998 is included, based on the entry and exit signals for 1998 from back testing.

Harding's STS methodology resulted in not only outperforming the market in the powerful bull market years but, unlike the market itself, not giving back the gains and going on to make further gains in the bear market.

TABLE 7-3

Seasonal Timing System Results, 1998–2002

YEAR	DJIA	STS Using a DJIA Index	S&P 500	STS Using an S&P Index Fund
1998	+ 18.0%	+33.2%	+ 28.7%	+ 41.8%
1999	+ 27.2%	+ 31.1%	+ 21.0%	+ 26.5%
2000	−4.7%	−2.6%	−8.9%	−7.3%
2001	−5.2%	+ 12.8%	−11.7%	+ 4.0%
2002	−14.8%	+ 8.8%	−21.6%	+ 6.6%
Compounded Total 5–Yr return	+15.5%	+ 114.1%	−1.8%	+ 84.3%

Source: Asset Management Resource Corp. Reprinted with permission.

In back testing for the 38-year period from 1964 through 2002, Harding reports that the strategy would have produced a total compounded return of 15,172 percent, using an index fund on the DJIA, compared to 4577 percent for buy-and-hold. Converted to dollars, STS would have turned a $100,000 investment in 1964 into $15,272,750 in 2002, compared to $4,677,170 for the buy-and-hold investor.

Harding points out that in addition to raising the odds in favor or realizing substantially more gains than a buy-and-hold strategy, the STS approach does so while reducing risk by approximately 50 percent, since an investor is in the market on average only half of the time. (While the average holding period of STS over the long term is still roughly six months, the starting and ending dates for the favorable seasons vary considerably. The lengths of individual favorable seasons have actually varied from four and a half months to seven months.)

Harding's *Street Smart Report* Web site describes STS as "a modified buy-and-hold strategy that buys and holds but only for each year's favorable seasonal when the market usually makes most its gains for the year, and is out of the market, safely earning interest on cash in the unfavorable season, when the market tends to suffer most of its corrections."

Harding's newsletter and Web site provide his subscribers with up-to-date information on his STS strategy, including ongoing research to provide further improvements. Also appearing is an "Aggressive STS Portfolio," which incorporates the use of leveraged positions on the DJIA or S&P 500 in the market's favorable season and bear-type mutual funds in the unfavorable season. The latter feature is based on nonseasonal market timing tools. For more about Harding's newsletter and Web site, see Chapter 12.

MARK VAKKUR'S CONTRIBUTION TO SEASONAL INVESTING

Mark Vakkur, M.D., mentioned in the beginning of this chapter, expanded upon Hirsch's BSM strategy. Vakkur compared six strategies to buy-and-hold and cash for the 1950–1995 period published in the June 1996 issue of the *Technical Analysis of Stocks & Commodities* magazine.[8] Vakkur did *not* include reinvested dividends, which would bolster the buy-and-hold results. The strategies tested by Vakkur included the following:

1. Avoid September entirely: Liquidate investments on the last trading day of August, and buy back on the first trading day in October. Then, don't sell again until the last trading day of August of the next year. Do the same for all subsequent years.
2. Invest using Hirsch's BSM strategy using November entry and April exit dates.
3. Invest during Hirsch's worst months using a May entry and an October exit date.
4. Adopt a switching strategy: Be 100 percent invested in the best six months of November, December, January, March, April, and July. Be 50 percent invested and have 50 percent in cash (T-bills) in the next best three months of February, August, and October. And be 100 percent in cash for the worst three months of May, June, and September.
5. Have a 2:1 leverage, where 50 percent is invested with margin (2:1 leverage) for the best six months. As defined in strategy number 4, 100 percent is invested in the next best three months, and 100 percent is in cash for the worst three months.
6. Invest in all months of the year with 2:1 leverage.

Results of Vakkur's Analysis

Table 7-4 contains the performance results of Vakkur's strategies. During this 45-year period simply buying and holding the S&P 500 Index with a $10,000 stake in 1950 resulted in a total ending principal in 1995 of $372,388, which is equivalent to an average annual return of 8.4 percent. Investing solely in cash (T-bills) for the entire 45 years, rather than in the S&P 500 Index, resulted in a total ending principal of $110,905. This provided a 5.5 percent annual return with $261,483, less than buy-and-hold. Cash is not a viable investment, especially when adjusted for inflation.

Now, let's review the results of not investing during September. By eliminating this one month each year, the total

TABLE 7-4

Vakkur's Seasonal Strategies Using the S&P 500 Index

January 1950–December 1995

Strategy Used	Value of $10,000	Average Annual Return	Standard Deviation	Risk-Adjusted Ann. Return	Maximum Annual Gain	Maximum Annual Loss
Buy-and-Hold	$372,388	8.40%	14.40%	7.30%	57.00%	–41.30%
Ignore September	$624,135	9.60%	13.90%	8.70%	56.80%	–33.50%
Nov.–April/T-Bills*	$703,935	9.90%	9.60%	9.50%	34.40%	–16.60%
May–Oct	$58,670	4.00%	8.60%	3.60%	32.90%	–26.90%
100% Cash	$110,905	5.50%	2.80%	5.50%	14.40%	N.A.
Switching†	$997,620	10.80%	10.40%	10.20%	40.20%	–24.70%
2:1 Leverage‡	$1,839,958	12.30%	21.50%	10.00%	79.10%	–49.60%
Jan–Dec. 2:1 Lev§	$54,903	3.90%	28.50%	–0.20%	119.40%	–70.60%

Dividends were *not* included in this analysis.

*Invested in T-bills for the remaining months.

† Fully invested during best 6 months, 50% invested and 50% in T-bills for next best 3 months, and 100% in T-bills for worst 3 months which are May, June, and September.

‡ 50% margin for best 6 months, 100% invested (no margin) for next best 3 months, and 100% T-bills for worst 3 months.

§ Always using 50% margin in all months. This equivalent to 2:1 leverage.

N.A. - Not applicable.

Source: "Seasonality and the S&P 500," Mark Vakkur, M.D., *Technical Analysis of Stocks & Commodities*, vol.14, no. 6, June 1996, pp. 38–47. © Technical Analysis. Inc. Used with permission.

proceeds were $624,135, or an annual average return of 9.6 percent which is $251,747 better than buy-and-hold. Moreover, the standard deviation (measure of volatility) and maximum 12-month loss encountered was lower than buy-and-hold. That means an investor was getting a higher return with less risk. That is the smart way to invest.

According to the *Formula Research* newsletter (August 21, 2001), September has been the worst month over the past 25, 50, and 100 years: "In a study of 20 global markets from 1970 to 1992, September was the only month with negative returns in all 20 cases."

The Hirsch BSM Strategy of being invested from November to April did even better, totaling $703,935, or a 9.9 percent average annual return. That performance was $331,546 better than buy-and-hold. This strategy also had a much lower standard deviation and lower maximum 12-month loss than buy-and-hold.

The opposite strategy of buying and remaining invested during the six unfavorable months of May through October resulted in only $58,670, or 4 percent annualized with a lower standard deviation and lower maximum 12-month loss than buy-and-hold. Clearly, the worst six months is consistently poor in all respects.

A switching strategy was also tested, where a 100 percent invested position was taken during the best six months, as determined in strategy number 4, mentioned previously. (Note that this is a variation of Hirsch's BSM strategy.) Also a 50 percent invested position and 50 percent cash position was taken for the next best three months, and a 100 percent cash position (T-bills) was taken for the worst three months. This strategy resulted in a nest egg of $997,620, with a 10.8 percent annual return, translating into $625,232 more than buy-and-hold. Moreover, this strategy had a lower standard deviation and lower maximum 12-month gains and losses. In essence, although the switching strategy is less risky than buy-and-hold, the former strategy has returned 2.7 times the principal of the latter. This is an outstanding compromise of risk versus return.

Investing with margin had been used as a more aggressive strategy during the best months. The strategy of 2:1 leveraging consisted of using 50 percent margin during the best six months, as defined in previous strategy number 4, 100 percent invested with no margin for the next best three months, and going into cash during the worst three months. This strategy has ended with $1,839,958 and provided a 12.3 percent annual return. That translates into $1,467,570 more than buy-and-hold, an astounding difference. Of course, this strategy was more risky than buy-and-hold because of the leverage, and it had a higher standard deviation and large yearly maximum gains and losses. But, remember that risk and reward usually go hand in hand. In this case, the higher risk turned into an exceptionally high reward, with a 394 percent increase in value.

Performance from January 1996 to March 2002

Vakkur updated his 1996 data by publishing an article in the September 2002 *Active Trader* magazine.[9] He does not provide the risk-adjusted return and 12-month maximum gain for this period, as he had in the prior article, nor does he include reinvested dividends in his calculations. And he doesn't include the more aggressive strategies in his latest analysis. Table 7-5 provides the data for this latest time period.

Again, buy-and-hold is beaten by both the November–April strategy and by the September avoidance strategy. In both instances the annual returns were greater than buy-and-hold, and

TABLE 7-5

Vakkur's 1996–2001 Study Results
January 1996–December 2001

Strategy Used	Value of $10,000	Average Annual Return	Standard Deviation	Maximum Annual Loss
Buy-and-Hold	$18,629	10.93%	19.03%	−14.90%
Ignore September	$19,411	11.69%	14.87%	−9.40%
Nov.–April/T-Bills*	$20,834	13.00%	12.60%	−10.00%
May–October	$11,984	3.06%	10.36%	−12.80%

*Invested in T-bills for the remaining months.

Source: "Mark Your Calendar," Mark Vakkur, M.D., *Active Trader*, September 2002, pp. 96–99. © Active Trader Magazine. All rights reserved.

the standard deviations and the maximum 12-month losses were lower as well. As expected, 100 percent cash fared poorly but better than investing during the weak monthly period of May to October. Moreover, the opposite strategy of buying in the weak period again showed the worst results. So, even during the last six years the seasonal strategies continue to work as expected. This is consistent with Vakkur's prior 1996 work.

Additional Testing of September Avoidance Strategy

FORMULA RESEARCH (August 21, 2001) also tested Vakkur's September avoidance strategy from 1950 through 2001.[10] This strategy with an initial $10,000 stake would have returned an annualized total return of 13.4 percent, worth $5.6 million. During this same period buy-and-hold would have generated a return of 12.5 percent and earned $3.9 million, while the Hirsch BSM strategy would have returned 12.1 percent a year, totaling $3.3 million. Clearly, the September avoidance strategy has significantly outpaced the other two strategies. And remember that in the month of September in the year's 2000, 2001, and 2002; the Nasdaq dropped –12.7 percent, –17 percent, and –10.9 percent, respectively. Another three years of bad Septembers.

Robert W. Colby also tested the September avoidance strategy using the DJIA over a 101 year period from 1900 through 2000. In addition, instead of going to all cash in September, Colby sold short on the last trading day in August and covered the short on the last trading day in September. Starting with $100 in 1900 this strategy resulted in a profit of $164,048 with was 644 percent greater than buy-and-hold (ending balance of $22,055).

Colby also tested a slight variation of this strategy which bought on October 27 (or the next closest trading day if on that day the market was closed), and sold on the next September 5 (or the next closest trading day if on that day the market was closed). The same short strategy was used on September 5 and covered on October 27. This slight adjustment to the original test provided a substantial increase in profits to $644,467 compared to $20,699 for buy-and-hold. Thus this strategy beat buy-and-hold by 3014 percent!

CONCLUSIONS

Now that you are thoroughly drained from reading everything about the BSM, you probably want to know how to go about using it to your advantage. You have a number of alternatives:

1. **Use Hirsch's** original **BSM strategy (without the MACD) and consult the calendar twice a year.** Invest in the stock market (for example, S&P 500 Index fund, Nasdaq Composite Index fund, or Total Stock Market fund) on November 1 of each year. Then sell on April 30 of the following year (and go into cash equivalents—a money fund or T-bills) until November 1 of the next year.

2. **Use Harding's adjusted BSM strategy.** Invest in the stock market (for example, a S&P 500 Index fund) on the last day in October of each year, and then sell on the fourth business day in May of the following year (and go into cash equivalents—a money fund or T-bills). This had better results than the original Hirsch BSM strategy.

3. **Use the MACD indicator in conjunction with the original Hirsch or the original Harding BSM strategy.** Use a free charting Web site such as *www.bigcharts.com*, *www.stockcharts.com*, or *www.clearstation.com* to chart the index you are tracking (for example, the DJIA or the Nasdaq Composite Index) for the past year using daily prices. Place the MACD indicator with settings of (12,25,9) on the bottom of the chart. In the April–June time frame look for a MACD crossover signal to the downside to sell your investments. Likewise in the October–December time frame look for a MACD crossover signal to the upside to get into the market.

4. **Avoid the stock market** entirely each **September.** Simply sell on the last day in August and buy on the first day in October. For the more venturesome investors follow Colby's September strategy of shorting during September and covering and going long in October. And you may want to consider using his other strategy of shorting on September 5 and covering the short on October 27 and then going long.

5. **Subscribe to** *Sy Harding's Street Smart Report* **monthly newsletter for his STS system signals for $225 a year.** He provides his newly revised methodology for the MACD-based signals via his hotline and on his Web site. This seasonal strategy is only one feature of this newsletter and hotline service. See Chapter 12 for complete information on the newsletter

6. **Subscribe to the monthly** *Stock Trader's Almanac Investor* **for $97.50 (for new subscribers), which includes the latest copy of the** *Stock Trader's Almanac, 2003.* Jeff Hirsch tracks the BSM and provides his MACD buy and sell signals when they occur via Web and phone access. This is only one feature of this newsletter.

Be aware that Harding and Hirsch use a different methodology for obtaining their MACD signals, so you have to decide which one has the best track record. In 2003, for example, Hirsch's MACD sell signal was triggered on April 10, while Harding's was hit on May 19. Harding's signal captured a higher return than Hirsch's signal.

It's your choice which alternative BSM to use, based on your ability to work with the MACD, charting software, and understanding of the strategy. As far as actually using the September avoidance strategy or the strategies with leverage as illustrated by Vakkur, that choice is solely up to you with your level of knowledge and comfort with the risks these strategies entail. As far as which investment vehicles to use, you can select from any of those mentioned in the previous chapters such as index funds, sector funds, leveraged funds, and ETFs. Be sure to use stop-loss rules in case the "buy" strategy does not work in certain years, which is always a possibility. You would re-enter the market on the next year's buy signal.

ENDNOTES

1. E. S. Browning, "Danger for the Economy—Yes: Rally for Stocks Now," *The Wall Street Journal*, November 4, 2002.

2. Jonathan R. Laing, "Merry Month," *Barron's*, May 7, 2001.

3. Mark Vakkur, M.D., "Mark Your Calendars: Stock Market Seasonality," *Active Trader*, September 2002, pp. 96–97.

4. *Stock Trader's Almanac, 2003*, published by the Hirsch Organization Inc. Their Web site is *www.stocktradersalmanac.com*.

5. Since investing in the DJIA as an index back in the 1950s was not possible (for example, Diamonds traded on the AMEX did not exist then) the results presented are theoretical in nature, based on back testing the data. Also, the almanac does not mention whether or not reinvested dividends have been included in the performance numbers.

6. *Stock Trader's Almanac, 2003*, p. 58.

7. Sy Harding, *Riding the Bear: How to Prosper in the Coming Bear Market*, Adams Media Corporation, Holbrook, MA, 1999.

8. Mark Vakkur, M.D., "Seasonality and the S&P 500," *Technical Analysis of Stocks & Commodities*, vol.14, no. 6, June 1996.

9. Vakkur, "Mark Your Calendar," pp. 96–99.

10. *FORMULA RESEARCH*, August 21, 2001, vol. 6, no. 11.

CHAPTER 8

Combining Presidential Cycle Years with Seasonality

Bulls and bears aren't responsible for as many stock losses as bum steers.

Olin Miller

PRESIDENTIAL CYCLE INVESTING

After spending time going through the numerous monthly seasonality strategies presented in the last chapter, you probably thought that's about all you can squeeze out of the calendar. Guess again. There are more profitable strategies in this chapter. Certain seasonal strategies will not be covered because they are more applicable to traders than to investors. If you are interested in pursuing seasonal strategies, as a trader or investor, be sure to get a copy of the Stock Trader's Almanac, available at 1-800-477-3400, or at their Web site: www.stocktradersalmanac.com.

Vakkur Tests Optimum Months Combined with Optimum Presidential Cycle Years

Mark Vakkur made another significant research contribution by publishing another seminal article in the October 1996 issue of *Technical*

Analysis of Stocks & Commodities.[1] In this nine-page article, Vakkur combined the optimum months with the optimum presidential cycle years. The results were outstanding; so let's get right to them.

The election cycle years are:

- Pre-election year: The year before the election year (for example, 1987, 1991, 1995, 1999, and 2003)
- Election year: The year of the election (for example, 1988, 1992, 1996, 2000, and 2004)
- Postelection year: The year after the election year (for example, 1989, 1993, 1997, 2001, and 2005)
- Midterm election year: Two years after the last election year and also prior to the next election year (for example, 1990, 1994, 1998, 2002, and 2006)

Historically, there is a four-year cycle in the stock market encompassing the presidential election years. Usually, the market rises more in the pre-election year than in the election year itself. The election year is the second best of those four years. And in the two years after the election, the market usually does not make much progress. Table 8-1 contains the data from 1950 through 1995 delineating the average monthly returns of the S&P 500 Index in each of the four years of the presidential election cycle, as compiled by Vakkur.

As the table indicates, the pre-election years' stock market returns are by far superior to any of the other three years of the presidential election cycle. The average annual return since 1950 was 18.72 percent and the market rose every pre-election year. The next best performing year was the election year, with an average annual return of 10.08 percent and a 91 percent success ratio.

Conversely, the worst performing presidential cycle year was the postelection year, with an average annual return of only 2 percent and with the markets rising only 45 percent of the time in those years. Next worst performance was the midterm year, which sported an average annual return of a meager 4.63 percent, with a positive market in 55 percent of the years.

Freeburg Tests Presidential Cycle Back to 1886

Nelson Freeburg tested the quadrennial presidential cycle back to 1886 through 2001, to double-check and expand upon the data tested

TABLE 8-1

Average Monthly Return of the S&P 500 (Dividends Excluded), 1950–1995

	Avg. Monthly Return of S&P 500	Percent +/– to all years	Percentage of Months Market Rose	Average Annual Return	Percentage of Years Market Rose
All Years	0.74%	NA	57%	9.00%	71%
Postelection	0.12%	−0.62%	49%	2.00%	45%
Midterm	0.46%	−0.28%	57%	4.63%	55%
Pre-election	1.50%	0.76%	66%	18.72%	100%
Election	0.84%	0.10%	62%	10.08%	91%

Source: Vakkur, Mark, M.D. "Seasonality and the Presidential Election Cycle," *Technical Analysis of Stocks & Commodities,* October 1996, vol. 14, no. 10, p.22. © 1996 Technical Analysis, Inc. Used with permission.

by Vakkur. In the May 31, 2002, issue of *FORMULA RESEARCH*, Freeburg provided the statistics for the DJIA (refer to Table 8-2).[2] Keep in mind that Vakkur used the S&P 500 Index (without dividends) in calculating his numbers (nominal return), while Freeburg used the DJIA (without dividends), since that index had a much longer price history available. Clearly, there has been a definite bias toward higher stock market returns in the pre-election and election years during the 45 years observed in Vakkur's analysis, as well as in Freeburg's more up-to-date and comprehensive analysis.

TABLE 8-2

DJIA Annual Gain by Year in Electoral Cycle, 1886–2001

Year	Annual Gain	Percent of Years Up
All years	7.60%	64%
Pre-election	11.10%	79%
Election	8.40%	69%
Midterm	4.00%	55%
Post-election	5.00%	52%

Source: FORMULA RESEARCH, May 31, 2002.

Vakkur's Leveraged Strategies Earn Millions

Refer to Table 8-3 to see how an investor fared by taking advantage of Vakkur's several strategies from 1950 to 1995.[3] First, let's get the lowdown on the returns from buy-and-hold. This often-touted simple no-decision strategy had an average annual return of 8.4 percent that turned a $10,000 initial investment into $372,388 with a 12-month maximum drawdown (or maximum loss of 41.3 percent during the test period). This means that the buy-and-hold investor sat through this loss without flinching. In reality, the average investor would have a hard time doing this.

Now compare those results with the simple strategy of investing only during the best performing two presidential cycle years—the pre-election and election years—and remaining in cash for the other two years. This strategy has an average annual return of 10 percent, which is 1.6 percentage points a year better than buy-and-hold. But over 45 years, that incremental difference resulted in the growth of the $10,000 investment to $733,605, compared to $372,388 for buy-and-hold. This translates into a 197 percent improvement over buy-and-hold, with a standard deviation of only 8.3 percent versus 14 percent for buy-and-hold, and a maximum 12-month drawdown of only 18.7 percent. So, on all counts, this presidential cycle strategy provided superior results with 50 percent less risk, since you were invested for only two years out of four. In my book, a higher return with less risk is always a win-win strategy.

You may be curious to see the results of investing only in the worst two performing presidential cycle years—the postelection and midterm election years. As expected, the performance results were much worse than buy-and-hold, with only a 3.9 percent average annual return and the same annual maximum drawdown of –41.3 percent. Even the lowly 100 percent cash portfolio (not investing at all) beat these two years' performance by generating an average annual return of 5.5 percent with no negative drawdown! When cash is able to beat buy-and-hold (for the worst two presidential cycle years), you know that you should avoid investing at all. Vakkur tested a number of different strategies to determine their profitability. The first strategy used was with 2:1 leveraging. This strategy used 50 percent margin in the pre-election year, invested funds with no margin in the election year, and was 100

TABLE 8-3

Comparison of Buy-and-Hold to Presidential Election Cycle Scenarios, January 1950–December 1995

Strategy Used	Value of $10,000	Average Annual Return	Standard Deviation	Risk-Adjusted Ann. Return	Maximum Annual Gain	Maximum Annual Loss
Buy-and-Hold	$372,388	8.40%	14.40%	7.30%	57.00%	−41.30%
100% Cash	$110,905	5.50%	2.80%	5.50%	14.40%	0.90%
Pre-election and Election yrs.	$733,605	10.00%	8.30%	9.70%	43.40%	−18.70%
Post-election and Midterm yrs.	$56,297	3.90%	11.80%	3.20%	38.90%	−41.30%
2:1 Leverage*	$1,272,369	11.40%	14.80%	10.03%	86.30%	−46.00%
Leverage Best Months†	$2,183,257	12.70%	15.20%	11.60%	64.20%	−21.20%
Optimal Months‡	$5,189,384	14.90%	15.50%	13.70%	60.10%	−21.00%

*2:1 leverage (50% margin) in pre-election year and 100% invested in election year.

†Leveraged 2:1 (November–April) in the pre-election and election years; 100% invested during these same months in the post-election and mid-term election years, and 100% invested during the May-October period during the same two years. The only time there would be a 100% cash allocation would be in the May-October postelection and mid-term election years.

‡Optimal Months:2:1 leverage in pre-election and election years in the following months in those years: January to April, July, November and December; 100% cash in May and September of all 4 years, and June and August of the postelection and midterm election years; and 100% invested in all the other months not mentioned: January to April, July, and October to December in the post-election/midterm years, and June and August in the pre-election years.

Source: Mark, Vakkur, M. D. "Seasonality and the Presidential Election Cycle," *Technical Analysis of Stocks & Commodities,* October 1996, vol.14, no.10. Copyright © 1996 Technical Analysis, Inc. Used with permission.

percent in cash for the other two years. As expected, this strategy quadrupled the return of buy and hold.

With an average annual return of 11.4 percent, and an ending balance of $1,272,369, this leveraged strategy provided an additional return of $538,764 over the nonleveraged pre-election and election-year strategy. Using this more aggressive strategy also resulted in more than doubling the maximum annual drawdown (largest loss incurred) to –46 percent from –18.7 percent in the prior strategy. Also, the maximum annual gain jumped about 100 percent, to 86.3 percent from 43.4 percent. And the standard deviation (variability around the 11.4 percent return) rose to 14.8 percent from 8.3 percent.

As Milton Friedman, the Noble Laureate economist, said, "There is no such thing as a free lunch." And as the saying goes, "no pain, no gain." As mentioned earlier, risk and reward go hand in hand. Investors who have a higher risk tolerance may want to consider using this leveraged strategy. However, they should use a stop-loss order to minimize the their risk of a large intra-year drawdown and avoid getting clobbered when the market goes against them.

Vakkur tested another leveraged strategy called the Leveraged Best Months (LBM) strategy. Here the best performing months (November to April) of the year were leveraged 2 to 1 (50 percent margin) in the pre-election and election years, 100 percent was invested during these same months in the postelection and midterm election years, and 100 percent was invested during the May–October period during the same two years. The only time that there would be a 100 percent cash allocation would be in the May–October postelection and midterm election years.

This strategy really hit pay dirt, with an annual return of 12.7 percent and total ending principal of $2,183,257. Moreover, both the maximum drawdown and the maximum yearly gain were reduced. And the standard deviation moved up only slightly to 15.2 percent from the previously reviewed 2:1 leveraged strategy of 14.8 percent. On a risk-adjusted basis the LBM strategy is the best tested so far. This strategy was less risky than the 2:1 leveraged strategy while providing an additional $910,888, quite an astounding difference in the bottom line.

Before reviewing another highly profitable leveraged strategy that more than doubled the LBM returns, let's look at Table 8-4 showing the monthly returns over 45 years in each of the four election cycle years. The best seven months in the pre-election year and election years were January, February, March, April, July, November, and December. The worst months in all the four election cycle years were May and September. Two more worse months occurred in June and August of the postelection and midterm election years. All the other months not mentioned—January, February, March, April, July, October, November, and December in the postelection/midterm years, and June and August in the pre-election years—were considered average months.

Using this information, Vakkur formulated another highly profitable strategy that he referred to as the "optimal months" strategy. Look at the footnote in Table 8-3, which provides the exact

TABLE 8-4

Monthly Results During Quadrennial Presidential Election Year Cycle, January 1950–December 1995

Month	Postelection Avg. S&P 500 Return (%)	Midterm Avg. S&P 500 Return (%)	Pre-election Avg. S&P 500 Return (%)	Election Avg. S&P 500 Return (%)
All	0.12	0.46	1.50	0.84
January	0.71	−0.90	5.38	0.87
February	−1.17	0.97	1.44	0.08
March	0.90	−0.36	2.29	0.19
April	0.24	0.39	3.27	0.93
May	1.00	−0.20	−0.14	0.01
June	−1.07	−2.12	1.59	2.00
July	1.10	1.27	1.65	1.10
August	−1.03	0.49	1.56	0.43
September	−1.28	−0.98	−0.40	0.27
October	1.45	2.51	−2.54	0.44
November	0.35	2.46	0.58	2.32
December	0.18	1.97	3.35	1.43
Nov. - Jan.	0.41	1.18	3.10	1.54
Nov. - Apr.	0.20	0.76	2.72	0.97
May - Oct.	0.03	0.16	0.29	0.71

Source: Mark, Vakkur, M. D., "Seasonality and the Presidential Election Cycle," *Technical Analysis of Stocks & Commodities*, October 1996, vol.14, no.10.,p. 30. Copyright © 1996 Technical Analysis, Inc. Used with permission.

"optimal months" strategy used. That strategy produced an annual return of 14.9 percent, or an astonishing $5,189,384 over the 45 years tested. With only a slightly higher 0.3 percent standard deviation than the LBM strategy and virtually equivalent drawdowns, this strategy added another $3 million to the bottom line. Also, on a risk-adjusted basis, this strategy had the highest annual return of all the strategies illustrated, at 13.7 percent.

Freeburg also tested the strategy of investing in the market (using the DJIA) only in the pre-election and election year from 1886 to 2001, and going into cash in the other two years.[4] He found that this strategy resulted in an annual return of 5.9 percent compared to 5.2 percent for buy-and-hold. This 70-basis-point difference, on a $10,000 initial investment, was valued at $8.4 million at the end of the test period, compared to $3.7 million for buy-and-hold.

The opposite strategy of investing in the two weakest performing years and going to cash during the two strong years since 1886 has returned 3.6 percent per year, worth $607,000. This is 93 percent less than the optimal strategy.

Freeburg ran additional leveraged tests of the data, using the strongest months in the strongest years, and they confirmed Vakkur's results. Since Vakkur analyzed the data through 1995, the question is how has the four-year presidential cycle (in particular using the strongest months in the strongest years) performed since then? Freeburg, who updated the data from 1995 through April 2002, found that using Vakkur's methodology produced an annual gain of 17.4 percent a year compared to 10.7 percent for the buy-and-hold S&P 500 Index. Even since 1886, use of the same methodology has given an annual return of 8.3 percent compared to 5.2 percent for the DJIA.

In conclusion, focusing on the optimal months in the presidential election cycle years really brings home the bacon. This strategy is far superior to just investing during the entire pre-election and election years, with outstanding return and risk parameters.

MIDTERM TO ELECTION YEAR PHENOMENA

Over the years, a number of analysts have scrutinized the presidential cycle years to look for patterns. One very consistent pattern that has been uncovered occurs from the lows of the midterm election cycle year to the highs of the following election year. These results are shown in Table 8-5, which was prepared by the Hays Advisory Group.[5] Of the 21 midterm years until the election years, 20 have produced gains. Although the S&P 500 Index gains have ranged from 18.4 percent to 121.9 percent, the average gain has been 56.8 percent. Excluding the only loss of 43.6 percent from 1930 to 1932, the average gain for the period has been 61.8 percent.

The Hays Advisory Group also provided data on the performance of the November through April time frame for each midterm election year from 1950 through 1998.[6] Figure 8-1 depicts the S&P 500 Index gains in the midterm (second) election year. As you can see every single year produced a gain. As of July 1, 2003, this midterm election year looks like another winner with the major averages up at least 10 percent for the year to date.

Table 8-6, also provided by the Hays Advisory Group, provides the S&P 500 data not only for the midterm year but the other surrounding years as well.[7] Just examining the midterm year November to April performance since 1950, we see that in every instance there was a positive return. The mean return was 18.1 percent, with the lowest return being 9 percent in 1994 and the highest 24.9 percent in 1970. The next best year was the pre-election year with a mean return of 6.3 percent, with only two years of small negative returns.

The election year November–April period returned an average 3.8 percent with three negative years. Lastly, the postelection year performance was the worst, with a 1.8 percent return with seven down periods.

CONCLUSIONS

Based upon the research by Freeburg, Vakkur, and the Hays Advisory Group, the intelligent investor should carefully consider the potential financial benefits of combining the strongest seasonal monthly and presidential cycle years.

By the time you read this book, you will probably have seen the 2003 market peak for the year, and then start its decline again. You may have been in cash for the first half or three-quarters of 2003. Don't be concerned, since the best six months strategy is coming up around November 1, 2003. And if you miss that time frame, the

TABLE 8-5

Presidential Election Cycle, Low to High

Mid-Year	Mid-Year Low	Election Year	Election Year-High	% gain or (loss)
1918	73.38	1920	109.88	49.7%
1922	78.59	1924	120.51	53.3%
1926	135.20	1928	300.00	121.9%
1930	157.51	1932	88.78	−43.6%
1934	85.51	1936	184.90	116.2%
1938	98.95	1940	152.80	54.4%
1942	92.92	1944	152.53	64.2%
1946	163.12	1948	193.16	18.4%
1950	196.81	1952	292.00	48.4%
1954	279.87	1956	521.05	86.2%
1958	436.89	1960	685.47	56.9%
1962	535.76	1964	891.71	66.4%
1966	744.32	1968	985.21	32.4%
1970	631.16	1972	1036.27	64.2%
1974	577.60	1976	1014.79	75.7%
1978	742.12	1980	1000.17	34.8%
1982	776.92	1984	1286.64	65.6%
1986	1502.29	1988	2183.50	45.3%
1990	2365.10	1992	3413.21	44.3%
1994	3593.25	1996	6560.91	82.6%
1998	7539.07	2000	11722.98	55.5%
		Avg. of All Years		56.8%
		Avg. of All Up Years		61.8%
2002	???	But What If???		
2002	7702.34	2004	12077.27	56.8%
2002	7702.34	2004	12462.39	61.8%

Note: DJIA is used as the index in these comparisons.

Source: Morning Market Comments, by Don Hays, September 16, 2002. Reprinted with permission of Hays Advisory Group.

worst six months period pops up around May 1, 2004. With seasonality investing there is always something happening, either on the long or the short side of the market, and you can invest on both the long and short sides of the market, if you know what you are doing.

Buy-and-hold is certainly not a recommended strategy in any circumstance, especially in light of the ability to use calendar-based

FIGURE 8-1

Seasonal Periods—Second Year of Presidential Cycle

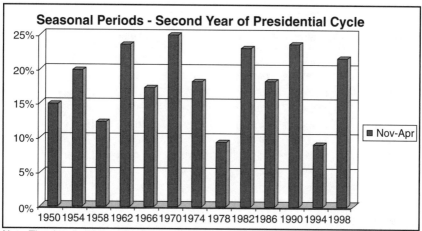

Note: The data in this bar chart is the S&P 500 Index percentage changes during
November through April of the following year.
Source: Mark Dodson and Hays Advisory Group. Morning Market Comments, September 26, 2002. Reprinted with
permission.

investing strategies to limit losses during the weak presidential
cycle years—the most recent of which were 2001 and 2002. And
true to form those two years provided negative returns to all buy-
and-hold investors. The next two weak presidential cycle years are
2005 and 2006, so be prepared for them. The recommended investment vehicles to use for both the seasonal and presidential cycle
strategies are index funds, leveraged funds and ETFs (such as the
SPY and QQQs). Of course, you will be paying capital gains taxes
if you are investing in nonretirement funds, and you won't be if
you are investing your retirement funds. Therefore, these strategies
are particularly attractive for your retirement accounts, where your
profits compound year over year tax-free.

ENDNOTES

1. Mark Vakkur, M. D., "Seasonality and the Presidential Election Cycle,"
   Technical Analysis of Stocks & Commodities, October 1996, vol.14, no. 10.
2. *FORMULA RESEARCH*, vol. VI, no. 12, May 31, 2002.

TABLE 8-6

Election Cycle and November–April Returns

Nov. - Apr.	Mid-term	Pre-elect.	Election	Post-elect.
1950	14.8%	1.7%	0.4%	15.2%
1954	19.8%	14.3%	0.4%	5.8%
1958	12.2%	−5.5%	22.3%	−4.9%
1962	23.5%	7.4%	5.0%	−1.5%
1966	17.2%	4.5%	0.3%	−16.1%
1970	24.9%	14.3%	−4.1%	−16.6%
1974	18.1%	14.2%	−4.3%	4.9%
1978	9.2%	4.4%	4.2%	−4.5%
1982	23.0%	−2.1%	8.3%	24.1%
1986	18.2%	3.8%	11.0%	−2.8%
1990	23.5%	5.7%	5.1%	−3.6%
1994	9.0%	12.5%	13.6%	21.6%
1998	21.5%	6.6%	−12.6%	1.6%
Mean	18.1%	6.3%	3.8%	1.8%
Geo. Mean	18.0%	6.1%	3.5%	1.1%
Std Dev.	5.2%	6.0%	8.5%	12.1%

The data in this table represent percentage changes for the S&P 500 Index.
Source: Mark Dodson, and the Hays Advisory Group. *Morning Market Comments*, September 26, 2002. Reprinted with permission.

3. Vakkur, "Seasonality and the Presidential Election Cycle."

4. *FORMULA RESEARCH*, May 31, 2002, p. 8.

5. Don Hays, *Morning Market Comments*, September 16, 2002. Reprinted with permission of the Hays Advisory Group.

6. Ibid.

7. Ibid.

CHAPTER 9

Using Moving Averages

> There is only one side of the market and it is not the bull side or
> the bear side, but the right side.
>
> *Jesse Livermore*

The objective of using a moving average on a price chart of a mutual
fund or ETF is to catch each major up trend and down trend. Using
moving averages properly will enable you to capture approximately
75 percent of the move in each direction. You miss the first part of the
move because a moving average is a lagging indicator that shows you
what has happened in the past and, if it continues, what the future
trend will be. Therefore, it has great market timing value, as we shall
see in this chapter, for when a moving average signal is given, this
adds puts the odds in your favor that your trade will succeed.

SIMPLE MOVING-AVERAGE BASICS

A simple moving average is calculated each day by adding the last
day's closing price to the total of all closing prices over the time
period chosen, and then subtracting the first day's closing price.
However, you need not calculate it for yourself because all the chart
services automatically do it for you once you indicate the time
frame you wish to graph.

FIGURE 9–1

200-and 50-day moving averages

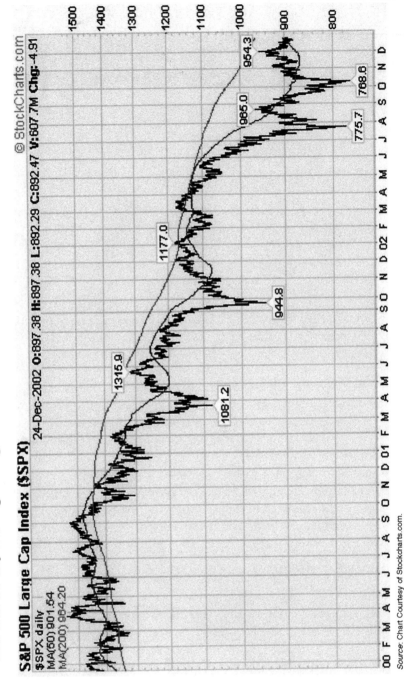

S&P 500 Large Cap Index ($SPX)

$SPX daily
MA(50) 901.54
MA(200) 964.20

24-Dec-2002 O:897.38 H:897.38 L:892.29 C:892.47 V:607.7M Chg:-4.91

© StockCharts.com

Source: Chart Courtesy of Stockcharts.com.

Securities prices, market indexes, and mutual fund prices vac-illate up and down from day to day, week to week and month to month. Because of this it often becomes difficult to discern which way the prices are actually moving. A moving average is therefore used to smooth the data so that the trend can be easily detected. A rising moving-average line indicates that prices are trending up, while a declining line indicates the opposite. A flat line indicates a market stuck in a trading range that can't seem to make up its mind where it is going.

You can create a moving average of any length (e.g., 10-day, 20-day, 50-day, 200-day) and for any time period (minutes, hours, days, weeks, months) depending upon what you are trying to achieve: for example, for trading the market over short time frames (minutes) or for investing (days or weeks).

Basically, when timing the market, you want to be long the market when the price of the stock or index crosses above the mov-ing average, and out-of-the market or short the market, when the price crosses below the moving average. To determine when this happens you would be following the price crossovers of the mov-ing averages for one or more of the major market indexes such as the DJIA, the Nasdaq Composite, the S&P 500, the Nasdaq 100, the Russell 2000, etc.

Referring to Figure 9-1, you can see that when the 50-dma crossed below the S&P 500 Index's price you would have been out of the market at the end of February 2001, missing the 239-point drop from 1320 to 1081.2, you would have been out of the market in mid-June 2001, missing the 275-point drop from 1220 to 944.8, and you would have been and out of the market from late April 2002, missing the 354 point drop from 1130 to 775.7. Just using the 50-dma in this example would have partially protected you from the fast-falling declines that occurred at those times.

Some of the more popular time periods used by market pro-fessionals for moving average crossovers are the 20-dma, the 50-dma, and the 200-dma. Keep in mind that to time the market using moving averages, it is critical to select an average that is not too sensitive to "whipsaws." This relates to rapid upswings in price above the moving average only to soon reverse and fall below the average, and to downswings which can do the same, first falling below the moving average and then soon turning up above the average. This situation is most common during a market that is in a sideways or trading range. Also, be aware that the shorter the time period chosen the more subject you are to whipsaws and false breakouts while the longer the time frame the slower the signal, meaning that you will miss a part of the move that had already begun. So, the time frame you will most likely choose will be relative to whether you are trading with a short-term or a long-term objective.

200-Day Moving Average

The 200-day moving average (200-dma) is considered the one most indicative that a real trend is in place because it covers a period of 40 weeks worth of trading. In Figure 9-1 you can see that the 200-dma (the upper line, beginning in November 2001) is slower moving and farther away from the prices, while the 50-day is a tighter fit. One popular strategy is to make your buy decisions when the faster (50-dma) moving average crosses above the slower (200-dma) moving average and to sell when the 50-dma crosses below the 200-dma. This strategy does not always produce the best results, however.

For example, in Figure 9-1 the 50-dma crossed the 200-dma to the downside in early November 2001. And that was the last signal given through year-end 2002. So you would have sold your investments when the S&P 500 Index was around 1430, and you would not have had your money at risk while the index plummeted 46 percent to 768 on October 9, 2002. Imagine how pleased you would have been to be in cash during this catastrophic bear market. And this could have been accomplished by using this simple technique, just by pulling up this type of chart once a week and looking for a crossover signal to occur.

50-Day Moving Average

Looking at Figure 9-1 again, just focus on the 50-dma for a moment—that is the more wavy line closer to the prices. You can see that you had many buy and sell signals (whipsaws using this moving average's crossovers, especially from January through

September 2000. And through the end of 2002 there were another 15 buy and sell signals given.

You must be especially careful in a sideways market because too many whipsaw buy and sell signals often lose money during trading ranges. In a sideways market you are better off in cash. The problem is that you do not know which signal will work out beforehand, so you have to take all of them. Otherwise, you do not have a strategy. You should never take some signals and avoid others. That is a path to confusion, loss of discipline, and ultimately, financial ruin.

Losing money some of the time is an integral part of any trading system if it is to work. You just need to remember to limit your loss to a maximum 10% on each trade and if you are stopped out, just sit tight and wait for the next signal before you jump back in.

How to Use Single and Dual Moving Averages

Here's how you use a single moving average timing system: If you are using an S&P 500 Index fund or SPYs, then you would buy when the SPY price pierces above the moving-average line. Likewise, you would sell the fund when the price declines below the moving average line. When you sell, you can either go into a money fund or, if you are an aggressive investor, go short using bear funds offered by Rydex or ProFunds, or you could simply short the SPY and ride it on the down leg. This is the way you would handle any investment vehicle, whether it be a stock, index fund, sector fund or exchange-traded fund. Whenever the price crosses the moving average line you act on that signal.

Another variation is to use a dual moving average crossover system. In a dual moving average crossing system which uses the 50-dma and the 200-dma a buy signal is given when the 50-dma crosses over the 200-dma and a sell signal is given when the 50-dma falls below the 200-dma. The difference between the single moving average system and the dual moving average system is that in the single system the trading signals are given when the price crosses the moving average line whereas in the dual system the signal is given when the faster moving average line (50-dma) crosses the slower moving average line (200-dma).

RESEARCHERS' MOVING-AVERAGE TESTS

Over the years, a number of researchers have tested various moving-average lengths. This section focuses on the work of Robert W. Colby, Michael McDonald, Paul Merriman, Dennis Tilley, and John J. Murphy.

Robert W. Colby's Moving-Average DJIA Tests

Robert W. Colby is the author of *The Encyclopedia of Technical Market Indicators* (McGraw-Hill, 2003). This 820-page book covers hundreds of technical market indicators that he back tested against a buy-and-hold strategy. As you may recall from previous chapters, back testing involves using a strategy with historical data to determine how an index of stocks would have performed in the past. The results do not mean that anyone could have achieved the results shown. Basically, back testing is used to test specific strategies certain to determine their validity on a theoretical basis. If the results were valid over long time frames, then they may work as well in the future.

Colby tested many simple moving average lengths, using DJIA daily closing prices, from 1900 through 2001. His assumptions in testing the data were that all profits were reinvested, but that dividends, transaction costs, and taxes were excluded in his calculations. A buy signal was generated when the DJIA price pierced the moving average (being tested) to the upside, and a sell signal was generated when the DJIA price declined below the moving average to the downside. All sell signals were used to short the market. Surprisingly, Colby found that all the simple moving averages between 1 day and 385 days beat buy-and-hold. In particular, he discovered that all the moving averages between 1 day and 100 days beat buy-and-hold by more than 7:1.

His best results were with the shortest lengths the 1-, 4-, and 5-dma, which produced outstanding results with net profits in the billions of dollars. For the intermediate-term lengths, the 66-dma was 31 times better than buy-and-hold over the 102-year test period. The price crossovers of the 66-day simple moving average generated a net profit of $639,933 on a $100 initial one-time investment, compared to $20,105 profit for buy-and-hold. Testing the popular 200-dma, Colby determined that the net profit was only $121,257, about 19 percent of the 66-dma's profit, but still six times better than buy-and-hold.

Of the long-term period lengths, Colby determined that the 126-dma was the most profitable strategy, with a net profit of $426,746. This was 2022.54 percent more profitable than buy-and-hold. Colby also noted that since the crash of 1987 the short-selling strategy on the sell signals has not been profitable. Interestingly, only 185 trades out of 886 (21 percent) were profitable over this 102-year time frame. But the average winning trade amount of $6886.30 compares very well to the average trade loss of –$1238.08. That is why overall, this strategy is profitable. The average number of days for each trade's length is 42.

You may be wondering why Colby's test results for the short-term moving averages had much higher returns than the returns for the intermediate and longer-term moving averages. Clearly, the faster moving averages (fewer days) react more quickly to changes in direction than longer-term moving averages; therefore overall the profits keep mounting and the losses are cut short more quickly. One downside of using short-term moving averages is the large number of trades during the year. For the average investor an intermediate to long-term moving average approach is much easier to implement and track.

Michael McDonald's Moving-Average S&P 500 Index Tests

Michael McDonald in his book *Predict Market Swings with Technical Analysis* (Wiley, 2002), back-tested numerous moving-average lengths to determine which ones provided the best performance compared to buy-and-hold against the S&P 500 Index including re-invested dividends. He found that superior results were obtained using the 72-dma and 132-dma. Remember that Colby, who did his back testing with the DJIA, found that the 66-dma and the 126-dma were high-profitability strategies. Results this similar on two different indexes for different time periods provide confirmation that these moving-average lengths are valid timing tools.

In 1983, McDonald back-tested all daily moving averages using the S&P 500 Index between 5 days to 200 days, in one-day increments, to determine the most profitable time frame. McDonald used the next day's closing price, after the signal was given, as the buy or sell price. This approach is a more conservative one than using the same-day price when the moving average crossovers occurred because acting on the same-day price usually provided increased profits for the investor. McDonald replicated his research in 1992 and in 1999, to confirm the results of his original study. To do this he divided the data into four distinct periods: the Great Depression, the 20-year post–World War II bull market, the 1966–1982 sideways market, and the 1982–1999 bull market. According to McDonald, the original results were confirmed by the later studies. Over the 71-year total test period the buy-and-hold strategy produced an average return of 10.3 percent a year, including reinvested dividends, whereas the shorter moving averages of 50 days or less produced average returns of 9.5 percent a year not keeping up with buy-and-hold. One of the best returns was obtained with the 130-dma that provided an annual return of 12.5 percent. Remember that Colby's short-term moving average results did not include reinvested dividends and used the DJIA instead of the S&P 500 Index; therefore, his results were different.

Paul Merriman's 100-Day Moving-Average Nasdaq 100 Index Tests

Paul Merriman, president of Merriman Capital Management Inc., is a well-known market timer, author, educator, and mutual fund manager who has conducted extensive back testing on market timing and diversification strategies.

Merriman wrote an article, "All About Market-timing" focusing on the 100-dma to make buy and sell decisions. You may read it on his Web site at *www.fundadvice.com*. Merriman tested what would have happened if you had invested $1000 at the beginning of 1942 and left the money untouched through year-end 2001, compared to what would have happened if you used the 100-day simple moving average to move in and out of the market. The simple 100-dma system was used to generate buy and sell signals on the S&P 500 Total Return Index (dividends reinvested) and on the Nasdaq 100 Index. The signals were initiated when the index prices crossed their respective moving average to the upside (a buy signal) and the downside (a sell signal).

Merriman compared the results to a buy-and-hold strategy, and a 50 percent (equivalent to a beta of 1.5) and 100 percent leveraged position (a beta of 2.0). On all sell signals, the proceeds were invested into a money market account. He did not go short on the sell signals. The data in these original studies ended at year-end 2000, but Merriman was kind enough to provide me with the updated data through year-end 2001. The results of the Nasdaq Index testing are presented here.

Merriman tested the 100-dma using the Nasdaq 100 Index over a 30-year period from 1972 to 2001 with and without leverage. From 1972 through 1999 this timing approach had only one loss in 1993 of −1.7%. That compared with five years of losses (1973, 1974, 1981, 1984, and 1990) for buy-and-hold. Moreover, even though 2000 was a big down year for buy-and-hold, at −36.8 percent, the moving average timing lost only −19 percent. In 2000, buy-and-hold lost −32.7 percent, while the 100-dma was up 1.7 percent. That is quite an accomplishment.

The buy-and-hold strategy for the Nasdaq 100 Index from 1972 through 2001 yielded an annualized return of 11.8 percent, compared to 18.9 percent for the 100-dma approach. Thus, the 100-dma approach beats buy-and-hold with a lower standard deviation: 19.3 percent versus 28.0 percent. This was coupled with less than half the drawdown levels (maximum loss) experienced by buy-and-hold during the worst months. Since 1972, a $1000 investment in the Nasdaq 100 Index would have accumulated to $28,396 with the buy-and-hold scenario, compared to $180,476 for the 100-dma approach without using leverage. Therefore, the 100-dma results were 534 percent better than buy-and-hold, with less risk—a great combination.

Using 50 percent leverage on the Nasdaq 100 Index using the 100-dma approach increased the annual return to 23.2 percent, with an ending value of $522,782. For the 100 percent leveraged case (a beta of 2.0 and similar to investing in the Rydex Velocity 100 Fund or UltraOTC ProFund), the annualized return was 26.9 percent, with an ending value of $1,270,131. In both leveraged cases, the standard deviations were higher than buy-and-hold, but both leveraged strategies had better drawdown numbers—certainly a desirable situation. Again, be aware that investing in instruments with higher betas entails much more risk and moves in either direction are much deeper and much faster.

Looking at the numbers on a risk-versus-reward basis, the 100-dma timing approach with the Nasdaq Composite Index is superior to buy-and-hold with regard to total return, being out of the market for 36.4 percent of the time, and for minimizing the losses in the bear market slaughters. Also, more aggressive investors may want to use the Rydex Velocity 100 Fund or the UltraOTC ProFund as their investing vehicle to replicate a leveraged strategy.

In his article, Merriman summed up what was learned about using the moving-average approach, he said:

> Contrary to [what] many of the critics of timing [say], a timing system can be "wrong" more than 60 percent of the time and still produce a phenomenal increase in return. ... [T]iming is more effective when it is applied to more volatile assets instead of less volatile ones. ... [T]iming is even more effective using leverage. And we saw that it always reduces risk by taking investors out of the market at least some of the time.

Dennis Tilley's 100-dma S&P 500 Total Return Index Tests

Dennis Tilley, Director of Research at Merriman Capital Management, Inc., has developed many timing systems and has updated many of the systems used at Paul Merriman's firm. In an article entitled "Will the Bear Be With Us for a Long Time?" published in November 2001 on *www.fundadvice.com*, Tilley wrote a segment on timing the market using the 100-dma with the S&P 500 Total Return Index (including dividend reinvestment). He divided the 58-year test period from 1942 through 1999 into four periods. Table 9-1 contains the statistics during those periods.

As Table 9-1 indicates, on an overall basis, the 100-dma approach provided an annualized return of 13.5 percent for the 58-year period. Buy-and- hold averaged an annual return of 13.8 percent. Thus, buy-and-hold had a slight advantage of 0.3 percentage points annualized. However, that was accomplished with more risk and higher drawdowns than the moving average strategy.

TABLE 9-1

Market Timing vs. Buy-and-Hold, 1942–1999

Type of market Length in years	1942–1999: Total Period, 58 yrs	1942–1965: Secular Bull, 24 yrs	1966–1981: Secular Bear, 16 yrs	1982–1999: Secular Bull, 18 yrs
Buy-and-Hold:				
Annualized Return of S&P 500	**13.8**	**15.7**	6	**18.5**
Annualized Return 30-day T-Bill	4.5	1.7	6.8	6.2
Inflation Index (CPI)	4.2	3.1	7	3.3
Standard Deviation	16.2	14.7	16.3	17.6
Ave. 5 Worst Drawdowns	−32.7	−20.3	−25.9	−20.6
Worst Drawdown	−45.0	−26.8	−45.0	−33.0
Timing				
Annualized Return of Timing	**13.5**	**13.9**	**10.5**	**15.8**
Standard Deviation	12.3	12.2	11.1	13.5
Ave. 5 Worst Drawdowns	−13.7	−12.6	−9	−11.4
Worst Drawdown	−19.9	−19.9	−10.7	−14.4
Risk Reduction, Stand. Dev.	−24.1	−17	−31.9	−23.3
Risk Reduction, Avg. 5 worst DD	−58.1	−37.9	−65.3	−44.7

Market timing was performed with a 100-day moving average using the S&P 500 Index.

Source: "Will the Bear Market Be With Us for a Long Time?" by Dennis Tilley, Director of Research, Merriman Capital Management, Inc., November 2002.

In the two secular bull markets (1942–1965 and 1966–1981) shown in Table 9-1, the 100-dma strategy performed 1.8 and 2.7 percentage points worse, respectively, on an annualized basis than buy-and-hold. That is a large difference in dollar terms, especially for a long time frame. However, to its credit, this timing strategy had lower risk and drawdowns.

In the secular bear market period from 1966 to 1981, the timing strategy really sparkled, with an annualized return of 10.5 percent compared to 6 percent for buy-and-hold. This difference over a 16-year period is a large one. If we assume that $1000 was invested in 1966, then it would have grown to $2540 by 1981 with buy-and-hold, and $4941 with the timing strategy, a 94 percent improvement over buy-and-hold. And to top it off, the risk and drawdowns were 32 percent and 65 percent less, respectively for the timing strategy compared to buy-and-hold. So here is a case of higher return with less risk, just the opposite of the conventional wisdom. And here is a case of market timing actually working.

What does Tilley's work prove? It demonstrated that market timing excelled in a long-term bear market with less risk but trailed in long-term bull markets, again with less risk. If we actually began a secular bear market in early 2000, then intelligent investors should be using a market timing strategy to protect their principal. Otherwise they may find that they have very little cash left when the next secular bull market starts.

Even if we are not in long-term bear market, there will be many 10 to 30 percent rallies in the markets that a savvy investor can take advantage of with market timing. The buy-and-hope investor will not have the good fortune of protecting his or her capital or benefiting from these rallies with more money to invest.

John Murphy's 50-dma–Nasdaq Composite Index Test

According to John J. Murphy, the chief technical analyst at StockCharts.com and president of MurphyMorris Money Management Co.: "In the 30 years from 1972 to 2002 a 'buy-and-hold' strategy reaped a gain of 1,105% in the Nasdaq. A simple timing strategy of selling whenever the Nasdaq fell under its 50-dma (and re-entering when it rose back above it) reaped a profit of 13,794%. In the 10 years from 1993 to 2002, a 'buy-and-hold' strategy yielded a Nasdaq profit of 93%. By utilizing the 'sell discipline' of the 50-day average, that Nasdaq profit jumped to 280%."[1]

TradeStation Moving-Average Tests

I tested the moving-average timing strategy using the Nasdaq Composite Index, first on a weekly basis by using the 25-week moving average (wma). This is a strategy that an investor with limited time can use. Since Merriman had excellent performance using the Nasdaq Composite Index with the 100-dma I used the 25-wma which is equivalent to a 125-dma which is also very close to McDonald's 132-dma. I used the TradeStation software to back-test this 25-wma on the Nasdaq Composite Index from February 5, 1971, through December 27, 2002.

25-Wma–Nasdaq Composite Index Test

TradeStation is a powerful trading platform with an extensive back-testing capability. Additional information about this software is provided in Chapter 13 on market timing software. TradeStation provides extensive performance reports and charts detailing all aspects of each strategy. The reports show all the pertinent statistics on the test period including the following:

- Every buy and sell signal delineated with dates and profits or losses
- Daily, weekly, and monthly performance in detail
- Annual net profits by year
- Win/loss ratio statistics
- Graphs of the equity curve
- Monthly net profit, average profit by month, and monthly rolling net profit

My buy and sell rules are shown in the box below. An initial $100,000 was invested at the first signal, and no additional funds were invested. All investments were made the same day as the moving average crossover signal was given. Dividends were not included in this analysis, since the TradeStation program did not provide that option.

Nasdaq Composite 25-wma Strategy

Buy signal. When the closing weekly price of the Nasdaq Composite Index pierces the 25-wma from below, a buy signal is given.

Sell signal. When the closing weekly price of the Nasdaq Composite Index drops below the 25-wma, a sell signal is given and a short position is taken.

Table 9-2 shows the key statistics of this simple strategy. Over the total 31-year time frame, buy-and-hold had a cumulative return of 968 percent. This did not even come close to the performance of the 25-wma strategy, which returned 4275 percent. In total dollars, the original $100,000 investment returned a profit of $4,274,870 compared to a profit of $968,400 for buy-and-hold. The annual rate of return for the 25-wma strategy was 13.52 percent. Unfortunately, TradeStation does not provide the buy-and-hold annual return.

The ratio of average winning dollars per trade compared to average losing dollars per trade was terrific, at 4 to 1, where the average winning trade amount was $157,052 and the average losing trade was $38,648. Only 42 percent of all trades were profitable, and the profit factor was 2.98. So, here again is a case where less than 50 percent of trades were profitable but buy-and-hold was still demolished.

In total, there were 97 trades over the 31 years averaging just over three trades a year, certainly a reasonable number.

Twenty-four years had profits and five years had losses. The worst years were 2000 and 1994, with similar losses—of about 16 percent. Two years with back-to-back losses were 1987 and 1988, with about a 7.5 percent average loss per year. And 1977 had a minor loss of 1.4 percent.

20-dma–Nasdaq Composite Index Test

The second back test of the Nasdaq Composite Index used a 20-dma with the same $100,000 starting capital. This is a much faster moving average than the 25-wma and a popular moving average among traders. Using the exact same 31-year test period from February 7, 1971 through December 27, 2002, and the same assumptions, the results are hard to believe.

The simple 20-dma Nasdaq Composite Index strategy produced a total profit of $46,563,046, which is over 10 times greater than the $4,274,870 realized from the 25-wma strategy (see Table 9-3). The buy-and-hold strategy for the 20-dma resulted in total return of $1,139,260. Thus, the 20-dma strategy beat buy-and-hold by a ratio of 46:1.

The percent of winning trades was only 38 percent. There were 664 trades during the test period or about 21 per year, compared to only 97 trades or 3 per year for the 25-wma strategy. Thus, this strategy had 567 more trades than the weekly strategy.

Look at the equity curve in Figure 9-2. The equity curve is a line graph that plots the continuous profit and loss of each trade. The graph indicates a slow but solid start, then around trade 190 a rise to a peak at trade 350, then a flat period until trade 500, then an upward surge punctuated by huge downswings after trade 600. Although this equity curve was not a smooth, upward-sloping curve, which would be the ideal scenario, at least it held its own during high volatility periods and the 2000–2002 bear market, and it ended at its high for the period.

Overall, the 20-dma strategy had only three negative years (–7 percent in 1977, –11 percent in 1993, and –1 percent in 1994) in its 31-year history. In the terrible bear market years of 1973 and 1974, this strategy had a 49 percent and 4 percent back-to-back *positive* return. In the 1987 bear market, it *gained* 46 percent. And in the 2000–2002 bear market, it gained 4 percent, 32 percent, and 16 percent, respectively.

Other Daily Moving-Average Back Tests

Using TradeStation, I ran an optimization analysis of daily Nasdaq Composite Index moving averages between 15 days and 125 days to determine any discernable profit patterns. The exact same test period as the other back tests was used: the 31-year period from February 7, 1971, through December 27, 2002, as were all the same assumptions Using an 18- to 22-dma, I found the total returns for the period to be in the $37 million to $56 million range. The 23- to 50-dmas produced returns in the $19 million to $28 million range. By contrast a 100-dma and 125-dma had total returns of about $6 million. Thus, my testing confirms Colby's findings that shorter moving averages have higher returns than intermediate and long-term moving averages.

The highest returns for the Nasdaq Composite Index were clearly in the 18- to 22-day range. The optimal strategy turned out to be the 18-dma, with a total return of $56.02 million, and an annualized return of 22.47 percent. This return was almost $10 million better than the 20-dma strategy which had a 21.74 percent

TABLE 9-2

TradeStation Strategy Performance Report

TradeStation Strategy Performance Report 25-Wma $COMPX-Weekly (2/5/1971-12/27/2002)

Strategy Analysis

Net Profit	$4,274,869.56	Open Position	$43,668.18
Gross Profit	$6,439,144.31	Interest Earned	$9,958.90
Gross Loss	($2,164,274.74)	Commission Paid	$0.00
Percent profitable	42.27%	Profit factor	2.98
Ratio avg. win/avg. loss	4.06	Adjusted profit factor	2.21
Annual Rate of Return	13.52%	Sharpe Ratio	0.79
Return on Initial Capital	4274.87%	Return Retracement Ratio	1.30
Return on Max. Drawdown	155.52%	K-Ratio	1.66
Buy/Hold return	968.40%	RINA Index	16.96
Cumulative return	4274.87%	Percent in the market	93.76%
Adjusted Net Profit	$2,980,030.80	Select Net Profit	$488,376.36
Adjusted Gross Profit	$5,433,518.92	Select Gross Profit	$2,652,651.10
Adjusted Gross Loss	($2,453,488.12)	Select Gross Loss	($2,164,274.74)

Total Trade Analysis

Number of total trades	97		
Average trade	$44,070.82	Avg. trade ± 1 STDEV	$288,308.04 / ($200,166.40)
1 Std. Deviation (STDEV)	$244,237.22	Coefficient of variation	554.19%

Run-up

Maximum Run-up	$3,425,832.55	
Average Run-up	$145,966.63	Max. Run-up Date	3/10/2000
1 Std. Deviation (STDEV)	$415,317.60	Avg. trade ± 1 STDEV	$561,284.22 / $0.00
		Coefficient of variation	284.53%

Drawdown

Maximum Drawdown	($556,526.87)	Max. Drawdown Date	7/14/2000
Average Drawdown	($30,712.31)	Avg. trade ± 1 STDEV	$0.00 / ($100,744.32)
1 Std. Deviation (STDEV)	$70,032.01	Coefficient of variation	228.03%

Reward/Risk Ratios

Net Prft/Largest Loss	7.75	Net Prft/Max Drawdown	7.68
Adj Net Prft/Largest Loss	5.40	Adj Net Prft/Max Drawdown	5.35

Outlier Trades

	Total Trades	Profit/Loss
Positive outliers	3	$3,786,493.21
Negative outliers	0	$0.00
Total outliers	3	$3,786,493.21

Created with TradeStation. Printed with permission.

T A B L E   9 - 3

TradeStation Strategy Performance Report
TradeStation Strategy Performance Report 20-dma $COMPX-Daily (2/25/1971-12/27/2002)

Strategy Analysis

Net Profit	$46,563,045.76	Open Position	$920,062.48
Gross Profit	$119,057,567.11	Interest Earned	$3,136.99
Gross Loss	($72,494,521.35)	Commission Paid	$0.00
Percent profitable	38.25%	Profit factor	1.64
Ratio avg. win/avg. loss	2.65	Adjusted profit factor	1.47
Annual Rate of Return	21.74%	Sharpe Ratio	1.19
Return on Initial Capital	46563.05%	Return Retracement Ratio	3.07
Return on Max. Drawdown	364.07%	K-Ratio	1.30
Buy/Hold return	1139.26%	RINA Index	(123.20)
Cumulative return	46563.05%	Percent in the market	98.03%
Adjusted Net Profit	$35,512,460.38	Select Net Profit	($19,312,535.48)
Adjusted Gross Profit	$111,587,230.95	Select Gross Profit	$53,181,985.87
Adjusted Gross Loss	($76,074,770.57)	Select Gross Loss	($72,494,521.35)

Total Trade Analysis

Number of total trades	664		
Average trade	$70,125.07	Avg. trade ± 1 STDEV	$908,816.90 / ($768,566.76)
1 Std. Deviation (STDEV)	$838,691.83	Coefficient of variation	1195.99%

Run-up

Maximum Run-up	$11,251,371.85	Max. Run-up Date	4/4/2001
Average Run-up	$436,199.97	Avg. trade ± 1 STDEV	$1,705,601.80 / $0.00
1 Std. Deviation (STDEV)	$838,691.83	Coefficient of variation	291.01%

Drawdown

Maximum Drawdown	($2,355,552.45)	Max. Drawdown Date	8/15/2002
Average Drawdown	($159,903.98)	Avg. trade ± 1 STDEV	$0.00 / ($497,609.31)
1 Std. Deviation (STDEV)	$337,705.33	Coefficient of variation	211.19%

Reward/Risk Ratios

Net Prft/Largest Loss	19.77	Net Prft/Max Drawdown	19.77
Adj Net Prft/Largest Loss	15.08	Adj Net Prft/Max Drawdown	15.08

Outlier Trades

	Total Trades	Profit/Loss
Positive outliers	14	$65,875,581.24
Negative outliers	0	$0.00
Total outliers	14	$65,875,581.24

Equity Curve Nasdaq Composite 20-dma

**Equity Curve
MovAvg Crossover**

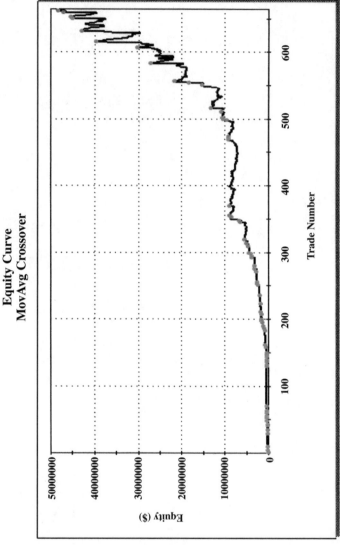

(Created with TradeStation. Printed with permission.)

annualized return. So as you can see, the selected Nasdaq Composite Index moving averages provided outstanding returns.

CONCLUSIONS

Using market timing on moving averages is quite simple in concept but often trying in practice as the price moves up and down crossing over and under the moving average line. As the research on moving averages indicates, there are profitable strategies whether you selected the Nasdaq Composite 20-dma or the 25-wma. Likewise the 66-dma and 132-dma also worked well, but with reduced profits. So it is your choice to select the most appropriate strategy that best fits your risk profile.

Keep in mind that when using shorter-term moving averages, you will have more trades than using longer-term moving averages. This will result in more smaller gains and losses than using longer-term moving averages. Moreover, be careful to assess your risk when using intermediate and long-term moving average. With these strategies, you should carefully consider implementing a stop-loss rule to protect your profits so that the investment does not go too far against you when the trend changes. For example, if you are making a profit of 50 percent on your investment after investing, you don't want to give it all back when the market reverses direction and goes all the way down crossing the moving average. So consider using an 8 to 10 percent stop-loss order to protect those profits. If you wait until the actual moving average sell signal occurs, then you could be giving back most of your profits. So use common sense in protecting your capital.

Once you select a moving-average strategy you can go online to any of the charting Web sites previously mentioned and bring up a two-year chart of the index you select with a selected moving average. For example, let's say you chose the Nasdaq Composite Index's 25-wma strategy. Each Friday afternoon before the market closes or on the weekend you would bring up the weekly chart to determine if the moving average crossed over or under the index's price. When a buy crossover occurs you could purchase the QQQs (Nasdaq 100) or a bullish Nasdaq fund such as Rydex OTC Fund. Then you would wait for the index's price to decline below the

moving average to either sell your position by going into cash or
going short the QQQs or with an inverse Nasdaq 100 fund such as
the Rydex Arktos Fund.

END NOTES

1. *The Money Show Digest (www.moneyshowdigest.com)* by Steve Halpern,
   February 21, 2003. Comments by John Murphy.

CHAPTER 10

The Value Line 4 Percent Strategy

The safest way to double your money is to fold it over once and put it in your pocket.

Frank McKinney Hubbard

Would you be interested in another simple market-timing strategy that signals you when to buy to take advantage of market up trends, and then signals you when to sell to take advantage of most of the market's down trends? All of the so-called experts on Wall Street will tell you that no strategy can do this consistently. Remember that in the last chapter we reviewed some simple moving-average strategies that do just that.

By using the Value Line 4 percent strategy (hereafter abbreviated VL4%), developed about 20 years ago, or a similar strategy dubbed the Nasdaq 6 percent strategy (explained in the following chapter), you can achieve the benefits of using market timing on a thoroughly tested and profitable strategy. Moreover, the strategies reduce your risk and beat buy-and-hold. The VL4% strategy presented in this chapter is for conservative investors with a low risk tolerance, while the Nasdaq 6 percent strategy presented in the next chapter is for more investors with a higher risk–reward tolerance. For the aggressive investor, just be aware that the higher the reward, the higher the risk.

HOW THE VL4% STRATEGY WORKS

The VL4% strategy uses a daily chart of the VLCI. The VL4% strategy is very simple: If the VLCI rises 4 percent from its last market low (for example, if it rises from 100.00 to 104.00 or higher), based solely on its weekly Friday closing price, that is a buy signal, and an investment is made in an appropriate index fund, sector fund, or ETF, as explained in Chapters 5 and 6.

If the VLCI declines from its last market top by 4 percent (for example, if it drops from 120.00 to 115.20 or lower), based on a weekly Friday closing price, that is a sell signal.

The proceeds of the sale can then be placed into a money market account. Alternatively, a more aggressive investor may short the market by using a bear (inverse) fund or shorting any ETF. Note that ETFs cannot be shorted in retirement accounts, but you can buy bear funds in retirement accounts.

Keep in mind that you cannot buy or sell the actual VLCI. It is an index that has not has been offered as a mutual fund index or ETF. Therefore, you can invest in an index fund or ETF instead. The VLCI is tradable as a futures and options on the Kansas City Board of Trade (KCBT). But trading in futures and options is not recommended for the average investor.

BRIEF HISTORY OF THE VL4%

On June 30, 1961, *The Value Line Investment Survey* instituted the Value Line Composite Index (VLCI), also known as the Value Line Geometric Index. It represents a geometrically weighted index of 1700 stocks in 90 industries and thus provides the "median" performance of all the stocks tracked.

The Value Line includes blue-chip, midcap, and small-cap issues. About three-fourths of the stocks are traded on the New York Stock Exchange, 20 percent are traded on the Nasdaq, and the remainder on the AMEX and in Canada.

This index has a different weighting scheme than the DJIA and the S&P 500 Index. The DJIA is price-weighted by each of the 30 components (the highest-priced stocks have the most impact on the average) and the S&P 500 Index is market-capitalization-weighted (the number of common shares outstanding multiplied by the stock's price). In the latter case, the big market cap stocks exert a larger influence on the index. I originally came across the VL4% strategy in Martin Zweig's *Winning on Wall Street*, published in 1986. According to Zweig, Ned Davis of Ned Davis Research developed the "Four Percent Model" using the Value Line Composite Index (VLCI). The model's goal was to help investors stick with the existing market trend, and not get shaken out of the market by small, random day-to-day fluctuations.

VL4% Experience from 1966 to 1988

The VL4% back-tested results in this chapter are only theoretical in nature, because the trades identified are not executable by an investor, because a trading vehicle mirroring the index does not exist. However, back testing of data against past years is a common and accepted practice used by researchers to determine the viability of specific trading strategies. Of course, back testing does not guarantee that the same performance that occurred in the past will occur in the future. But, if the same strategy that was tested and worked well in past years still works well today, then that performance says something about the strategy's longevity and validity. The VL4% fits this paradigm.

According to *Winning on Wall Street*, Ned Davis back-tested the VL4% strategy from May 6, 1966, through December 27, 1988. Davis went long on the buy signal and short on a sell signal. He could have gone into cash and waited for the next buy signal, but he decided to go short. That decision, as we'll see, paid off with better results. The results were published in the first (1986) and second (1990) editions of Zweig's books. The data presented on the next page are from the later edition.

In the 22.7 years of the time period studied by Davis, a one-time initial investment of $10,000 had an ending value for the hypothetical investments made with the VL4% strategy of $233,981, which meant that the investment provided a 14.9 percent annualized return. Buy-and-hold produced a meager return of $17,242, or 2.4% annualized. Neither dividends nor transaction costs were factored into this analysis, in either case.

The breakdown on the long and short side of the signals is as follows:

Longs (buys): Fifty trades were made, averaging 97 days each, producing an annual profit of 16.6 percent. Twenty-six of these trades produced losses averaging –3.9 percent, while 24 trades produced gains averaging 14.6 percent.

Shorts (sells): Fifty-one trades were made, averaging 67 days each, producing an annual profit of 12.5 percent. Twenty-seven of these trades produced losses averaging –3.5 percent, while 24 trades produced gains of 9.3 percent.

Total Trades: One hundred and one trades were made, averaging 82 days, producing an annual profit of 14.9 percent. Fifty-three trades showed losses averaging –3.7 percent, while 48 trades showed gains averaging 11.9 percent. The ratio of percentage profits to losses was better than 3:1. This is a great example of cutting losses and letting profits run.

In summary, the VL4% strategy, tested by Davis, was a simple timing system that worked well during the 1966 to 1988 time frame. Even though 52 percent of the trades were unprofitable, the average loss of –3.7% was far less than the 48 percent of profitable trades, where the average gain was 11.9 percent, a win-to-loss percentage ratio of 3.22, which is excellent.

VL4% Experience from 1961 to 1992

Nelson Freeburg published an updated analysis of VL4% in his November 30, 1992, newsletter *FORMULA RESEARCH*. Freeburg back-tested the period April 19, 1985, through November 6, 1992, a full four years beyond Davis's test period.

Freeburg found that the VL4% strategy gained 168 VL points over that seven-year time frame, while the index itself gained only 57 points under a buy-and-hold scenario. On an annualized basis, excluding dividends, the VL4% strategy returned 8.5 percent, compared to 3.5 percent for buy-and-hold.

Freeburg even tested the period prior to Davis's research, going back to July 1961 and testing through mid-1966. During this five-year mostly bullish period, VL4% provided an annual return of 10.7 percent, compared to 5.5 percent for buy-and-hold. Thus, the VL4% strategy performed well in three different time frames, confirming its consistency and usefulness as a profitable strategy.

Over the entire expanded period from 1961 through 1992, VL4% rose an annualized 13.6 percent, compared to about 3 percent for buy-and-hold. This accomplishment is impressive—doubly so, as 60 of the 127 buy-and-sell signals were profitable only 47 percent of the time.

Not satisfied with only testing a fixed 4 percent up or down move on the VLCI, Freeburg tested every percentage point swing from 1 percent to 8 percent for both the long and short trades, to determine if the strategy would still be profitable. After testing 64 parameter sets over 31 years, Freeburg found that all of the parameter sets tested exceeded buy-and-hold results by a minimum ratio of 2:1.

The greatest gain in VL points occurred with a buy signal set at 4 percent and a sell signal set at 2 percent, i.e., a buy if VLCI rises 4 percent from a bottom and a sell if VLCI drops 2 percent from a top. This produced 645 VL points compared to 149 points for buy-and-hold. Other top combinations were +2 percent and –2 percent, producing 588 points, and the standard strategy of +4 percent and –4 percent, producing 584 points. The worst strategy tested produced 313 points, which was still better than double the buy-and-hold approach! According to Freeburg, this consistent performance over many different percentage point parameters indicates the strength and soundness of the VL4% strategy.

David Penn, a staff writer for *Technical Analysis of Stocks & Commodities* magazine wrote an article in the May 2002 issue titled "Trends and the 4% Solution." He reviewed the VL4% weekly strategy from 1985 to 2000. Penn tested the VL4% strategy using the Nasdaq Composite Index and the S&P 500 Index as the investment vehicles. He found based on the VL4% buy and sell signals, that investing in the Nasdaq Composite Index produced triple the gain of an investment in the S&P 500 Index. Penn did not provide detailed data regarding his analysis in his article. Also, Penn did not provide any performance results or using only the actual VLCI as the index to invest in. So his results cannot be compared to Freeburg's work, which only measured VLCI point changes.

MORE RECENT TESTING

I used TradeStation, a popular trading platform, to bring the test period current through November, 2002. All the tables in this chapter are from TradeStation. Neither dividends nor taxes were figured into any of the strategies tested with this software, as that was not a testing option of the software.

VL4% VLCI Weekly Tests from 1992 to 2002

Using TradeStation, I ran the Four % Model strategy available on the TradeStationWorld Web site. This model is actually the VL4% weekly strategy, as first developed by Ned Davis. I updated the VL4% strategy using the VLCI from December 25 1992, through November 29, 2002—a period containing bull and bear markets.

The VL4% model was set up with an initial capital of $100,000. The strategy went long the VLCI on a weekly buy signal and it went short the VLCI on a weekly sell signal. On each buy and sell signal, all the proceeds of the previous closed transaction were fully reinvested, so that the funds were never in cash.

During this 10-year time frame, the VL4% strategy produced a net profit of $81,998, (refer to Table 10-1) and a cumulative return of 82 percent. This result compares favorably with a small loss of −1.32 percent for buy and hold.

The equity curve in Figure 10-1 shows the investment value after each trade was made. As you can see, there was a big drop after the twenty-first trade and the fall continued through trade 36. Of these 15 trades, 14 were losers from January 28, 2000, through January 12, 2001. If you looked at a chart of the VLCI during this time frame, then you would see that the VLCI was in a trading range of 980 to 1180 with numerous up and down moves in price. And each of these trades resulted in a loss. Shortly after you went long on a buy signal, the market reversed down and a sell short signal occurred at a lower price resulting a loss. Similarly, right after you went short, the market reversed up, and that was offset by a buy signal at a higher price resulting in a loss. All these whipsaws in price resulted in losses that overcame all the profits built up over the previous years. Actually, the total capital did drop below the original $100,000 investment during this period. From the twenty-first to forty-fifth trades the VL4% VLCI weekly strategy made no progress, as the equity curve shows. This was a disturbing and costly problem. On the positive side, substantial positive annual returns of 32 percent a year for 2001and 2002 were impressive because these were down years for the market. And by the end of 2002 the equity curve was at an all-time high.

However, despite this large loss and recovery, the VL4% strategy continued to beat the buy-and-hold benchmark in all the time frames tested by Davis, Freeburg, and me. The cumulative returns for the period 1993 through 2002 may appear to be very low, but remember that we are only measuring the performance of the VLCI itself during this period. If you would have used the VL4% buy and sell signals to trade index funds that tracked the DJIA or Nasdaq Composite Index, your results would have been better. Recall David Penn's study earlier where he tested the Nasdaq Composite Index using the VL4% signals, producing excellent results.

Development of the VL Arithmetic Index

On February 1, 1988, Value Line published a new index dubbed the Value Line Arithmetic Index (VLAI). It is an equally weighted index of 1700 stocks. This index provides the average (rather than median) performance of all stocks in the index. It is based on summing up the percentage price increase in every stock each day and dividing that total by the number of stocks in the index. So each stock has equal weighting, whether high or low in price.

VL4% VLAI Weekly Test

I wanted to determine if substituting the more recently developed arithmetic index produced different results than using the VLCI. I reran the VL4% analysis, substituting the VLAI weekly data for the VLCI weekly data for almost the same time 10-year period: December 25, 1992, through November 29, 2002.

The VLAI produced a 51 percent improvement in net profit to $123,915 compared to $81,998 for the VLCI, as Table 10-2 shows. The VLAI annual return was 9.88 percent compared to the VLCI return of 7.25 with a 123.9 percent VLAI cumulative return compared to the VLCI's 82 percent cumulative return. Just by substituting the arithmetic for the geometric index using the VL4% strategy dramatically improved the results. The VLAI buy-and-hold performance produced a 145 percent cumulative return as

TABLE 10-1

TradeStation Strategy Performance Report
Four % Model VLCI-Weekly (12/25/1992-11/29/2002)

Strategy Analysis

Net Profit	$81,998.28	Open Position	$21,772.92
Gross Profit	$213,665.24	Interest Earned	$6,315.07
Gross Loss	($131,666.96)	Commission Paid	$0.00
Percent profitable	42.22%	Profit factor	1.62
Ratio avg. win/avg. loss	2.22	Adjusted profit factor	1.05
Annual Rate of Return	7.25%	Sharpe Ratio	0.58
		Return Retracement Ratio	0.29
Return on Initial Capital		K-Ratio	0.62
Return on Max. Drawdown	90.38%	RINA Index	24.42
Buy/Hold return	-1.32%	Percent in the market	87.29%
Cumulative return	82.00%	Select Net Profit	$81,998.28
Adjusted Net Profit	$7,158.10	Select Gross Profit	$213,665.24
Adjusted Gross Profit	$164,647.07	Select Gross Loss	($131,666.96)
Adjusted Gross Loss	($157,488.97)		

Total Trade Analysis

Number of total trades	45		
Average trade	$1,822.18	Avg. trade ± 1 STDEV	$11,864.82 / ($8,220.45)
1 Std. Deviation (STDEV)	$10,042.63	Coefficient of variation	551.13%

Run-up

Maximum Run-up	$42,640.00	Max. Run-up Date	7/26/2002
Average Run-up	$10,669.97	Avg. trade ± 1 STDEV	$21,353.21 / $0.00
1 Std. Deviation (STDEV)	$10,683.24	Coefficient of variation	100.12%

Drawdown

Maximum Drawdown	($10,521.90)	Max. Drawdown Date	4/28/2000
Average Drawdown	($3,847.26)	Avg. trade ± 1 STDEV	($691,82) / ($7,002.69)
1 Std. Deviation (STDEV)	$3.155.43	Coefficient of variation	82.02%

Reward/Risk Ratios

Net Prft/Largest Loss	8.12	Net Prft/Max Drawdown	7.79
Adj Net Prft/Largest Loss	0.71	Adj Net Prft/Max Drawdown	0.68

Outlier Trades

	Total Trades	Profit/Loss
Positive outliers	0	$0.00
Negative outliers	0	$0.00
Total outliers	0	$0.00

Created with TradeStation. Printed with permission.

FIGURE 10-1

Equity Curve for the VL4% VLCI Weekly Strategy 1992-2002

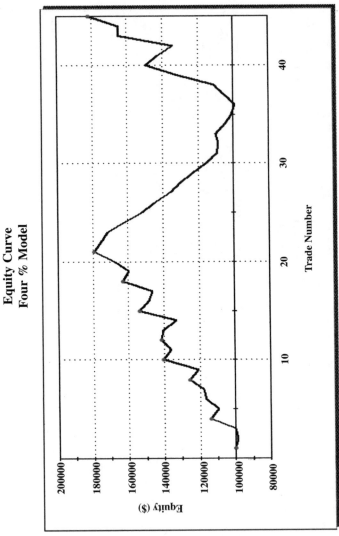

Equity Curve
Four % Model

Created with TradeStation. Printed with permission.

opposed to a −1.32 percent loss with the VLCI buy and hold. Therefore, the VLAI's cumulative return of 123.9 percent did not beat buy-and-hold's 145 percent return. It is interesting to note the different results with the geometric and arithmetic averages. So, as you can see, the index used to obtain the signal had a major impact on the performance statistics, including the buy and hold results.

Ultra 7 Test of VL4% Weekly VLCI

Using Ultra 7 software from Ultra Financial Systems Inc. (covered in Chapter 13), which offers market-timing strategies with an historical database. I was able to test the VLCI on a weekly basis. However, when sell signals were given, the proceeds were invested in a money market account, since this software did not offer shorting capability. I ran an analysis from December 1, 1974, through January 17, 2003. The following are the results:

Same day's price (today's price used on the signal date)

Total gain with VL4%: 4101 percent

Compounded annual return: 14.23 percent

Percent of time invested: 65.3 percent

Buy-and-hold VL: 1147 percent

Compounded annual return: 9.39 percent

So, even though shorting was not used, the VLCI weekly strategy was 3.6 times better than buy-and-hold. This result was produced despite the fact that it was invested only 65.3 percent of the time. If the entry or the exit price were delayed until one day after the signal was triggered, the total gain was reduced by about 1400 percentage points. Even so, it still beat buy-and-hold by more than double:

Next day's price (next day's price after signal used)

Total gain with VL4%: 2795 percent

Compounded annual return: 12.7 percent

Percent of time invested: 65.2 percent

Buy-and-hold VL: 1147 percent

Compounded annual return: 9.39 percent

TABLE 10-2

TradeStation Strategy Performance Report
Four % Model, VLAC-Weekly (12/25/1992-11/29/2002)

Strategy Analysis

Net Profit	$123,915.18	Open Position	$32,252.16
Gross Profit	$260,243.41	Interest Earned	$6,315.07
Gross Loss	($136,328.24)	Commission Paid	$0.00
Percent profitable	43.90%	Profit factor	1.91
Ratio avg. win/avg. loss	2.44	Adjusted profit factor	1.21
Annual Rate of Return	9.88%	Sharpe Ratio	0.77
Return on Initial Capital	123.92%	Return Retracement Ratio	0.69
Return on Max. Drawdown	169.26%	K-Ratio	1.45
Buy/Hold return	144.95%	RINA Index	28.37
Cumulative return	123.92%	Percent in the market	87.29%
Adjusted Net Profit	$34,148.81	Select Net Profit	$123,915.18
Adjusted Gross Profit	$198,903.45	Select Gross Profit	$260,243.41
Adjusted Gross Loss	($164,754.64)	Select Gross Loss	($136,328.24)

Total Trade Analysis

Number of total trades	41		
Average trade	$3,022.32	Avg. trade ± 1 STDEV	$15,492.43 / ($9,447.78)
1 Std. Deviation (STDEV)	$12,470.11	Coefficient of variation	413.60%

Run-up

Maximum Run-up	$51,690.00	Max. Run-up Date	7/26/2002
Average Run-up	$13,930.98	Avg. trade ± 1 STDEV	$27,242.31 / $619.64
1 Std. Deviation (STDEV)	$13,311.33	Coefficient of variation	95.55%

Drawdown

Maximum Drawdown	($18,157.44)	Max. Drawdown Date	10/9/1998
Average Drawdown	($5,004.38)	Avg. trade ± 1 STDEV	($561.51) / ($9,447.24)
1 Std. Deviation (STDEV)	$4,442.86	Coefficient of variation	88.78%

Reward/Risk Ratios

Net Prft/Largest Loss	9.44	Net Prft/Max Drawdown	6.82
Adj Net Prft/Largest Loss	2.60	Adj Net Prft/Max Drawdown	1.88

Outlier Trades

	Total Trades	Profit/Loss
Positive outliers	0	$0.00
Negative outliers	0	$0.00
Total outliers	0	$0.00

Created with TradeStation. Printed with permission.

165

And if we use a beta of 2.0 (leverage of 2:1), with the same day's price, the results are superb, producing a gain of 24,821 percent, or six times greater return than if no leverage were used at all. That shows the power of compounding coupled with a solid strategy. You can achieve a beta of 2.0 by investing in leveraged funds. Using a beta of 2.0 produced the following results:

Same day's price (today's price today used) with beta of 2.0

Total gain with VL4%:   24,821 percent

Compounded annual return: 21.7 percent

Percent of time invested: 65.3 percent

Buy-and-hold VL: 1147 percent

Compounded annual return: 9.39 percent

VL4% DAILY TESTS

All the published research performed on the VL4% by Davis, Freeburg, and Penn used weekly VLCI data. I have not seen any published findings of research in which VLCI daily data or VLAI weekly or daily data were used. Therefore, I decided to run the VL4% strategy using TradeStation with daily data for both the VLCI and VLAI.

VL4% VLCI Daily Analysis from 1992 to 2002

With the use of daily data, I expected to find more frequent buy and sell signals with improved performance over the weekly data. That is because daily data, in theory, should provide faster buy and sell signals and therefore should produce greater annualized returns than if weekly data were used.

I tested VL4% with the original VLCI, *daily* from December 4, 1992, through November 29, 2002, which resulted in a total profit of $111,234 (as opposed to $81,998 on VLCI weekly test) The annual rate of return for the daily VLCI was 8.14 percent compared to 7.25 percent for the weekly VLCI. The cumulative daily VLCI return was 111.23 percent compared to a meager buy-and-hold return of daily VLCI of 4.57 percent so, the daily VLCI strategy was better than the weekly VLCI by approximately $29,236 during the test period. Unfortunately, if you looked at the equity curve, it still had a big drop in the 2000 time period, where 18 out of 20 trades were losers. So the daily signals still could not overcome the whipsaws and thus produced losses.

VL4% VLAI Daily Analysis from 1992 to 2002

Next, I substituted the VLAI for the VLCI and reran the VL4% strategy on a daily basis with all the same parameters as before. The time frame for this test was December 23, 1992, through November 29, 2002.

Table 10-3 indicates that an initial investment of $100,000 in the VLAI resulted in a net profit of $266,792 at the end of the test period, which translates into a cumulative return of 267 percent that greatly exceeded the buy-and-hold return of 140 percent. Remember that daily VLCI produced only $111,234 net profit.

Figure 10-2 is the equity curve for the daily VLAI showing the continuous value of the initial $100,000 investment throughout the entire time period. It depicts a closing value of $366,792. As you can see the strategy was in an up trend through the twenty-eighth trade, went into a slight downtrend, then flat through trade 48 (March 16, 2000, through July 10, 2001), and then up and away to new highs. Finally, this VL4% strategy using the daily VLAI performed well and did not have the large losses that plagued the other VLAI and VLCI weekly and daily tests.

A profitable market-timing strategy has an upward-sloping equity curve, which was the case here, except for a one-year interruption. And in light of the severe bear market from early 2000 through October 9, 2002, this daily strategy produced remarkable results. While the daily VLAI performance was down 31 percent in 2000, it was up 54 percent in 2001 and almost 50 percent for 2002 (through November 29, 2002).

To give you a visual aid to see how accurate the timing of the buy and sell signals (up arrows are buy signals and down arrows are sell signals) were, look at the chart from TradeStation (Figure 10-3) for the period July 2001 through November 2002. You'll notice well-timed buy signals at market bottoms in September 2001 and February, July, and October 2002, and well-timed sell signals in July 2001 and May and August 2002. I did not include a chart showing all the signals from 1993 to 2002, simply because of space limitations.

TABLE 10-3

TradeStation Strategy Performance Report
Four % Model, VLAI-Weekly (12/23/1992-11/29/2002)

Strategy Analysis

Net Profit	$266,792.32	Open Position	$26,703.75
Gross Profit	$458,121.84	Interest Earned	$6,301.37
Gross Loss	($191,329.52)	Commission Paid	$0.00
Percent profitable	50.82%	Profit factor	2.39
Ratio avg. win/avg. loss	2.32	Adjusted profit factor	
Annual Rate of Return	16.24%	Sharpe Ratio	1.00
Return on Initial Capital	266.79%	Return Retracement Ratio	1.42
Return on Max. Drawdown	313.19%	K-Ratio	1.82
Buy/Hold return	139.82%	RINA Index	47.07
Cumulative return	266.79%	Percent in the market	87.32%
Adjusted Net Profit	$149,579.38	Select Net Profit	$205,477.28
Adjusted Gross Profit	$375,840.73	Select Gross Profit	$396,806.79
Adjusted Gross Loss	($226,261.35)	Select Gross Loss	($191,329.52)

Total Trade Analysis

Number of total trades	61		
Average trade	$4,373.64	Avg. trade ± 1 STDEV	$19,428.81 / ($10,681.52)
1 Std. Deviation (STDEV)	$15,055.16	Coefficient of variation	344.22%

Run-up

Maximum Run-up	$74,506.68	
Average Run-up	$15,128.31	Max. Run-up Date	7/24/2002
1 Std. Deviation (STDEV)	$16,073.16	Avg. trade ± 1 STDEV	$31,201.48 / $0.00
		Coefficient of variation	106.25%

Drawdown

Maximum Drawdown	($18,775.44)	
Average Drawdown	($4,998.95)	Max. Drawdown Date	9/30/2002
1 Std. Deviation (STDEV)	$4,442.41	Avg. trade ± 1 STDEV	($556.54) / ($9,441.36)
		Coefficient of variation	88.87%

Reward/Risk Ratios

Net Prft/Largest Loss	15.49	Net Prft/Max Drawdown	14.21
Adj Net Prft/Largest Loss	8.68	Adj Net Prft/Max Drawdown	7.97

Outlier Trades

	Total Trades	Profit/Loss
Positive outliers	1	$61,315.05
Negative outliers	0	$0.00
Total outliers	1	$61,315.05

FIGURE 10–2

Equity Curve for the VL4% VLAI Daily Strategy 1992–2002

Equity Curve
Four % Model

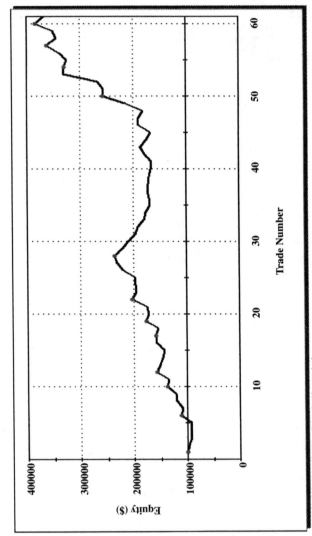

Created with TradeStation. Printed with permission.

Table 10-4 delineates the performance for the VL4% VLAI daily and weekly, on an annual and cumulative basis. Clearly, the daily strategy has a $136,934 advantage over the weekly strategy. The annual performance of the actual VL Arithmetic Index and the S&P 500 Index is shown for comparative purposes. The only time that these two indexes had fairly close performances was from 1995 to 1997. Otherwise, there has been a wide variance. The VL4% daily strategy also beats buy-and-hold by $159,596, while the VL4% weekly strategy beats buy-and-hold by $17,532. Therefore, after performing the daily and weekly tests on the VLCI and VLAI, the preferred VL4% strategy is the daily VLAI.

Combining the VL4% VLAI Daily Strategy with the 20-dma

Based on the large loss of –30.5 percent for the year 2000 time frame for the VL4% VLAI strategy, I want to suggest a way to improve the results by adding the 20-dma to this strategy. This additional price filter provided much better overall results, while also reducing the year 2000 loss to only –14.42 percent (refer to Table 10-5).

The combined strategy works as follows:

1. A buy signal occurs when the VLAI rises 4 percentage points from a bottom.
2. A buy signal occurs when the VLAI pierces its 20-dma to the upside, from below
3. The earliest buy signal occurring on either strategy would be taken first, whether from the VL4% or the 20-dma. Then, if the other strategy issued a buy signal while the current buy signal was in place, no action would be necessary.
4. A sell signal occurs when the VLAI declines 4 percentage points from a top.
5. A sell signal occurs when the VLAI drops below its 20-dma to the downside, from above.
6. The earliest sell signal occurring on either strategy would be taken first, whether from the VL4% or the 20-dma. Then, if the other strategy issued a sell signal while the current sell signal was in place, no action would be necessary.

FIGURE 10–3

VL4% VLAI Daily Strategy Charted on TradeStation
July 2001- November 2002

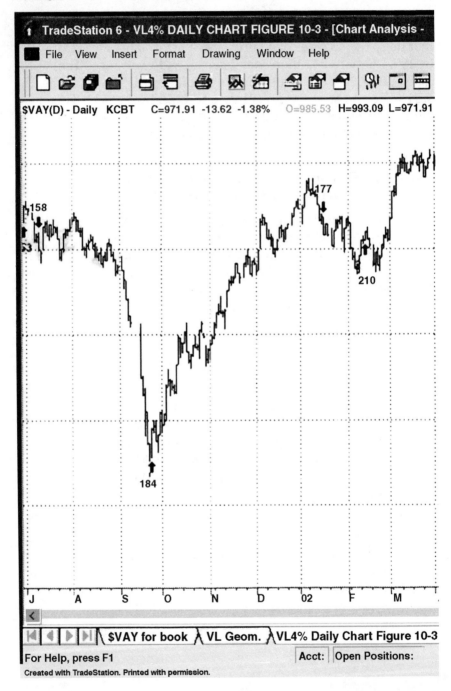

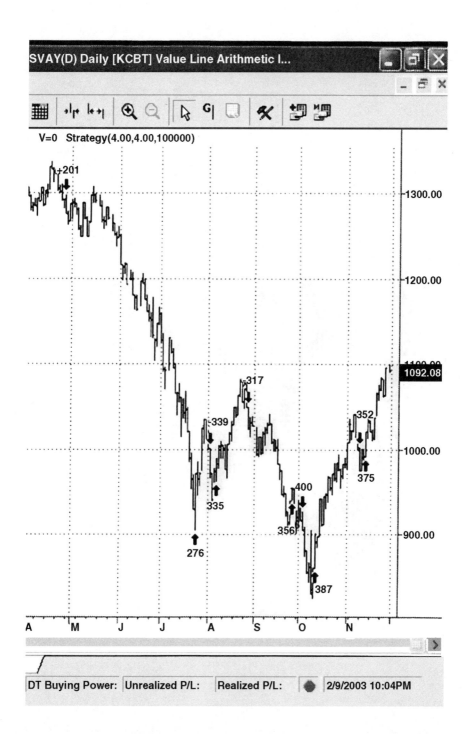

TABLE 10-4

VL4% Weekly and Daily Comparison—Annual Performace
Summary - VL Arithmetic Index 1992 - 2002

	VL4% Daily		VL4% Weekly		VL Arithmetic Index	S&P 500 Index
	Net Profit*	Percent Gain/Loss	Net Profit†	Percent Gain/Loss		
2002	$130,522	49.85%	$50,856	24.77%	-12.40%	-18.50%
2001	$92,197	54.11%	$79,822	63.61%	10.88%	-13.04%
2000	($74,857)	-30.52%	($61,419)	-32.86%	8.65%	-10.14%
1999	$44,973	22.46%	$15,905	9.30%	9.48%	19.53%
1998	$59,304	42.07%	$22,496	15.15%	5.82%	26.67%
1997	$5,327	3.93%	$19,468	15.09%	28.45%	31.01%
1996	$25,289	22.92%	$16,916	15.09%	19.77%	20.26%
1995	$17,904	19.36%	$14,955	15.39%	25.94%	34.11%
1994	($7,544)	-7.54%	($2,832)	-2.83%	-0.73%	-1.54%

Net Profit	$293,115	$156,167
Interest	$6,301	$6,315
Total Profit	$299,416	$162,482
Buy-and-hold	$139,820	$144,950
VL4% vs. B&H	**$159,596**	**$17,532**

Note: Initial investment for each strategy was $100,000.

Note: The net profit for 2002 for both VL4% daily and weekly contains the profit of the open position of $26,704 and $32,252.

* Through December 23, 2002

† Through December 25, 2002

VL Arithmetic annual data provided by Value Line, Inc.

Note: The first year in which signals occurred was 1994.

Source: TradeStation Strategy Performance Report, Annual Trading Summary.

The objective in using this combined strategy is to react quicker by taking the first signal that comes along from either strategy on both sides of the market. Although more trades occurred, the overall strategy performed very well, as follows:

- The VL4% VLAI daily strategy where the trades are triggered when the VLAI rises or falls 4 percent from bottoms and peaks is shown in the section just before this one. It produced a gain of $266,272 for an annualized return of 16.24 percent, with 61 trades.
- The VL 20-dma strategy entailing trading as the VLAI crosses above and below its 20-dma produced a gain of $425,744 with an annual return of 19.50 percent with 201 trades.
- The two strategies combined—meaning buy or sell at the first of the two signals given by the 4 percent move or the 20-dma crossover—produced a total gain of $521,632, for an annualized return of 21.67 percent with 207 trades.

The annual performance of this combined strategy was as follows:

2002	46.7 %
2001	42.7 %
2000	−14.4 %
1999	19.7 %
1998	58.3 %
1997	26.7 %
1996	21.3 %
1995	18.8 %
1994	10.4 %
1993	4.5 %

The equity curve for this strategy is shown in Figure 10-4. In summary, the combined strategy doubles the total gain of the VL4% VLAI daily strategy, reduces the 2000 loss to half its previous loss but has an additional 146 transactions. Not a bad price to pay for reduced losses, reduced risk, and higher returns.

TIMING THE MARKET WITH THE VL4% VLAI STRATEGY

If you decide to time the market with the VL4% VLAI strategy, you first must decide on either the daily or weekly approach. Based on the analysis presented in this chapter, I recommend using the daily VL4% VLAI strategy combined with the 20-dma (as just discussed). That assumes that you are able to check a chart which includes the 20-dma of the VLAI each day and can preferably make your trades the same day when a buy or sell signal is given or on the next day. If you prefer not to include the 20-dma with the daily VLAI VL4% strategy, then use daily VLAI alone, but remember the possibility of a period of poor results caused by market whipsaws as occurred in the year 2000.

If you are the type of person who prefers a weekly approach, then use the VL4% VLAI weekly strategy. With that approach, you can calculate the VLAI percentage change from the previous high or low, as the case may be, once a week (on Friday evening or over the weekend), and then make your investment on Monday. If at all possible, try to make the investment on Friday, if you have access to the information, as that timing will produce better results than waiting until Monday.

If you are using the weekly strategy for the first time and you are currently in cash, then look for a buy signal when the weekly price goes up by 4 percent from any previous weekly close. Alternatively, a sell signal is generated when the index closes down 4 percent from a prior high. At that point, you can go short or stay in cash, if that is your preference.

Once a buy signal is given, you can go long the market with an index fund, an ETF (for example, a DIA or QQQ), or an investment vehicle of your choice, as previously discussed. When a sell signal occurs, then you go into cash or buy an inverse (bear) fund (for example, Rydex Ursa) or short an ETF, depending on your risk tolerance. Remember you cannot short an ETF in a retirement account, but you can buy a bear fund.

You don't even need a PC to use either the daily or weekly VLAI VL4% strategy. The VLAI is published weekly in the *Value Line Investment Survey*, to which most libraries subscribe. In addi-

TABLE 10-5

TradeStation Strategy Performance Report
VL4% Daily + 20–dma (12/23/1992-11/29/2002)

Strategy Analysis

Net Profit	$521,631,91	Open Position	$64,941.96
Gross Profit	$971,629.49	Interest Earned	$2,890.41
Gross Loss	($449,997.58)	Commission Paid	$0.00
Percent profitable	35.75%	Profit factor	2.16
Ratio avg. win/avg. loss	3.88	Adjusted profit factor	1.76
Annual Rate of Return	21.67%	Sharpe Ratio	1.30
Return on Initial Capital	521.63	Return Retracement Ratio	4.71
Return on Max. Drawdown	674.46%	K-Ratio	2.87
Buy/Hold return	162.92%	RINA Index	50.33
Cumulative return	521.63%	Percent in the market	94.19%
Adjusted Net Profit	$369,662.54	Select Net Profit	$145,653.36
Adjusted Gross Profit	$858,679.85	Select Gross Profit	$595,650.94
Adjusted Gross Loss	($489,017.32)	Select Gross Loss	($449,997.58)

Total Trade Analysis

Number of total trades	207		
Average trade	$2,519.96	Avg. trade ± 1 STDEV	$16,679.03 / ($11,639.11)
1 Std. Deviation (STDEV)	$14,159.07	Coefficient of variation	561.88%

Run-up

Maximum Run-up	$134,865.81	Max. Run-up Date	7/24/2002
Average Run-up	$10,289.26	Avg. trade ± 1 STDEV	$28,359.98 / $0.00
1 Std. Deviation (STDEV)	$18,070.72	Coefficient of variation	175.63%

Drawdown

Maximum Drawdown	($30,800.16)	Max. Drawdown Date	9/30/2002
Average Drawdown	($3,072.54)	Avg. trade ± 1 STDEV	$0.00 / ($7,155.95)
1 Std. Deviation (STDEV)	$4,083.41	Coefficient of variation	132.90%

Reward/Risk Ratios

Net Prft/Largest Loss	18.46	Net Prft/Max Drawdown	16.94
Adj Net Prft/Largest Loss	13.08	Adj Net Prft/Max Drawdown	12.00

Outlier Trades

	Total Trades	Profit/Loss
Positive outliers	6	$375,978.55
Negative outliers	0	$0.00
Total outliers	6	375,978.55

FIGURE 10-4

VL4% VLAI Daily Strategy Using 20-dma July 2001 - November 2002

**Equity Curve
MovAge Crossover**

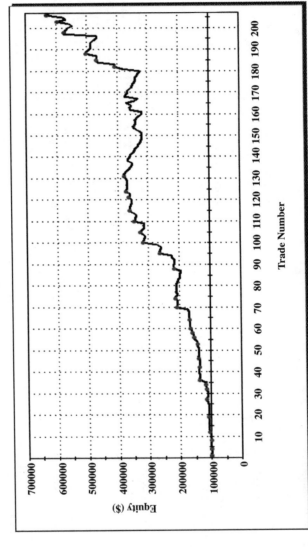

tion, the index can be found in *The Wall Street Journal, Investor's Business Daily,* and on many of Web sites previously mentioned and in the end-of-book bibliography.

The simplest approach is to obtain the Friday closing price and compare it to the previous high and low to determine if a 4 percent signal is given. Use a one-year weekly chart to pinpoint the last high and low price close.

Another approach is to write down the most recent VLAI high and low price. Then calculate 4 percent from each level, wait for that price to be hit, and then take action. Just watch the daily financial papers or check the Net daily. If possible, you should put in your market order on the day of the signal. If you can watch the market on Fridays at around 3:30 P.M. EST, check the VLAI price. If it looks that the signal will be given that day, put in your buy or sell order that afternoon. Otherwise, you will get the Monday night's close, where the price could have advanced further in the direction of your signal.

Print a chart of the VLAI, place your targeted buy and sell signals on it and wait for the signals to be triggered to place your trade. Or if you have software such as TradeStation or MetaStock, you can probably program in the VL4% strategy and run the program weekly or daily, whatever your preference, and wait until a signal is automatically generated.

The market can move 5 to 20 percent, either up or down, for or against you, within a particular week or month. That movement may result in your getting out of the market on a Friday (or the following Monday) with a larger loss than you had planned for. That's to be expected because you can't be perfect all the time, and the chances of such a large move occurring within a single week is very rare. But to prevent a large loss you should always use a stop-loss order around 8 to 10 percent below your trade execution price. Of course, it is up to you to select the percentage loss you are willing to tolerate. Be sure you cut your losses quickly; otherwise small losses can turn into big losses.

Of course, if you are long when the market jumps 5 to 30 percent or short or in cash when it falls by the same amount, then you reap the rewards, since you were on the right side of the market at the right time. Using daily prices instead of weekly prices will provide a quicker buy and sell signal, and as we saw, it can produce higher profits and minimize any potential intra-week losses.

CONCLUSIONS

The use of a mechanical or automatic trading strategy, such as VL4% VLAI daily or weekly, or the VLAI daily strategy combined with the 20-dma, will hopefully take the emotion and uncertainty out of your investing decision. All serious investors should use a systematic investing approach to improve their results. The VL4% weekly strategy requires minimal time to track the signals, provides less risk, and produces a better return than buy-and-hold.

Just observing the VL4% signals during the devastating 2001–2002 bear market clearly indicates why this strategy made money: It was short most of the time when the market crumbled. Although the strategy lost around 30.5 percent in 2000, it did reverse and earned back-to-back 25 percent annualized return in 2001 and 2002. That is what market timing is all about—being on the right side of the market at the right time.

Simple strategies do work. This VL4% VLAI daily strategy, especially with the 20-dma, is a keeper. Investors who had been using the VL4% daily strategy during the past decade most likely would have performed better than 99 percent of the financial gurus and investors.

The Nasdaq Composite 6 Percent Strategy

Even being right three or four times out of ten should yield a person a fortune if they have the sense to cut losses quickly.

Bernard Baruch

Forecasting is very difficult, especially if it involves the future.

Casey Stengel, former manager, New York Yankees

What would happen if the logic behind the VL4% strategy, as presented in the previous chapter, were used instead on two Nasdaq indexes? Using TradeStation, I back-tested the VL4% strategy using both weekly and daily prices of the Nasdaq Composite Index (COMPX), and the Nasdaq 100 Index (NDX). The results of these four tests are presented in the sections that follow.

TEST 1: WEEKLY NASDAQ COMPOSITE 6 PERCENT STRATEGY (NC6%)

The COMPX contains a much different mix of stocks than the Value Line indexes. The COMPX contains about 3500 companies compared with 1700 in the Value Line indexes. Also, the COMPX tends to be more volatile and has wider price swings than the VLCI and VLAI.

Because of the higher volatility of the COMPX, I arbitrarily changed the testing percentage used to 6 percent instead of 4 percent. Therefore, the first strategy tested set the weekly buy and sell signals at 6 percent. That means, that if the COMPX rises 6 percent from a previous low, then a buy signal is generated on that Friday. Likewise, a 6 percent drop from a previous high generates a sell signal on that Friday. On the sell signal the strategy went *short* instead of going into cash. This is the same approach used in the previous chapter for the VL4% strategy except for the change in the signal parameter to 6 percent instead of 4 percent.

The first test period tested the COMPX from its inception on February 5, 1971, through November 29, 2002. An initial investment of $100,000 was made on that beginning date, and no further funds were invested. After each trade, all the proceeds were reinvested in the next trade. This strategy produced an annualized return of 18.77 percent and a profit of $15,209,502 compared to a $1,273,310 gain for buy-and-hold—thus producing an additional profit of $13,936,192 over buy-and-hold.

There were a total of 94 trades over the 32-year test period, averaging about 2.94 trades per year. However, only 54.3 percent of the trades were winners, but the ratio of average winners to losers was 2:1 and the profit factor was 2.37, both reasonable ratios. The long trades had a profit factor of 1.41 versus 2.78 for the short side meaning a 41% profit for the longs and a 178% profit for the shorts. There were 59.6 percent profitable trades on the long side and 48.9 percent on the short side.

The only negative performance years for the NC6% were 1973 (–3.3 percent), 1984 (–0.1 percent), and 1994 (–11.8 percent). In 90 percent of the years tested, there was a profit. And there were gains in the bear market years of 1974 (34.2 percent), 1987 (11.3 percent), 2000 (9.8 percent), 2001 (39.5 percent), and 2002 (22.4 percent). That is what market timing is all about: protecting you from bear market devastation while making positive returns.

Figure 11-1 provides the equity curve for this strategy. As you can see the slope of the curve is upwards and to the right with drops between trades 73 and 91, and then a resumption of the trend to new highs in November 2002. The TradeStation chart in Figure 11-2 shows the buy and sell signals (up and down arrows) of this strategy during the past two years. You can see how well the signals caught the market turns.

FIGURE 11-1

Nasdaq Composite 6% Weekly-Feb. 1971–Nov. 2002

**Equity Curve
Six % Model**

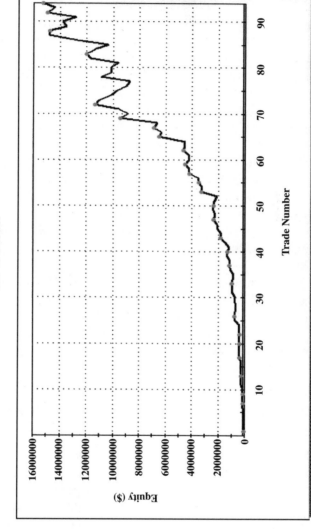

Created with TradeStation, which is a registered trademark of TradeStation Group Inc. Printed with permission.

TEST 2: WEEKLY NDX 6 PERCENT STRATEGY (NDX6%)

Next, the Nasdaq 100 (NDX6%) strategy was tested over a 12-year period, November 11, 1990, through November 29, 2002 – its entirety. This weekly strategy produced an annual return of 22.34 percent, with a net profit of $599,337, for a cumulative return of 599.3 percent. This compares with buy-and-hold which had cumulative return of 220.8 percent, with a net profit of $220,790. Although only 47 percent of the 55 trades were profitable, the ratio of winning trades to losing trades was 2.38, and the profit factor of 2.13, made this strategy a winner. All the years produced positive returns and the equity curve parallels the NC6% curve.

I used TradeStation to run an optimization of the parameters and found that the 6 percent buy and sell signals actually provided one of the most profitable combinations. Only two strategies did better than the 6 percent strategy. The 5 percent off the low and 6 percent off the high strategy earned a profit of $770,317, and the 5 percent off the low and 8 percent off the high earned a profit of $721,387.

I was curious to see how the NDX6% did in comparison to the NC6% over the same time period and found that the NDX6% earned about $51,000 more in profit than the NC6% strategy ($599,337, compared to $548,663). I also ran the actual VL4% daily strategy over the same 13-year time period and it came out with a profit of only $363,682.

TEST 3: DAILY NASDAQ 6 PERCENT STRATEGY (NC6%)

Based on the exceptional results of the NC6% weekly strategy, I decided to run the same strategy on a daily basis for comparative purposes. This change produced a meager profit of only $15,040 over the entire 13-year period. Profits started slowly, reached a nice peak, and then deteriorated. So, using daily data instead of weekly data produces very poor results. Using the optimization feature of TradeStation, the optimal daily parameters for both the buy and sell signals turned out to be 11 percent, and that strategy produced a total profit of only $341,411 over the 13 years, still not a good showing. In conclusion, the NC6% daily strategy does not cut the mustard, and should be discarded.

TEST 4: DAILY NDX 6 PERCENT STRATEGY (NDX6%)

I also tested the daily NDX6% data for the same 13-year time frame. The results were disastrous, with a *loss* of $88,806 for the entire period, or a negative –17.4 percent annual return. The optimal parameters turned out to be 12 percent for both the buy and the sell side, producing a gain of $75,436. This strategy is completely unstable, as a 1 percentage point change can drastically alter the results. Also, the equity curve is downward-sloping right from the start, a bad sign. In conclusion, this daily strategy should be avoided at all costs.

CONCLUSIONS

In so far as the Nasdaq indexes are concerned, the weekly 6 percent signals are clearly superior to the daily 6 percent buy and sell signals. The daily signals are much more frequent because of the volatility of their respective indexes. Moreover, both weekly strategies NDX6% and NC6% significantly beat the VL4% strategy.

I also back-tested the S&P 500 Index with various buy and sell filters, but the results were poor for both the weekly and daily signals. Based on the back-test results shown in this chapter, I recommend that either the NC6% (Nasdaq Composite Index) or the NDX6% (Nasdaq 100 Index) weekly strategy be used for market timing, because of their exceptional performance: 18.8 percent annualized and 22.3 percent annualized, respectively.

FIGURE 11–2

Nasdaq Composite 6% Weekly TradeStation Chart Analysis
2000–2002

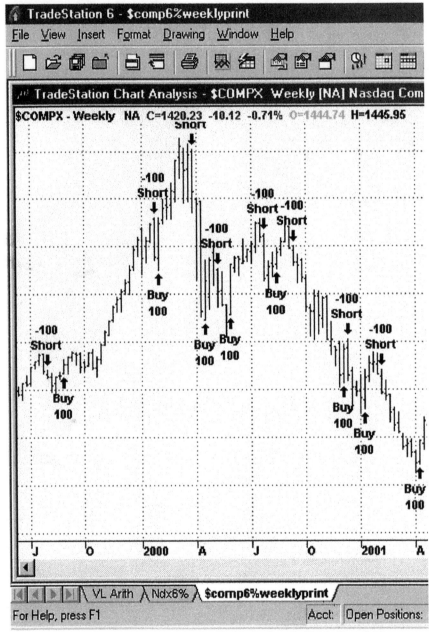

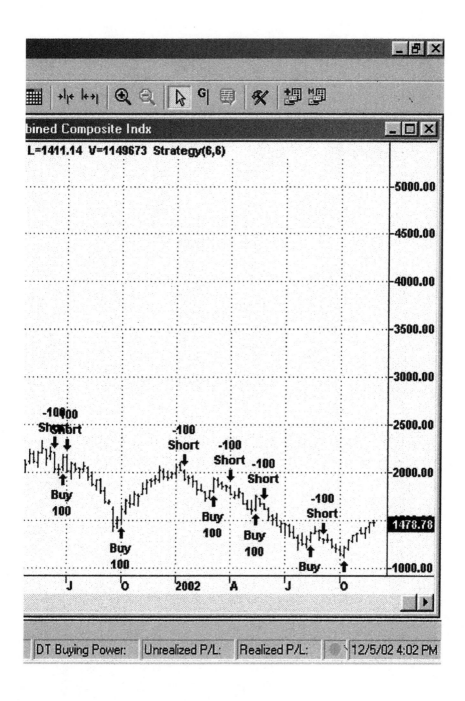

Market-Timing Resources

PART 3

MarketTiming Resources

CHAPTER 12

Market-Timing Resources

Newsletters, Web Sites, and Advisors

Ignorance is not knowing something; stupidity is not admitting your ignorance.

Daniel Turov (Turov on Timing*).*

If we don't change the direction we're going, we're going to end up where we're headed.

Chinese Proverb

There is no shortage of market-timing newsletters, and advisors available to take investors' money. The problem is that most of them are worthless and dangerous to your wealth. One way to engage in market timing without doing the work yourself is to subscribe to a market-timing newsletter and scrupulously follow its buy and sell signals. Another approach is to hire a market-timing advisor to manage your funds with mutual funds.

The first part of this chapter will cover market-timing newsletters, the second part will focus on market-timing advisory services that manage your funds for you, and the third part will provide other related resources. Today there are well over 100 market-timing newsletters published in hardcopy or on the Web. New ones appear all the time, and old ones with miserable track records disappear into the night. The problem is determining which, if any, newsletters meets your specific needs.

MARKET-TIMING NEWSLETTERS

In general, to locate timing newsletters, you can go to a search engine such as *www.google.com* and type in market-timing newsletters. That will get you over 100 items to review. You will find advertisements, as well as the good, the bad, and the ugly among these hits. You can then go the Web sites of the newsletters you've selected and read about what they offer, see a sample newsletter, and perhaps review their track record against a comparable benchmark. Be careful doing so, since some unscrupulous individuals provide inaccurate track records, and some services have only back-tested and optimized a trading system that has minimal real-time performance statistics. And the advertising claims of many of the purveyors are outrageous. Caveat emptor!

Another option is to use the services of The Select Information Exchange. The firm offers a Web site (*www.stockfocus.com*) that provides trial subscriptions to 169 newsletters and advisory services, of which 37 focus on market timing. Access their Web site and go to the center of the screen to the box "browse by topic," then highlight "market-timing" and you'll get a list of all market-timing newsletters to which they offer trials. You can then decide if you are interested in a trial of four newsletters for five months for $69. They can also be reached at (800) 743-9346, and they send out a hardcopy brochure periodically.

Independent Newsletters Tracking Market-Timing Newsletters and Specialized Newsletters

Nevertheless, after scrutinizing Google's offerings and reviewing those of The Select Information Exchange, you may still find yourself unsure of what to do. The marketing hype and testimonials of many newsletters are oftentimes grossly misleading. Fortunately, two independent newsletter services are available that verify the performance of timing newsletters. They publish their results every three or four weeks, respectively, for subscribers. Having these services is just like having *Consumer Reports* for newsletters—getting the facts rather than the hype. You need the truth, not the baloney sandwich.

Timer Digest

The *Timer Digest* newsletter, edited by Jim Schmidt since 1987, tracks the performance of over 100 market-timing models published in newsletters. Schmidt follows the timing signals in each newsletter, as would a typical subscriber, including those provided by email or a telephone hotmail service. All newsletter signal changes are bench-marked against the S&P 500 Index. All market-timing newsletters are ranked against each other and the timers are listed in each issue of *Timer Digest*.

Timer Digest is published every three weeks in newsletter format (via hardcopy or via a PDF file that can be downloaded off a Web site at *www.timerdigest.com*). This information is supplemented by a biweekly hotline service (accessed via the Web site or telephone), which is updated on Wednesday and Saturday nights. The hotline reports any signal changes from the timers as well as their latest opinion. The digest ranks the top stock, bond, and gold timers based on their latest 52-week performance.

The top timers are those with the best stock market performance over the past 52 weeks, compared to the S&P 500 benchmark. The latest market call (bullish or bearish), performance data, and signal date from each of these timers is printed in the newsletter, along with the timer's latest market commentary (one to two lines). Over time, since the evaluation encompasses a rolling 52-week period, there are different top timers. So, only those with the best performance out of the 100-odd timers are highlighted. In addition, the "Top 5" Bond and Gold Timers are shown, with their performance, buy and sell signals, and brief market comment.

"Top 10" *Timer Digest* Consensus tells the current recommended position of the majority of these stock timers—that is, either a bullish or bearish call on the market. In addition to providing the top timers for the past 52 weeks, the digest also lists the stock timers for the most recent six months and three months, with their timing performance compared to the S&P 500 benchmark, and the date of their most recent signal. Additionally, the "Top 5" bond and gold timers are ranked and a consensus reading (bullish or bearish) is also provided with the same information just mentioned.

How have the 100 timers tracked by *Timer Digest* performed over the past four years? Publisher Jim Schmidt indicates that less than 5 percent of the timers beat the S&P 500 Index in 1999, which was up 19.5 percent, but approximately 65 percent beat that benchmark in 2000 (S&P –10.1 percent), 45 percent beat it in 2001 (S&P –13 percent), and 80 percent beat it in 2002 (S&P –23.4 percent). The relative performance of all the timers monitored versus the benchmark was excellent considering the extended bear market. This doesn't necessarily mean that the timers actually had positive returns but that they lost less than the S&P 500.

For the year ending in 2001, the "Top 10" Timers Consensus as a group had a performance index of 100.4 compared to the S&P performance index of 86.96. The performance index is set at 100.0 at the beginning of each year for each timer and for the index. And timing signals assume either long or short positions in the S&P. So, for the one-year period ending in 2001, the top 10 timers performed 13 percentage points better than the benchmark.

For the year ending 2002, the "Top 10" *Timer Digest* Consensus as a group had a performance index of 126.23 compared to the S&P performance index of 76.63. So for the one-year period, the top timers performed almost 50 percentage points better than the benchmark, certainly an outstanding performance, and one of the record variances for a one-year period since *Timer Digest*'s inception.

Look at Table 12-1. Here the performance of the top timers is shown, relative to the S&P 500 benchmark at year-end 2002. Overall, the Top 10 Consensus designated as "T.D. Consensus" in the table beat the S&P Index in all time periods. However, only four timers exceeded the benchmark over 8 years, and only three did so over 10 years. These results are not unexpected in big bull markets. Timing does not usually beat buy-and-hold in that environment. But in bear markets, timers tend to excel, as I pointed out a few paragraphs earlier.

The "TD Consensus" performance was more than double the benchmark for three years, and between 50 and 100 percentage points higher for the 5-, 8- and 10-year time frames.

The following is a look at some of the top timers and the lists they appeared on in the year ending in 2002, as shown on Table 12-1:

1-, 3-, 5-, 8- and 10-year lists
Dan Turov, *Turov on Timing*
Mark Leibovit, *VRTrader.com*
Jim Tillman, *Cycletrend*

TABLE 12-1

Top 10 Timers Performance vs. S&P 500 Index,
Years Ending 12/31/02

	1 Year Perf. Index	3 Years Perf. Index	5 Years Perf. Index	8 Years Perf. Index	10 Years Perf. Index
T.D. Consensus	126.23	132.74	155.59	317.47	306.65
S&P 500	76.63	59.88	90.66	191.57	201.93
Top Timer	178.64	223.91	246.2	285.19	267.48
10th Top Timer	126.84	130.89	126.76	128.14	102.1

Note: Only 4 timers beat S&P 500 in 8-year performance, and only 3 did so over 10 years.

Source: Timer Digest, "Special Annual Report," January 27, 2003.

Information printed with permission of *Timer Digest.*

3-, 5-, 8-, and 10-year lists
Doug Jimerson, *National Trendlines*

5-, 8-, and 10-year lists
Steve Todd, *The Todd Market Forecast*

1-, 3-, 10-year lists
Arch Crawford, *Crawford Perspectives*

5- and 8-year lists
Tom McClellan, *The McClellan Market Report*

3- and 5- year lists
Craig Corcoran, *Craig Corcoran Futures*

1- and 3-year lists
Joseph Granville, *The Granville Market Letter*
Christopher Cadbury, *Cadbury Timing Service*

Timers who can maintain such consistent standings, year after year, are exceptional. The longer they remain as top performers on the three-year lists and longer, the more credibility their forecasting recommendations have. As I pointed out above, the timers may not beat buy-and-hold in all time frames, but they are worth their weight in gold during bear markets.

How has the *Timer Digest* "Top 10" Consensus performed? Over the last 10 years ending March 31, 2002, *Timer Digest* was ranked second out of 26 timing newsletters for performance. For the 10 years ending June 30, 2002, *Timer Digest's* average annual return for the "Top 10" Consensus was 12.5 percent compared to 4.3 percent for buy-and-hold (Hulbert uses the Wilshire 5000 as the benchmark, not the S&P 500). Schmidt's Fidelity Select program (buying the strongest single select fund based on a proprietary evaluation) was up an average of 16 percent for this same period (but had more risk), and the Dow Jones strategy (buying the strongest DJIA stocks) was up 9.6 percent.

Timer Digest is a comprehensive newsletter and timing service that offers investors unbiased information at a reasonable price ($225 annual subscription cost). For more information, contact the newsletter at (203) 629-3503, or at its Web site: *www.timerdigest.com*.

Mutual Fund Prospector

Eric Dany has published the *Mutual Fund Prospector* newsletter since December 1998. His goal is to provide a simple mutual fund timing strategy that provides solid long-term returns. His research indicated that "equity style timing" is a strategy that produces excellent returns. Rather than focusing on the more traditional market timing approaches, Dany concentrates on selecting actively managed mutual funds that are performing well not only in the large-cap, small-cap, mid-cap areas and international areas, but more importantly whether "value" or "growth." is the dominant theme. Then he selects the appropriate funds to take advantage of the situation.

Each month, Dany publishes his 12-page newsletter containing his current portfolios, his view on the market, latest news about the funds that he follows, as well as a detailed six-page listing of the top performing funds in all the asset classes mentioned earlier. He then assigns a score to each that he refers to as "nuggets". The higher the nugget rating the better.

The *Mutual Fund Prospector's* model portfolio consists of about eleven funds with one core broadly-based market fund. accounting for about 40% or so of the weighting, with the remainder invested in actively managed funds. The percentages in the active funds can vary based upon Dany's analysis of market conditions and which equity styles are outperforming the market. The model portfolio has outperformed the market since its inception (12/31/98-12/31/04), returning 80% versus a market gain of 14.8%. Hulbert Financial Digest also tracks the performance of *The Mutual Fund Prospector.*

There are also other portfolios for investors including an Aggressive portfolio without a core index fund, a three-fund Fidelity sector portfolio, and a super aggressive ProFunds 2.0 Beta portfolio.

For more information about the *Mutual Fund Prospector,* contact Dany at:

editor@propectornewsletters.com or toll-free: Toll-free: 866-541-5299. The newsletter cost $129 year; or $199 two years in North America.

FORMULA RESEARCH Newsletter

For those investors interested in learning about the latest in timing models, one newsletter provides unique, time-tested, profitable models. That newsletter is *FORMULA RESEARCH.* Since October 1991, Nelson Freeburg has been its editor and publisher. Freeburg is a master systems builder and developer of systematic timing models and trading systems for stocks, T-bonds, sector funds, regular mutual funds, futures, and commodities. He provides research to over one thousand clients—institutional and individual—in over twenty-five countries. As you will recall, Freeburg's extensive model testing was frequently referenced in Chapters 7, 8, and 10. Freeburg also actively trades the markets and is a popular speaker in the United States and abroad.

FORMULA RESEARCH is neither a stock tip sheet nor a market-timing service. It offers neither investment advice nor opinions of where the markets are going. Freeburg's sole objective is finding, developing, and rigorously testing market-timing models and strategies using standard statistical testing routines. His extensive research, published over many years, has produced a large number of timing models that produce consistent performance while outperforming the S&P 500 Index.

Each issue of the newsletter provides a proprietary trading system with high performance and limited risk. His writing is crisp and to the point. If he is testing a system developed by someone else, he provides complete attribution and credits the individual for his work, then he does his own research using different sampling periods and other variations to improve upon the originator's work. For more information on the newsletter, contact :

FORMULA RESEARCH

4646 Poplar Avenue Suite 401
Memphis, TN 38117
(800) 720-1080
(901) 756-8607
Subscription: $295 for 12 issues
E-mail: *sigma20@midsouth.rr.com*

Individual reports of trading models from past issues are available for $25 for subscribers, $30 for trial subscribers, and $45 for nonsubscribers.

Sy Harding's Street Smart Report

Sy Harding, mentioned in Chapter 7 for his contribution to seasonal investing, also provides investment and market-timing advice via his newsletter *Sy Harding's Street Smart Report*, published every three weeks, for 16 years. A typical newsletter includes the following:

- ◆ 2-page commentary on current market conditions
- ◆ 1-page review of Harding's Seasonal Timing System (STS) status with charts
- ◆ 2-page commentary and charts of Harding's nonseasonal timing strategy covering the S&P 500, DJIA, and Nasdaq Composite indexes
- ◆ 1-page of commentary and charts on the gold sector
- ◆ Update on bonds with charts
- ◆ Review of current portfolio holdings and performance

Harding provides subscribers with two stock market strategies:

- ◆ **Seasonal Timing Strategy.** This strategy is based on strong seasonal patterns. Two portfolios are offered: one for average risk investors and one for aggressive investors.

+ **Regular market-timing strategy.** This strategy is based on technical analysis, overbought/oversold conditions, investor sentiment, etc. Two portfolios are offered—one for mutual fund switching and one for equities.

Street Smart Report can be obtained in hardcopy or online :

+ The hardcopy newsletter is published and mailed every three weeks. Included are telephone hotline updates, and online Internet access. The cost is $250 per year.
+ The online Internet newsletter alone includes updates, additional commentaries, and other educational materials from the Street Smart School, and Street Smart Library. The cost is $225 per year.
+ Both subscriptions include a copy of Sy Harding's book, *Riding the Bear: How to Prosper in the Coming Bear Market.*
+ For further information on the newsletter, contact:

Asset Management Research Corp.

505 East New York Avenue, Suite 2
DeLand, FL 32724
(386) 943-4081
Web site: *www.StreetSmartReport.com*

MARKET-TIMING WEB SITES

In addition to the previous two newsletter rating services and two specialized newsletters there are other resources that you may want to check out. The four mentioned below are Web-based advisory services. Of course there are many other resources available, and you can find them by going to the Google search engine and doing your homework. Also, look in the bibliography for a listing of useful Web sites.

www.haysmarketfocus.com

The Hays Advisory Group offers *www.haysmarketfocus.com*, a Web site that provides thrice-weekly financial commentary and investing strategy for individual investors and professionals. Each commentary explains and interprets the current economic and financial news, the short- and long-term stock market outlook, and the impact of news affecting the stock market.

In addition to the commentary, the Web site contains numerous updated charts so subscribers can observe the current situation. Some of the indicators tracked in chart form are sentiment indicators, market breath and overbought/oversold indicators, market trends in major averages, market valuation, and monetary indicators. The Web site also provides subscribers with sector and industry analysis with weekly updates and a list of recommended stocks in top-performing industries.

If you remember the presentation of sentiment and internal market indicators in Chapter 4, you'll remember that a number of charts were provided by the Hays Advisory Group.

A yearly subscription costs $159 and includes the following:

- Market commentaries are posted to the Web site three times a week.
- Access to proprietary market research and studies, including:
  - Charts of market indicators
  - Asset allocation recommendations
  - Studies of industries and sectors
  - Stock screening

There is a also five-week complimentary subscription on the Hays Advisory Group's Web site to try out their service without any risk. For additional information contact the firm at:

Hays Advisory Group

P.O. Box 158548
Nashville, TN 37215-8548
Web site: *www.haysmarketfocus.com*

www.fundadvice.com

Paul Merriman offers a complimentary online mutual fund newsletter that contains in-depth and comprehensive information. Over 100 articles are on the site (in their archives, and articles are updated as needed with the latest annual statistics) on all aspects of investing including market timing, buy-and-hold, and investment psychology. The following information is available at this information-packed site:

+ Current market-timing signals for U.S. stocks and bonds
+ Model portfolios and performance statistics
+ Audio archives of the weekly *Sound Investing* radio show
+ Investment calculators
+ Latest articles on investing
+ Library of archived articles—12 articles on retirement investing, 35 articles on market timing, 18 articles on buy-and-hold, 24 articles on the psychology of investing, and much more
+ Merriman University—audio clips on important investing subjects

By signing up at the site, investors will be sent an email message whenever new articles are published and whenever a new timing signal occurs. Additionally, Merriman writes an investing column, which can be found at *www.cbs.marketwatch.com*.

For more information, contact the firm at:

Merriman Capital Management, Inc.

1200 Westlake Avenue North, Suite 700
Seattle, WA 98109
Phone: (800) 423-4893
Web site: *www.MerrimanCapital.com*

www.timingcube.com

TimingCube® is an Internet-based market timing service for long-term investors. It uses a mechanical computer-based trend-timing model, based on a proprietary formula, to determine market buy and sell signals. The Nasdaq Composite Index is used to determine any changes in the model's market trends. On average, there are three to five signals a year. The model data was back-tested to January 3, 1989, and the first real-time signal was on June 18, 2001. *TimingCube®* is a good example of a market timing service that has consistently outperformed buy and hold.

Subscribers receive same day e-mail notification of Buy, Sell or Cash signals, *as* well as have phone access. Also, subscribers can also check the website daily for any signal changes. Each Friday there is a "Weekly Market Update" covering the market's action for the previous week and educational perspective in its "Trend Timing School" editorials.

Investors can use one or more of the four strategies provided, and then use the signals to make their buy and sell decisions. The strategies provided include:

1. Long only   3. Long and Short
2. Long with margin   4. Long and short with margin

The website tracks the Nasdaq 100, the Russell 2000, and the S&P 500, since they are highly correlated with each other. Specific exchange-traded funds, and enhanced funds from the ProFunds and Rydex funds families are recommended for the different strategies. The site clearly explains all the strategies and which ETFs or funds to use to implement each one.

Hulbert Financial, Digest and TimerTrac.com independently verify *Timing*Cube's trades and returns. *Timing*Cube®, was developed and co-founded by two computer scientists Frank Minssieux and Dr. Serge Dacic. The service cost $29.95 per month or $299.95 annually. First time subscribers are provided with a 30-day unconditional money back guarantee.

For more information about *Timing*Cube®, contact them at: sunport@timingcube.com

David Korn's Advisory Service

The last item in this section is an unusual Web-based service that is neither a market-timing newsletter nor a market-timing advisory service. However, it offers interesting market insights and it tracks the recommendations and commentary of *Bob Brinker's Moneytalk* weekly radio show which can be heard on radio stations across the country on weekends. Brinker, a long-time market timer and publisher of *Bob Brinker's Marketimer*, has been around for over 15 years. He was *Timer Digest's* top 10-year long-term timer for the year ending December 31, 2002. His return over that period was 244.58, compared to 210.94 for the S&P 500 benchmark. He was also the third best timer for the five years ending December 31, 2002, and was the 2000 Long-Term Timer of the Year.

David Korn, an attorney by profession, and an avid stock market buff, decided about four years ago to offer a fee-based commentary service on the stock market and in particular, on *Bob Brinker's Moneytalk*. For 15 years, Korn has been reading Brinker's newsletter, and listening to his radio show. Korn's Internet-based service came about because of demand from investors who wanted his interpretation of Brinker's comments. Korn's service, known as "David Korn's Stock Market Commentary," contains interpretation of *Moneytalk*, (Bob Brinker, Host), financial education, helpful links, guest editorials and special alert e-mail service, Korn's own market insights, and a model portfolio. He also follows other market timers, and he keeps his subscribers apprised of the changing financial and economic environment.

In the year 2000, Korn's subscribers wanted a Web site where they could meet to discuss the stock market, Bob Brinker, and whatever other financial topics were of interest. Thus, Korn's discussion threads sprung up on his Web site, *www.begininvesting.com*. Subscribers post questions on all aspects of investing, including the workings of the stock market, technical analysis, market timing, bonds, real estate, and anything else they can think of. Korn responds to all subscribers' questions with detailed answers.

A subscription to David Korn's stock market commentary, interpretation of the *Moneytalk* radio program hosted by Bob Brinker, financial links, and special alert e-mail service and Web site, and *www.begininvesting.com* is $2.50 a week.

For more information on Korn's services, contact him at:

David Korn, L.L.C.

P.O. Box 58076
New Orleans, LA 70158-8076
Web site: *www.begininvesting.com* (click on the site to send an e-mail to him)

MARKET-TIMING ADVISORS

If people conclude that it's not what we make that counts but what we keep, or that it's not just how we do in the good times that mat-

ters but how we do in the bad times, I think they'll see timing is a
valuable tool. It's just a question of whether they want to do it
themselves or whether they want someone to do it for them.

Paul Merriman, founder and president of Merriman Capital Management Inc., *The
Value Line No-Load Fund Advisor*, "Interview with Paul Merriman" May, 1995.

Some investors may neither be interested in timing the market for
themselves, using the market-timing strategies presented in this book
or elsewhere, or using a market-timing newsletter to get their timing
signals. The last alternative is to hire a market-timing investment
advisor to actually make the buy and sell decisions in the investor's
account under a limited power of attorney. In that case, the question
becomes who to hire.

The MoniResearch Newsletter

For those investors seeking to engage a market timer to manage their
mutual fund investments, there is an unbiased source of information
that has been offering audited performance statistics on market
timers since March 1986. That service is called *The MoniResearch
Newsletter*, edited and published by Steve Shellans, who has actually
been tracking market timers for 22 years. Shellans earned a B.S.
degree from M.I.T., and an M.S. degree in computer science from the
Stevens Institute of Technology. He has more than 30 years of investment experience.

Shellans accepts no fees from timers that he measures nor
does he receive any remuneration from them based on the amount
of business generated for them by the newsletter. He does, however, charge every timer a fixed annual tracking fee of $275.
According to Shellans, "the performance data in his newsletter is
factual, impartial and unbiased." He will not track any firm he
does not trust.

About 100 market timers are covered with alternating newsletter issues tracking classic market timers and dynamic asset allocators
in the six newsletters published a year. Classic market timers invest
in U.S. equity mutual funds when they receive their buy signals, and
they invest in money market funds when they get sell signals from
their timing models. On the other hand, dynamic asset allocators
invest in a mix of asset classes such as domestic and international

stocks, bonds, or gold. This strategy is basically a diversified play on the market to take advantage of the changing environment.

MoniResearch tracks neither market-timing "newsletters" nor market-timing "hotline services" but only professional timers who manage actual client funds and permit access to client statements for audit performance purposes by MoniResearch. All performance data shown in the newsletter for each timer is net of their management fees. So it is a true representation of actual performance. There are no theoretical or back-tested performance numbers in this newsletter.

Most of the timers covered by Shellans invest only in mutual funds, and mostly in no-load funds, but some new timers have been added that time the ETFs. That means that the investor who decides to engage one of the timers would set up an account (to buy and sell mutual funds) with his own investment or brokerage firm or directly with the fund family (for example, Rydex or ProFunds); he would then provide the timer with trading authority (limited power of attorney) over the account. The timer has no ability to take funds out of the account, because the account is owned by the investor. A few firms operate as hedge funds or limited partnerships, and investors who participate in these do not own their own account—funds are commingled.

In most cases, the classic timers use a proprietary timing model and the firm will only give investors a general idea as to what factors are used to determine their buy and sell signals. Therefore, it is critically important to check the track record of performance over the longest time period available as well as during the most recent years.

Refer to Table 12-2 from the November/December *MoniResearch Newsletter* to see the performance statistics for the March 2002 Quarter and for one-, two-, three- and five-year periods, for timers who use only Rydex, ProFunds, or Potomac Funds as their investment vehicles. As you recall, these funds were set up specifically for market timers. The ending date of the measurement period was September 30, 2002, exactly nine days before the low for the year. As you scan the table, you will note that some timers are listed more than once. This is because they had more than one portfolio measured by the newsletter.

For the one-year period ending September 30, 2002, of the 32 timer portfolios measured, 22 percent (7 portfolios) did worse than the Nasdaq or S&P 500 (dividends reinvested). These indexes were

T A B L E   12-2

Advisor Rydex Performance/ProFunds Performance
Period Ending: September 30, 2002   Issue: Nov. / Dec. 2002

| | Fund Family Used | | Style | Performance | | | | | Ulcer Index (Risk) | Notes |
| | Rydex | ProFunds | L=long, Sh=Short, Sc=Sectors, B=Bonds, G=Gold | Annualized | | | Actual | | | |
				5-yr	3-yr	2-yr	1-yr	3Q 2002		
Benchmarks										
Nasdaq Composite Index				-7.0	-24.7	-43.5	-21.8	-19.9	107.1	
S&P 500 with dividends reinvested				-1.6	-12.9	-23.6	-20.5	-17.3	44.1	
Firm / Program *The Following Firms are Listed Alphabetically*										
Advisor's Capital / Switching Strategy	√	√	L, Sh	7.9	-1.2	-6.1	8.3	9.4	74.4	2, 8
Appel Asset Mgmt	√		L	-3.0	-5.1	-15.7	-8.7	-0.3	69.1	
Aurum Capital Mgmt Corp		√	L	Not avail.		See Note				3, 9
Capital Growth Mgmt (CGM)			All		5.5	5.9	-3.8	3.5	34.0	
Christie Mgmt Services	√		L, Sh, Sc	19.2*	21.9*	23.3*	6.1	10.1*	14.2	
CM Capital Mgmt	√		L, Sh		14.9	11.8	12.2*	9.0	9.8	3
Cook (Michael R)	√		L, Sh, B			19.7	6.0	0.1	2.6*	3
Cooper Linse	√		L, Sh, Sc, G	-4.5	-11.5	-25.6	-2.5	-1.1	63.8	
Dorset Financial Services / Discretionary	√		All			19.8	5.4	9.3	9.3	3, 4
Dorset Financial Services Corp / Gold	√		G		0.5	-8.6	-29.5	-3.4	33.3	3, 7
Financial Growth Mgmt	√		L, Sh, Sc	-3.5	-10.2	-12.9	-9.1	-3.0	57.9	1, 8

Fund	*	Category							
Flexible Plan Investments / Classic	✓	L, Sh, B	-15.9	-30.7	-42.0	-35.3	-23.9	85.8	3, 9
Flexible Plan Inv. / VR Aggres Growth	✓	All		10.3	19.0	3.3	3.6	14.3	3
Global Invest. Solutions / McClellan	✓	L, Sh		-4.2	-0.3	-3.7	-8.8	37.9	3
Global Trends Investments	✓	L		-41.6	-54.4	-31.9	-21.5	208.1	
Index Asset Mgmt	✓	L, Sh	-3.4	-14.5	-26.8	-36.4	-15.9	48.5	3
Key Market Research / Index	✓	L		1.3	-5.0	-6.4	-7.1	20.9	3
Key Market Research / Sectors	✓	Sc				-9.4	-2.1	17.2	3
KFCM Market Research / OTC Timing	✓	L, Sc		-0.7	-8.9	-4.2	-5.1	82.4	3
KFCM Market Research / Sector Tim.	✓	Sc, G		-2.9	-13.7	-13.9	-7.3	71.1	3
Landmark Investment Co.	✓	L, Sh, B	-2.3	-8.3	-8.7	-6.2	-7.2	58.5	
Marathon / Sector Rotation	✓	L, Sh, Sc		11.0	0.8	7.2	2.2	35.7	3
National Invest. Adv. / Insured OTC	✓	L		7.2	-7.0	-11.2	0	65.0	2, 3
Pankin (Mark) / NDX Trading	✓	L	-3.2	-15.5	-28.5	-8.9	-8.6	91.7	
Pankin (Mark) / Rydex Sectors	✓	Sc	-3.4	-14.2	-31.9	-23.8	-9.5	97.0	5
Potomac / Index Plus	✓	All	-3.6	-11.6	-17.6	-6.6	-0.4	79.7	
Potomac / Bull & Bear	✓	L	0.7	-5.1	-9.9	0.5	-0.4	54.4	
St. Louis Financial Planners / S&P 500	✓	L	Not avail.						3, 11
Schreiner Capital Mgmt	✓	L	-0.2	-13.3	-21.8	-23.3	-15.7	51.0	
Sovereign Wealth Mgmt	✓	L, Sh		2.5	-15.7	8.3	-14.9	14.8	3
Spectrum Financial / Sector	✓	Sc, Sh	4.3	-24.9	-32.4	-17.7	-11.2	50.4	
Spectrum Finan. / Short term	✓	L	-6.4	-44.9	-40.8	-20.4	-4.7	95.1	
Trusskey Investment Advisors / Group 8	✓	L, Sh			-17.3	-48.5	-23.1	212.3	3, 9
Trusskey Investment Advisors / Group 9	✓	Sc				-15.7	-11.1	76.4	3

*Leader for this time period

both down around –21 percent. That is what a buy-and-hold strategy would have returned, if the investor were invested in those indexes. Interestingly, 78 percent of the timer portfolios exceeded those benchmarks, with seven timers actually showing positive returns for the year. The others had smaller losses than the benchmarks. The leading timer for most all time frames was Christie Management Services, with positive results in every time frame measured over the past five years.

Over the two-year time frame, 28 timer portfolios were analyzed, with 25 percent (seven timers) underperforming their index benchmark, and 75 percent beating it.

Over the three-year time frame, 25 timer portfolios were analyzed, with 70 percent beating the buy-and-hold strategy using the S&P 500, and 84 percent of the timers beating the Nasdaq Composite buy-and-hold strategy. Eight funds had a positive return, compared to losses in the benchmarks. Over the five-year time frame, 13 timers were analyzed, with two funds underperforming their benchmark, and the remaining, 85 percent, beating it.

Usually, timers charge a 1 to 3 percent annual fee for their services on a sliding scale (higher balances pay a smaller fee), based on the value of the portfolio. The minimum account size a classic timer will accept is usually $25,000. A very few firms will accept accounts as low as $1000 and $5000. For the dynamic asset allocators, $100,000 is the more typical minimum, and again a few firms will accept as little $10,000 and $25,000.

The MoniResearch Newsletter contains additional information besides the performance ranking of the timers. Sections in the newsletter include articles about market timers and market timing, a table listing which market timers are long or short the market, the asset classes in which they are invested, the timing of those investments, and their future market outlook. Also shown is a list of all the market timers, their contact information, their minimum account size, the assets under management, and their fee structure. An annual subscription to the newsletter is $159 for six issues. For further information on *The MoniResearch Newsletter,* contact the firm at:

The MoniResearch Newsletter

P.O. Box 1907
Woodland, WA 98674

E-mail: Moninews@compuserve.com
Phone: (800) 615-6664
Web site: *www.moniresearch.com*

Select Advisors

Another service available to investors who want to hire a market-timing advisor to manage their funds exclusively with the Rydex Funds family is *Select Advisors*. Schreiner Capital Management, Inc. (SCM), a SEC registered investment advisor, is a manager and the sponsor of the *Select Advisors* program.

Select Advisors requires a minimum $100,000 to open an account and charges a 2.50 percent annual fee for participating in the program, which includes the market-timing advisor fees. If an investor retains an individual advisor independently of *Select Advisors*, he would find fees ranging from 1 percent to 3 percent and higher, with investment minimums ranging from $25,000 to $250,000.

The *Select Advisors* program has created a wrap account with a single management fee and low minimum where assets can be moved anywhere within the Rydex Fund family without additional fees. Fees are paid at the end of each quarter. Of course the Rydex Funds levy their own internal fees (such as their annual expense ratio, and some fund classes also charge 12b-1 fees included in the expense ratio). Additional information about the Rydex Funds can be found on their Web site at *www.rydexfunds.com*, as well as in Chapter 5.

Select Advisors operates it's own Web site and investment platform at *www.select-advisors.com*. They provide performance data on almost 300 market timers (who manage 569 programs) who use the Rydex Funds as their investment vehicles.

There are few caveats of which you should be aware. First, only those advisors who agree to open accounts with *Select Advisors* are monitored and tracked in the program's online database. Second, *Select Advisors* has only three years of performance history on 109 timing programs that joined their service in 1999. For the last two years there is performance history on 258 programs, and for the year 2002 there is performance history on 440 programs. *Select Advisors* requires real-time performance and will not accept performance histories reported by the managers they track. SCM established real accounts with its own money and tracks the daily performance of each program. This process began in 1999, hence the reason for the limited track records.

This short performance history does not mean that the individual managers do not have longer performance histories. But it does mean that *Select Advisors* only provides the history that they can validate by their own tracking accounts. Investors who are considering a manager from the *Select Advisors* database should request a complete performance history from that advisor before filling out any paperwork to open an account.

If an investor signs up with *Select Advisors*, he is given free access to the online performance database of managers, which is updated daily. Investors can monitor their manager's performance against all other managers in multiple time frames, including 3 months, 6 months, 9 months, 1 year, quarter-to-date, year-to-date, 2000 and 2001.

Performance of Advisors in Select Advisors Program

You may be wondering about the performance of the market-timing advisors in the *Select Advisors* program. Table 12-3 compares the composite performance and volatility results of the advisors against the S&P 500, Nasdaq Composite, and Nasdaq 100 Indexes over one-, two-, and three-year periods ending December 31, 2002. A few caveats need to be kept in mind:

- Data performance history goes back for three years, from 2000 through 2002. Most of this period was a bear market. In this type of market environment, timers should outperform the market averages if they are worth their salt.
- The data in the table does not break out what percentage of the advisors should be compared against which benchmark. For example, if 50 percent of the advisors had Rydex programs that should be compared against the S&P 500, and if 50 percent had programs that should be compared to the Nasdaq Composite Index, then it would have been helpful to see those breakdowns. That assumes it is possible to determine each advisor's fund mix and appropriate benchmark.
- The average percentages in the table do not show how the best or worst advisors performed in their quartile. So for

TABLE 12-3

Performance Results of Advisors in Select Advisors Program
Year Ending December 31, 2002

Indices and Universe Averages When Ranked by Performance and Std. Dev.	12 Months 440 managers		24 Months 258 managers		36 Months 109 managers	
	Performance	Std. Dev.	Performance	Std. Dev.	Performance	Std. Dev.
S&P 500	−23.37%	5.70%	−18.32%	5.62%	−40.12%	5.35%
Nasdaq COMP	−31.53%	8.40%	−26.41%	10.71%	−67.18%	11.33%
Nasdaq 100	−37.58%	10.35%	−35.09%	12.77%	−73.45%	12.62%
Avg Top 25%	16.10%	1.30%	0.95%	1.38%	−5.10%	3.99%
Avg Top 50%	5.01%	2.69%	−2.27%	3.70%	−9.75%	5.05%
Avg Bottom 50%	−32.40%	12.46%	−23.41%	10.28%	−29.37%	13.68%
Avg Bottom 25%	−45.90%	17.76%	−39.32%	18.52%	−35.65%	18.98%
Average All	**−13.70%**	**7.57%**	**−16.56%**	**8.55%**	**−19.65%**	**9.46%**

Source: Theta investment research. Printed with permission.

example, for the past 12 months, in the "Avg Bottom 50%" the worst managers could have been down much more than 45.9 percent. And in the "Avg Top 25%," the best managers could have been up much more than 16.1 percent.

On an overall basis, for 2002 (shown as 12 months in the table), all 440 programs monitored had a negative 13.7 percent performance with a standard deviation (variance from the average return or investment risk) of 7.57 percent. This performance clearly outpaced the three benchmark averages. The managers performed almost 10 percentage points better than the S&P 500, and 17.5 percentage points better than the Nasdaq Composite Index.

Interestingly, the top 25 percent (110 programs) turned in an average positive performance of 16.1 percent, with a low standard deviation of 1.3 percent. The top 50 percent (220 programs) also had a positive performance with an average gain of 5 percent. The bottom quartile of programs really got killed, down an average 46 percent. Not the performance you want to see from an advisor who you are paying to perform better than the market.

Looking at the performance for 24 months (2001 and 2002), and for 36 months (2000 to 2002), the top 50 percent (129 programs for two years and 55 programs for three years) had negative returns, but they performed much better than all three benchmarks, with lower volatility. Overall for both the two- and three-year time frames, the managers' performance, although negative, was still much better than the benchmarks. For example, the three-year average return was a negative 20 percent, which was half the 40 percent drop of the S&P 500, and nearly 70 percent better than the Nasdaq Composite Index.

This performance data indicates that there are some exceptionally good and some exceptionally poor managers in the market-timing community. By using a service such as *Select Advisors* you can discover for yourself the most consistent managers and monitor their risk levels. *Select Advisors* can help you make a more informed decision. You may want a manager who has returns comparable to the benchmark but with lower risk. Other investors may want to use a Rydex sector fund manager who has the highest returns with reasonable risk parameters.

For more information on the *Select Advisors* program, contact them at:

Select Advisors

111 Summit Drive
Suite 100
Exton, PA 19341
Voicemail: (610) 524-7310
Fax: (610) 524-4050
E-mail: *info@scminvest.com*
Web site: *www.select-advisors.com*

CHAPTER 13

Market-Timing Software

Ninety percent of the people in the stock market, professionals and amateurs alike, simply haven't done enough homework.

William J. O'Neil, founder, Investors.com, September 6, 2002

Investors who prefer to develop their own market-timing systems or use the timing signals of an online timing service have various options. This chapter focuses on four readily available software packages in the marketplace today. All of the packages have a different focus, but they all provide market-timing capability, and they are used by both active traders and investors alike. Some of the software provides the ability to test many different strategies and technical indicators (for example, MACD, RSI, and moving averages), as well as the ability to build custom market-timing system. Other software mentioned automatically provides the timing signals with no input from the investor. I have personally used the software reviewed in this chapter, and my comments are based solely on my own knowledge and experience.

VECTORVEST

VectorVest was offered to the public in 1995 by Bart A. DiLiddo, Ph.D., a former chemical engineer, business executive, and investor with 40 years of experience. VectorVest is a software program developed to evaluate stocks, industry groups, sectors, ETFs, index, and closed-end funds, both on a fundamental and technical basis. The program evaluates a universe of 7,686 stocks every day to determine which ones are rated a buy, sell, or hold. The same approach is used to rate the industries and sectors.

DiLiddo developed a software program that measures each stock's relative value, relative safety, and relative timing. Each stock is measured on each of these factors as well as measured in combination to come up with a single rating known as "VST"—VectorVest's master indicator. VST stands for Value, Safety and Timing. The highest-rated VST stocks are usually "buys" and the lowest VST valued stocks are "sells."

The reason VectorVest is being mentioned in this chapter is not because of its stock rating capabilities, which by the way are high powered, but for its market-timing methodology. The chart in Figure 13-1 shows the major-timing signals issued on the VectorVest Composite Index (VVC) since 1998. The up-and-down arrows indicate the buy and sell dates. As you can see, the buy and sell signals, although not perfect have been on the money.

The VVC Index is composed of all the 7,686 stocks tracked by VectorVest. The prices of all the stocks are added together and then divided by the total number of stocks to obtain its daily value. It is simply an arithmetic average of the price of all the stocks, not market-capitalization weighted like the S&P 500.

A "Market Timing Indicator" (MTI) calculated by the program measures the strength or weakness of the overall market. This indicator (refer to bottom graph on Figure 13-1) combines the trends of the VVC price, the relative timing (direction, magnitude, and dynamics of price history) and the buy/sell ratio (number of stocks on VectorVest buy signals divided by the number of stocks on VectorVest sell signals) into a single indicator.

As you can see on the chart, the MTI fluctuates between a scale of 0 to 2, with 1 being a neutral reading. Readings above 1 indicate a rising market, and readings below 0 indicate a declining market. These readings are plotted on the chart. Since space is limited, this chart is plotted weekly, but it can be plotted in daily mode as well.

Since 1996, when the MTI readings have risen to an extreme high point approaching 1.5 to 1.75, that has turned out to be the time to consider selling stocks (going into cash or going short). Recent high readings occurred on December 2, 2002, at 1.65, and prior to that on December 7, 2001, at 1.76. Compare those high MTI readings with the price of the VVC on the upper chart to see that high MTI readings coincided with high VVC price levels. (Note: It may be hard to match up these points, as the chart is compressed.)

On the other hand, extreme low MTI readings of 0.3 to 0.5 have been shown to be the time to go long the market. Recent low readings occurred on July 23 to 25, 2002, at 0.34, and on October 9, 2002, at 0.40, both excellent entry points. Compare those low MTI readings with the price of the VVC on the upper chart to see that low MTI readings coincided with low VVC price levels.

The VectorVest program does not really focus on these extreme values, nor does it make buy and sell recommendations based on them. I found them to be effective buy and sell points just by eye-balling the data since 1996. Instead, VectorVest provides its daily VectorVest "Views," which provide the current market's situation and the strategy for investors.

For potential new customers, VectorVest offers a 30-day money-back trial of their software for $9.95. The description of the product in this chapter represents a small part of the software's total capability. So, try it out if you are interested in seeing how it works. If you decide to invest in ETFs, this software tracks them. For more information about the different levels of service (which range in price from $29 to $69 per month), you can contact the firm at:

VectorVest, Inc.

20472 Chartwell Center Drive Suite D
Cornelius, NC 28031
Phone: (704) 895-4095
(888) 658-7638
E-mail: sales@vectorvest.com
Web site: *www.vectorvest.com*

ULTRA FINANCIAL SYSTEMS

If you want to test prewritten and thoroughly reviewed market-timing systems, consider ULTRA 7 software from ULTRA Financial Systems (UFS). Steve Hunter, systems strategy tester, researcher,

FIGURE 13–1

VectorVest® Timing Signals Chart and the Vector Vest Composite

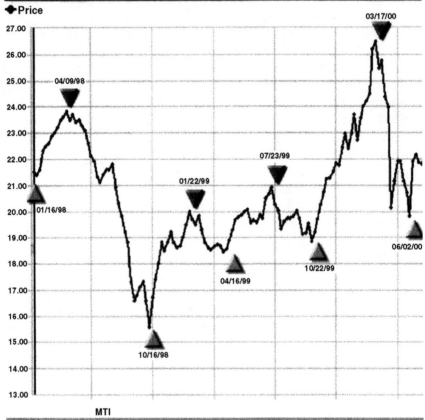

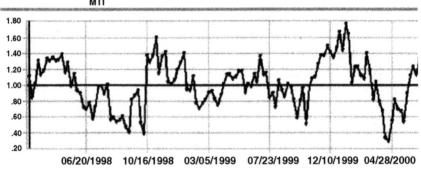

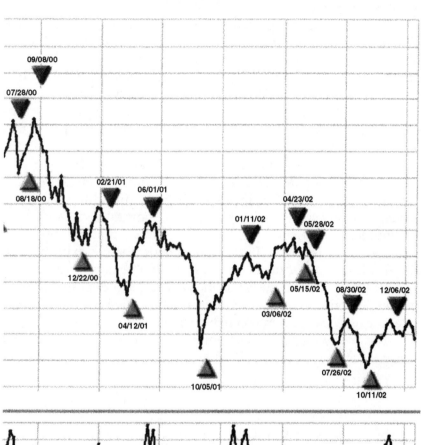

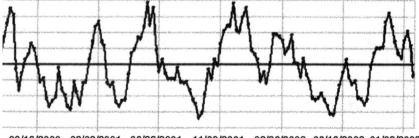

programmer, and owner of UFS, has compiled over 85 different market-timing systems that have been developed by other researchers, enhanced by others, or written by him. After testing hundreds of systems Hunter has retained the best-performing systems for this software package. New systems are added periodically in software updates.

The $349 software package called ULTRA 7 provides access to 48 intermediate-term stock timing systems (including VL4%), 15 short-term stock market timing systems, 8 seasonality systems (including presidential cycle and best six months strategy), 8 Nasdaq 100 systems, 6 bond timing systems, and 2 gold timing systems.

UFS offers a data updating service that can be purchased for $99 a year that updates the entire database including every system using an automated Internet download. All upgrades to ULTRA 7 are provided without charge for 12 months after purchase.

ULTRA 7 has an historical database from 1942 encompassing the following: 10 market indexes, 12 NYSE breadth statistics, 8 Nasdaq breadth statistics, 9 interest rates, short sales statistics, S&P 500 dividends and earnings, CPI, CRB, Gold Mining Index, Spot Gold, and the cash Swiss Franc. Also, the database is exportable to any ASCII format for further analysis with other software.

ULTRA 7 is a well-designed and easy software package to install and use. If you want to do your own system testing with mostly predetermined systems, then you may want to give this software a try.

The following is contact information for ULTRA Financial Systems Inc.:

ULTRA Financial Systems Inc.

P.O. Box 3938
Breckenridge, CO 80424
Phone: (970) 453-4956
Web site: *www.ULTRAfs.com*
E-mail: support@ULTRAfs.com

TRADESTATION

TradeStation is a software product that I've used for over seven years, mostly for trading the markets in real time. Besides offering an outstanding platform including a plethora of technical indicators and strategies to monitor and trade different markets, the software offers an extensive system back-testing capability that more advanced investors may find useful in their search for timing models. As you may recall, I used TradeStation to test the Value Line 4% strategy, the Nasdaq Composite 6% strategy, and a 25-week moving average strategy on the Nasdaq Composite Index. TradeStation provided all the performance reports for these strategies that were previously exhibited.

TradeStation is not suited for every investor, as it requires time and patience to learn all its features. When running back-testing strategies the software provides 11 different performance reports to help the user analyze all risk-versus-reward aspects of the strategy's performance history. These extensive reports indicate if your strategy was profitable or unprofitable in the past, its annual rate of return, the number of winning and losing trades, the average winning trade in dollars, the average losing trade in dollars, and much more.

Historical data goes back at least 30 years for stocks and indexes that were in existence at that time. TradeStation collects, stores, and maintains this database on its network. Delivery is quick, via the Internet.

One unique feature of TradeStation is its proprietary technology called EasyLanguage. This is a specially designed English language–based programming language that can be used to develop customized trading strategies. Although the software provides many built-in strategies and indicators, many traders and investors prefer to develop and test their own formulas. TradeStation offers another site *www.tradestationworld.com*, where numerous contributors have provided additional indicators and strategies that can be downloaded at no charge and immediately imported into the TradeStation software for immediate viewing and testing. Additional strategies and indicators discussed in monthly magazine articles such as *Technical Analysis of Stocks & Commodities,* and *Active Trader* are translated into TradeStation EasyLanguage available in the magazine or on TradeStation's Web site.

For investors and traders, the real-time pricing is $199 a month. TradeStation no longer offers its end-of-day version at $49.95 a month. Traders who utilize TradeStation Securities for their trading may be able to obtain the software at $99 per month, and there may be additional price concessions based upon trading volume. For more information contact the Sales Department at (800) 808-9336. Contact information for TradeStation is as follows:

TradeStation Group, Inc.

8050 SW 10th Street, Suite 4000
Plantation, FL 33324
Web site: *www.tradestation.com*

BUSINESSWEEK INVESTOR TOOLBOX

The BusinessWeek Investor Toolbox gives investors a one-stop resource to quickly search for and track suitable stock and option investments that meet their specific investment criteria. The Toolbox database universe consists of over 12,000 U.S and Canadian stocks, U.S. equity put and call options, mutual funds, and exchange-traded funds. The major components of the Web site include portfolio management, graphs, searches, industry groups, news, strategies, and mutual funds.

The online service provides a suite of easy-to-navigate screens and proprietary tools. A full complement of fundamental screens and built-in searches allow investors to slice and dice the data to come up with a customized portfolio to meet their individual needs, and risk parameters.

The Toolbox provides a spreadsheet of 246 industry groups ranked by relative price performance for the latest week and the past 11 weeks, on a scale of 0 to 99. This spreadsheet can be sorted by rank or industry name, depending on the preference of the investor.

Moreover, the Toolbox Industry Group Indexes can be further analyzed by volume, insider trading, and market capitalization. Technical indicators can be used with the indexes to determine the best time to buy or sell specific industries. For investment purposes, many industries are represented by broad-based ETFs or sector mutual funds.

The Toolbox also offers the "Mutual Fund Prospector," which has over 60 search criteria for mutual fund selection, mostly fundamental-based, including risk, value, standard deviation, relative performance (1-day, 1-week, 6-weeks, and 26-weeks), return, alpha, net assets, and annual return. Each Monday, the best-performing searches are ranked over the past 12 months for their performance. The search criteria can be reviewed with a mouse click, and the top 25 mutual funds meeting the criteria of the top search are automatically shown. Funds meeting the other top-performing search strategies can be accessed as well.

Once the top funds are selected they can be technically screened with an array of technical indicators. The proprietary Market Forecast tool can also be accessed to help determine the short and intermediate market trends.

Another market-timing tool offered by the Toolbox is the use of three technical analysis tools in combination, to determine buy and sell signals on specific ETFs or mutual funds, for example. The signals (up and down arrows) are automatically provided on each chart.

The BusinessWeek Investor is only offered to investors who have completed the BusinessWeek Investor Workshop. There is a complete money-back guarantee at the end of the first day, if all the workshop materials are returned. For complete information on the workshop, and monthly online access fees to the Investor Toolbox, contact *BusinessWeek* at *www.toolbox.businessweek.com* or (800) 301-9449 or 1221 Avenue of the Americas, New York, NY 10020.

OTHER SOFTWARE PACKAGES

The software packages mentioned in this chapter represent a small sampling of what is available in the marketplace. Other well-known packages include Equis International's MetaStock, eSignal, AIQ, Wealth-Lab, NeuroShell Trader, TickQuest's NeoTicker, Investor/RT, TradingSolutions, RTR Software, and FastTrack. For more information, view their Web sites listed at the end of the book.

The magazines *Technical Analysis of Stocks & Commodities,* and *Active Trader* provide the code for strategies and indicators for articles printed in their magazines and for software packages mentioned here.

CONCLUSIONS

For self-directed investors with a penchant for performing their own research, the software packages mentioned will provide the ability to back-test most of the strategies covered in this book, and many others. The software covered in this chapter provides a sampling of what's available in the marketplace. Half of the packages listed above did not exist five years ago. New software appears all the time. If you are new to back-testing strategies, you should read a few books and articles on the subject. Check out the resources and books in the bibliography.

When selecting software, be sure to check the vendor's Web site, obtain any brochures that are available, evaluate the product's features, data update reliability, and total monthly charges. Most software firms offer free trial periods for a few weeks to a month. Definitely take the trial period to test the software from all perspectives. Make sure you don't have to sign up for a one-year deal without being able to get out of the contract without a penalty.

Testing requires some care. For example, you can optimize strategies and obtain phenomenal results in back testing. But if these results cannot be replicated over multiple time frames, they may not provide any benefit in the real world. If a strategy is improperly back-tested or you use faulty logic this will result in spurious results. Do not invest your money in any strategy that is not properly and thoroughly tested over long time frames. Even then, consider paper trading before actually putting any dollars in the market.

You can observe a lot just by watchin'.

Yogi Berra

The future is never clear, you pay a very high price in the stock market for a cheery consensus. Uncertainty actually is the friend of the buyer of long-term values.

Warren Buffet

Numerous stock market "experts" fill the airwaves, magazines, and newsletters with the assertion that market timing doesn't work. They profess, until they are blue in the face, that buy and hold is a far superior strategy over the long run. Of course, we all know that a bull market makes geniuses out of everyone who follows the buy-and-hold approach. But what about what the consequences of the inevitable and recurring bear markets? This book has provided you with the facts on both sides of the argument, so that you can decide for yourself whether or not market timing has merit.

The purpose of *All About Market Timing* is not to provide a comprehensive statistical compilation of the performance of a myriad of market-timing models and strategies. But rather, the purpose is to provide you with several step-by-step time-tested easy-to-use strategies to successfully time the market so you can protect your investments and enhance your investment performance. These strategies include seasonality, presidential year cycles, moving averages, and fixed-percentage entry-and-exit systems. And to pique the systems you are using I have shown you how to use specific internal market and sentiment indicators so you know when the market is about to change and you can keep on the right side of the trend.

You may want to embrace market timing, but you may not have the time, skill, or temperament to do it yourself. For those investors, there is detailed information on market-timing newsletters and professional market-timing advisors who can make the market-timing decisions for you. And for the more venturesome self-directed investor, who wants to develop a more personalized timing approach, there is a chapter on market-timing software.

To be a successful investor you must decide on your investing objectives, then get a strategy that will work for you, and most importantly, establish rules for limiting your losses that you will adhere to. Don't leave it to chance or you'll be left with chump change. Don't rely on gurus, brokers, or financial advisors to maximize your returns. They have already set the stage and are just waiting for you to come along. And they won't be there to tell you when it's time to get out.

Instead, think long and hard about selecting a mechanical, nonemotional market-timing approach that you can master so you can make your own independent selection of investment vehicles and your own buy and sell decisions. You should feel comfortable with the strategy you select. Make sure you use it with the proper risk-control measures, which means cutting losses quickly.

No one but you has your best interests at heart. You didn't depend on someone else to tell you how to earn your money, and you don't need to depend on some disinterested "expert" to tell you how to manage it. Remember that the overwhelming majority of financial advisors pay little heed to the market's health and they hardly ever tell you when to sell and never ever tell you to go into cash. They don't believe in market timing or technical analysis; but focus exclusively on the "story" and the fundamentals (i.e., current earnings, the forecasted earnings, and revenues) that don't work and can frequently backfire on you.

Over the long-run, the key to investment success is to protect your capital in the short run by cutting your losses and having a strict sell discipline so that small losses don't cascade into monstrous losses. I would bet that less than 5 percent of all investors follow this approach.

Hardly any of the mutual fund managers follow buy-and-hold for their fund's portfolio. According to Morningstar, the average portfolio turnover of a diversified stock mutual fund is 111 percent a year. That means that on average every stock in the mutual fund portfolio is sold each year and replaced by new ones. So, if it looks like market timing and smells like market timing, then it is market timing and should be acknowledged as market timing as practiced by the mutual fund managers. And, what's good for the goose should be good for the gander.

Some critics of market timing point out that unless your winning percentage is 70 percent or more, you have no chance of equaling or beating buy and hold. That is not true. You should cut your losses to a maximum of 7 to 8 percent below your purchase price, according to Bill O'Neil, the founder of *Investor's Business Daily*. Several of the strategies presented in this book only have winning percentages around 40 percent or less, and they still beat buy and hold. Remember the sage advice of financier Bernard Baruch, who said:

> Even being right three or four times out of 10 should yield a person a fortune if they have the sense to cut losses quickly.

The market-timing strategies I have presented all have, as the centerpiece of their performance, the concept of being out of the market when the market is falling or expected to fall. The main concern is to protect your capital and to cut your losses.

Investors will always be moved by fear and greed. When the market is rising, they look for more and more profits. When the market is falling they become so fearful that they freeze and do nothing. They rationalize it by saying that it is only a "paper" loss, and that history shows that the market "always comes back." They stay the course when they should have acted and acted fast. They put their heads in the sand and pretend that the mounting losses are not happening to them. They think this will blow over and that everything will be fine.

But the losses are real, not paper. For the day comes when they get so frightened or so tired of waiting for the turnaround or they become so enamored of the latest "fad" stock that they simply must get in on before it gets away from them that they bite the bullet and "take" the loss that had actually been incurred all along. That is the psychological nature of the investor and that is how it has always happened.

Market timing attempts to avoid all that. Be true to your timing principles and be true to yourself and market timing can work for you. If by now you are convinced that market timing is the way to go, you have three options:

1. Consider using one or more of the strategies in this book, if you are comfortable that the strategy works and will work for you. Be sure to use stop-loss orders to prevent your drawdowns from getting out of hand. Protecting your principal and reducing your risk should be your main goals.

2. Subscribe to a market-timing newsletter and follow the signals given religiously. But first you should check the newsletter's performance from independent sources and request the complete actual real-time buy and sell signals that occurred in the past.

3. Hire an advisor to time the market and invest on your behalf in a fund family such as Rydex Funds.

In summary, if you use a reliable, time-tested, unemotional market-timing approach, then the odds will be in your favor that you can avoid the brunt of future bear markets. Additionally, you can retain your profits during bull markets while reducing your risk. These benefits are hard to beat. And over the long term, you will substantially outperform the outdated, and potentially lethal, buy-and-hold strategy.

I hope that this book will help you to think and invest for yourself. May your time be well spent, and may you enjoy many successes in the future. The next step is yours!

I'd like to hear from you with questions, comments, and your experiences with market timing. You can email me at *lesmason@frontiernet.net*.

Books on Investing, Timing, and Technical Analysis

Alexander, Colin, *Street Smart Guide to Timing the Stock Market*, McGraw-Hill, New York, 1999.

Arnold, Curtis M., *Timing the Market: How to Profit in Bull and Bear Markets with Technical Analysis*, Revised Edition, McGraw-Hill, New York, 1995.

Baer, Gregory A., and Gary Gensler, *The Great Mutual Fund Trap: An Investment Recovery Plan*, Broadway Books, New York, 2002.

Bulkowski, Thomas N., *Encyclopedia of Chart Patterns*, Wiley, New York, 2002.

Colby, Robert W., *The Encyclopedia of Technical Market Indicators*, Second Edition, McGraw-Hill, New York, 2003.

Dorsey, Thomas J., *Point and Figure Charting: The Essential Application for Forecasting and Tracking Market Prices*, Second Edition, Wiley, New York, 2001.

Ferri, Richard A., Jr., *All About Index Funds: The Easy Way to Get Started*, McGraw-Hill, New York, 2002.

Harding Sy, *Riding the BEAR: How to Prosper in the Coming Bear Market*, Adams Media Corporation, Holbrook, MA, 1999.

Headley, Price, *Big Trends in Trading: Strategies to Master Major Market Moves*, Wiley, New York, 2002.

Hirsch, Yale, and Jeffrey A. Hirsch, *Stock Trader's Almanac 2003*, The Hirsch Organization Inc., Old Tappan, NJ, 2002.

Lloyd, Humphrey E.D., *The RSL Market Timing System: How to Pinpoint Market Turns in Mutual Funds, Futures, and Options*, Windsor Books, Brightwaters, NY, 1991.

McDonald, Michael, *Predict Market Swings with Technical Analysis*, Wiley, NY, 2002.

Merriman, Paul, and Merle E, Dowd, *Market Timing with No-Load Mutual Funds*, Backwater Books, Mercer Island, Washington, 1985.

Merriman, Raymond, *The Ultimate Book on Stock Market Timing: Cycles and Patterns in the Indexes*, Seek-It-Publications, West Bloomfield, MI, 1997.

Murphy, John J., *Technical Analysis of the Futures Markets*, New York Institute of Finance, New York, 1986.

O'Neil, William J., *How to Make Money in Stocks: A Winning System in Good or Bad Times*, Mc-Graw-Hill, New York, 2002.

Pring, Martin J., *Technical Analysis Explained*, Fourth Edition, McGraw-Hill, New York, 2002.

Sosnowy, John K., *Lasting Wealth Is a Matter of Timing*, 21st Century Publishers, Cheyenne, WY 1997.

Zweig, Martin, *Martin Zweig's Winning on Wall Street*, Warner Books, New York, 1986

Articles on Market timing

Thomas Basso, Timing the Market Revised," *Financial Planning*, Feb. 2001, vol. 31 Issue 2, pp. 104–110.

Gary Brinson, Brian D. Singer, and Gilbert L. Beebower, "Determinants of Portfolio Performance II: An Update," *Financial Analysts Journal*, May–June 1991.

William H. Dare, "To Hold or Not to Hold," *Journal of Financial Planning*, July
    1995, pp. 123–126.
W.G. Droms, "Market Timing as an Investment Policy," *Financial Analysts
    Journal*, January/February 1989, pp. 73–77.
Paul Merriman, "Market Timing's Bad Rap," *www.fundadvice.com*.
    http://www.fundadvice.com/FEhtml/MTStrategies/0208.htm
W. Sy, "Market Timing: Is it a Folly?" *Journal of Portfolio Management*, Summer
    1990, pp. 11-16.
Jerry C. Wagner, "Why Market Timing Works," *The Journal of Investing*, Summer
    1997.

Papers on Market timing

"Behavior and Performance of Investment Newsletter Analysts," (EFA 2002
    Berlin Meetings Presented Paper) Alok Kumar (University of Notre Dame
    – Mendoza College of Business) and Vicente Pons-Sanz (Yale School of
    Management), November, 2002.
    http://papers.ssrn.com/sol3/papers.cfm?abstract_id=302888
"On the Timing Ability of Mutual Fund Managers," Assistant Professor Nicolas
    P.B. Bollen of Vanderbilt University and Assistant Professor Jeffrey A.
    Busse, Goizueta Business School, Emory University, *The Journal of Finance*,
    June 2001.
    http://papers.ssrn.com/sol3/papers.cfm?abstract_id=245790
"The performance of professional market timers: daily evidence from executed
    strategies," Professor Don M. Chance, Department of Finance at Virginia
    Tech, and Professor Michael L. Hemler, Department of Finance and
    Business Economics at the University of Notre Dame, *Journal of Financial
    Economics*, Vol. 62, Issue 2, November 2001, pp. 377–411.

Web Sites

Charting and Technical Analysis Sites

www.bigcharts.com
www.clearstation.com
www.decisionpoint.com
www.dorseywright.com (point-and-figure charting)
www.investorsintelligence.com (point-and-figure charting)
www.prophetfinance.com
www.stockcharts.com
www.wallstreetcity.com

Software

www.vectorvest.com
www.tradestation.com
www.ultrafs.com
www.metastock.com
www.esignal.com

www.aiq.com
www.wealth-lab.com
www.neuroshell.com
www.tickquest.com
www.linnsoft.com (Investor/RT)
www.tradingsolutions.com
www.rtrsoftware.com
www.fasttrack.net

Advisory Service or Newsletters

www.begininvesting.com
www.elliottwave.com
www.fundadvice.com
www.haysmarketfocus.com
www.investorsintelligence.com
www.robertwcolby.com
www.streetsmartreport.com
www.stocktradersalmanac.com

Funds for Market Timers

www.rydexfunds.com
www.profunds.com
www.potomacfunds.com

Sector Funds and Index Funds

www.indexfunds.com
www.fidelity.com
www.vanguard.com

ETFs

www.amex.com
www.indexfunds.com
www.etfconnect.com
www.ishares.com
www.nasdaq.com

Independent Rankings of Market-Timing Advisors

www.moniresearch.com
www.select-advisors.com

Independent Ratings of Market Timers

www.timerdigest.com
www.hulbertdigest.com (now part of *www.cbs.marketwatch.com*)

Commentary, Financial News, and Investor Surveys

briefing.com
cbs.marketwatch.com
www.gallup.com
www.prudential-yardeni.com

Other Useful Sites

www.aaii.com
www.bankrate.com
www.barra.com
www.bloomberg.com
www.businessweek.com
www.cboe.com
www.federalreserve.gov
www.gomezadvisors.com
www.ici.org
investor.msn.com
www.investorlinks.com
finance.yahoo.com
finance.lycos.com
www.hoovers.com
www.mfea.com
www.momentumcd.com
money.cnn.com
www.moneycentral.com
www.morningstar.com
www.quicken.com
www.riskgrades.com
www.sec.gov/investor.shtml
www.wilshire.com

SAAFTI (Society of Asset Allocators and Fund Timers, Inc.)

SAAFTI is the premier organization for investment advisors who believe in utilizing investment strategies designed to protect clients against market downturns and capitalize on up trends in the market. SAAFTI regular members are registered investment advisors, actively managing assets for clients using dynamic asset allocation, market timing, and other active management strategies. Collectively, they manage an estimated $14 billion in client assets. For information on SAAFTI, call (888) 261-0787 or visit the association's home page at www.saafti.com.

Index

Leslie N. Masonson is president of Cash Management Resources, a financial consulting firm, based in Monroe, New York, that he founded in 1987. Masonson's 36-year working career has spanned investing, banking operations, management, teaching, and cash/treasury management consulting. He has worked for three banks—Citibank, Bank of America, and Irving Trust Company—before starting his own firm.

In 2001, Masonson authored *Day Trading on the Edge: A Look-Before-You-Leap Guide to Extreme Investing* published by AMACOM. In 1990 he authored *Cash Cash Cash: The Three Principles of Business Success and Survival*, published by HarperBusiness. And in 1985, he co-authored *Corporate Cash Management: Techniques and Analysis*, published by Dow-Jones Irwin. Since November 1998, Masonson has been editor of the *Corporate Treasury Management Manual*, published by A.S. Pratt & Sons, which is updated twice a year.

Masonson has been interviewed on business radio stations, as well on the Financial News Network and CNBC. He has been interviewed by the *Las Vegas Review Journal*, *Boardroom Reports*, and *Pensions & Investment Age*. Furthermore, he has written over 50 articles, including trader interviews and product and book reviews for numerous financial publications such as *Technical Analysis of Stocks & Commodities, Active Trader, Futures Magazine,* and *Pensions & Investment Age.* In November 2000, he was a speaker at the Online Investor Expo, where he spoke on "Successfully Trading Stocks for a Living."

Masonson has been studying the stock market for over 45 years. He has invested and traded in mutual funds, stocks, options, futures, and commodities. The author has read over 500 books on investing and trading, and he is proficient in technical analysis. Masonson has used many investing and trading software programs over the years, including Telescan, OmniTrader, DTN, TradeStation, ULTRA, VectorVest, and has used many charting, investing, and trading sites on the Internet.

Masonson is a permanently Certified Cash Manager (CCM). In 1989 he was elected to the American Management Association's "Wall of Fame" for his contributions to teaching financial management principles to corporate financial managers since 1978. He has prepared and delivered seminars on cash management to participants at the American Management Association, Association for Financial Professionals, Center for Professional Education, the Institute of Management Accountants, and the Financial Executives Institute.

Masonson has a BBA in Finance and Investments from the City College of New York, and an MBA in Operations Research from the Bernard M. Baruch College. The title of his master's thesis was "The Relative Strength Concept of Common Stock Selection."